THE REALLY PRACTICAL GUIDE TO PRIMARY GEOGRAPHY

Marcia Foley and Jan Janikoun

Stanley Thornes (Publishers) Ltd

Acknowledgements

The authors would like to thank the following people for their help, support and forbearance during the writing of this book: David Carter, Mike Foley, Graham Matthews and Jeff Lord.

The publishers would like to thank Danson Primary School, Bromley for permission to reproduce the charts on pages 39, 42, 50 and 60. Efforts have been made to contact copyright holders and we apologise if any have been overlooked.

Text © Marcia Foley and Jan Janikoun 1992

Original line illustrations © Stanley Thornes (Publishers) Ltd 1992

The right of Marcia Foley and Jan Janikoun to be identified as authors of this work has been asserted by them in accordance with the Copyright, Designs and Patents Act 1988.

First published in 1992 by:
Stanley Thornes (Publishers) Ltd
Ellenborough House
Wellington Street
CHELTENHAM GL50 1YD
England

Reprinted 1993 (twice), 1994

A catalogue of this book is available from the British Library.

ISBN 0 7487 1496 0

Prepared by *specialist publishing services*, Milton Keynes (090 857 307)
Printed and bound in Great Britain at The Bath Press, Avon

Contents

How to use this book

Our aims when writing this book were three-fold:

- To help teachers become aware of all aspects of primary geography
- To promote good geographical practice in primary schools
- To help teachers implement National Curriculum geography.

It has been written for a wide professional audience: teachers, headteachers, students in initial teacher training, those returning to the profession and other interested LEA colleagues.

We have tried to make the text as practical as possible, dealing with the various aspects of planning and implementing primary geography in as much depth as space constraints would allow. We do not envisage that you will read the whole book from cover to cover in one sitting. It can be read as a whole but has also been designed so that individual chapters can be read separately if you wish to inform or update yourself on a particular aspect of geography and curriculum planning. Cross references are given so that you know to which other chapters you might need to refer.

Geography is the focus of this book, but we recognise that it is but one part of the whole primary curriculum. Nevertheless we have presented a full model for planning, developing and implementing geographical learning in the primary school. By highlighting the nature of geography we hope you will come to a better understanding of the subject that will help you develop geography in your school, whatever your role.

Schools are at many different stages of development with primary geography. Each school's needs are unique but we hope that within the range of the book you will find clarification and practical assistance – whether you are beginning to think about primary geography or refining your expertise. We have used the term 'coordinator' throughout the book. We recognise that this might be one individual with just that curriculum responsibility; it could be somebody looking after a number of subjects; or a curriculum team. We also recognise that smaller schools might find it difficult to identify with any of these models. The important idea is that there is a way of organising planning and support for colleagues as geography develops.

The current notation for National Curriculum attainment targets is used throughout this book, e.g. geography attainment target 1, level 3, statement of attainment b, is shown as Gg1, 3b.

Everything in this book has either been done by ourselves whilst teaching, or developed for, or during, in-service training, or from working alongside colleagues in and outside classrooms. So we would like to thank all those teachers and children with whom we have had contact and who have shared our thinking and helped us develop our ideas.

1

GOOD PRACTICE IN PRIMARY GEOGRAPHY

Geography is the study of people and places, and the interaction between them. All primary teachers teach some geography even though they may be surprised to realise it; many have had little formal geographical education beyond the age of 13 or so and therefore do not consciously recognise the subject matter. Those of you who teach geographical matters well (whether as part of a broad topic or as a specific geography topic) do so because you are able to recognise geographical concepts and skills and thus the subject's contribution to children's learning.

Geography is not merely the ability to memorise the names of places and locate their position on the earth's surface. Knowing the name and location of places and features (sometimes referred to as 'capes and bays geography') is an integral but small part of a much larger and more fascinating area of learning. Geography consists of knowledge and understanding of concepts and skills, all of which relate to the physical and human environment and the interaction between them. Geography is also an enquiry-based subject and any questions raised whilst teaching geography will be related to one of a number of key areas of enquiry.

There are seven key questions which are fundamental to children's learning about geography:

- Where is this place?
- What is this place like?
- Why is this place as it is?
- How is this place connected to other places?
- How is this place changing?
- What is it like to be in this place?
- How is this place similar to, or different from, another place?

In order to teach and learn about geography, it is good practice to bear in mind these key questions. Asking children about any place brings out the essential learning about it, be it a feature – such as a mountain, a quarry, a village, a country – or a natural region, such as a desert. If the use of key questions is new to you, then Figure 1.1 gives some examples of how the answers to such questions can develop key geographical concepts and vocabulary.

Working through a key question approach helps children build up an understanding of processes and places. It provides a framework of knowledge in which to develop key geographical concepts.

Figure 1.1

Key geographical concepts and questions

Question 1: Where is this place?
Question 2: What is this place like?
helps develop the concept of location and a sense of place.

'My village is in the country, on a hill top, in East Sussex, England. It is called Rotherfield. It is small with a food store, a post office shop, a school, a garage and some pubs ...'

Question 3: Why is this place as it is?
helps develop the concepts of spatial pattern and process.

'... the village is difficult to drive through and dangerous to walk through because the main streets are narrow. They cannot be widened because the old houses, some of them very old indeed, do not have front gardens ...'

Question 4: How is this place connected to other places?
helps identify relative location and build up the idea of spatial patterns.

'... the railway was closed a long time ago, so to travel to London my dad must drive to the nearest town. There are a few buses every day, so it is not convenient for my mum if she wants to go to the supermarket ...

Question 5: How is this place changing?
helps identify changes occurring in patterns, process and systems; can bring up issues to be discussed.

'... they built a new estate of thirty houses and now there is more traffic turning onto the main road from it. But there are more children for our school, too ...'

Question 6: What is it like to be in this place/live here?
develops the concept of place and helps us to think about attitudes and values.

'It's good! I like it. We can play on the recreation ground opposite my house.'

Question 7: How is this place similar to/different from another place?
develops the concept of similarity and difference, as well as location and place by comparison.

'... it's smaller and quieter than where I lived before in the suburb of a big town. But my friends don't all live here so I have to rely on them coming to see me, unless it's the weekend when I can travel to see them by car.'

Geographical concepts

The key concepts of geography are:

- Location and place
- Spatial pattern
- Process
- Systems
- Similarity and difference.

Asking children key questions when they approach geographical work helps them progress towards the ultimate understanding of key geographical concepts.

Figure 1.2 shows how particular key questions relate to the first four concepts, and how each concept can be broken down into sub-concepts.

The final concept, similarity and difference, relates to all the other aspects of geography. In learning about different places, patterns, processes and systems children should be encouraged to compare and contrast so that they build up a more complex knowledge and understanding of place and space.

The important question which children can ask – What is it like to be in this place? – relates to attitudes, values and issues.

Figure 1.2

Key questions help develop key concepts		
Question	**Main concept**	**Subconcepts**
1 Where is this place?	Location	Relative location: where is it, related to another place?
2 What is this place like?	Spatial pattern Location	Patterns in physical landscape Patterns in human landscape
3 Why is this place as it is?	Spatial pattern Process Systems and location	Inputs, outputs, interaction
4 How is this place connected to other places?	Locations Systems Pattern	Position, relative location Networks
5 How is this place changing?	Process Systems	Change over time: development, rural, urban Cycles (rock, weather, water) Interaction
6 What is it like to be in this place?	Place	Leads to understanding attitudes, values, beliefs within issues
7 How is this place the same as, or different from, another? Extension/Overarching question	Similarity and difference	Assumes comparisons based on above six questions, relating to two or more places

Attitudes, values and issues

The people who live in any place have feelings about its features, and attitudes towards the processes and systems that arise from their set of values. They also have attitudes towards local issues. By asking primary children 'What would it feel like to be in this place?' after they have some knowledge and understanding of it, we can help develop their understanding of the range of attitudes, values and beliefs contained in any issue. We are asking pupils to try to put themselves as far as possible in the situation of the people and places they are studying.

As soon as children begin to consider this question, they may ask: 'How are decisions made about this place?', questioning the concepts of people's rationale and motives. 'Why has the factory been built here, when some residents were against it?'

Once questions about decision-making arise, an opportunity to build on an issue for enquiry may result. With primary children the issue will usually be a local one, as first-hand investigation or fieldwork will make the issue vital. However, it is possible to generate excellent work on issues through role-play activities. Hypothetical issues avoid the sensitivity of local issues in which pupils' parents may be involved.

Some teachers shy away from dealing with issues in geographical work because they immediately raise questions about children's and adults' attitudes and values. Their own attitudes and values may be questioned, too. Good teachers recognise however, that good geographical work cannot avoid dealing with such matters. Children need to know and be able to accept that society is so complex that people do not always come up with 'right' or 'wrong' answers. Most solutions are a compromise and will go against some people's wishes whilst fulfilling those of others. The DES HMI series Matters for Discussion, number 5, *The Teaching of Ideas in Geography 1978* states that:

> "*Geography offers the opportunity of situations where responsible efforts can be made to help pupils understand the nature of values and attitudes and their importance in making decisions.*"

This is not a matter of indoctrination but of raising the possibility of helping children from a young age independently to make some sense of the world around them. Although the influence of the school is slight compared with that of the home environment, media and society in general, primary teachers through geography, can help children to develop:

- A respect for evidence
- An awareness of biased information and intolerance
- An awareness that simple explanations rarely tell the whole tale
- An interest in other people and places
- Empathy with other life styles and cultures, including minority groups in the United Kingdom
- A concern for the quality of rural and urban environments
- The ability to appreciate other points of view and to reach compromise solutions
- The concern to value and conserve resources.

The enquiry process

Good geographical teaching and learning uses the enquiry process to motivate children to find out about the physical and human environment and their interrelation. We can pare down these seven key questions depending on what we are finding out about.

What does the enquiry process involve?

HMI explain that:

> "*Pupils should not be primarily passive recipients of information, but should be given adequate opportunities to carry out practical investigations, to explore and express ideas in their own language...and to reflect on other people's attitudes and values.*"
>
> *Geography from 5 to 16*, HMSO 1986

How do we go about the enquiry process?

Figure 1.3 shows examples which could be used with infants and juniors, depending on the sophistication of data collected. At key stage 1 the context is the school grounds, whilst at key stage 2 it is the local area.

Figure 1.3

Enquiry process in theory	Enquiry process in action in school grounds KS1	Enquiry process in action in a local area KS2
Recognise an issue or focus for enquiry	Where shall we have a compass rose sited in our school grounds?	A large new pub is to be built on a local derelict site.
Ask some relevant questions or make a statement to be investigated (one or several as appropriate)	Should it be painted on tarmac, or bricks on the grass? In an open or exposed site? Near our classroom or not?	Is this the best use for the site? What services and leisure activities already exist in our place? Are people happy with these?
Collect relevant data	Check proposed sites for sun/shade – take wind, temperature judgements (for infants), measurements (for juniors), etc. Check sites for flatness, drainage. Do a 'route' survey – would the proposed sites be in the official rights of way - on the football pitch, etc?– on the shortest route from hall to another building, etc?	Make up questionnaires to address these questions. Questionnaires to parents/other classes/local residents depending on time constraints. Visit locality to survey and plot leisure facilities and services on map. Write to/visit/invite into school (according to time constraints, etc.) Planning Department official, brewing company representative, etc.
Interpret and analyse data	Using data collected begin to decide on best location for compass rose.	Using data collected (via IT data base if possible) work out whether survey is in favour of new pub.
Present findings	Use plans, maps, diagrams to compare pros and cons of various sites.	Examine alternative suggestions and reasons. Produce 'public enquiry' role play to illustrate findings (this could be presented to another class, in a school assembly or before the class's parents).
Draw conclusions	Decide on final siting – propose site to headteacher	Write to local planning department with results of findings.
Evaluate enquiry	See how well the actual site works out in practice – is it accessible, not too exposed, etc? This would be monitored over a term or a year!	Evaluate what was learned about local area.

How many questions do we ask or expect children to formulate for an enquiry?

There is a temptation to think that many questions must be asked. However, it is sufficient to ask one question only – the age and experience of the children; the experience of the teacher in using the enquiry process and the time available can be the only guidance for the teacher's professional judgement.

Figure 1.4 lists further questions and statements which can trigger good geographical work. These questions are suitable for key stages 1 and 2, depending on the level to which they are developed.

Figure 1.4

Enquiry questions	
Where shall we have a compass rose painted on our playground?	What is the best shop/new building(s) to put on our nearby derelict site?
Where is the best place to site the new flower bed/seats/trees in our school grounds/park?	How many routes are there from place A to B (within school grounds as well as in a town)?
Where are the traffic or crossing danger points in our local streets/my route to school and how could we suggest improvements?	Why are the goods in the supermarket laid out in the order they are? Is it planned or random?
How can we improve our school grounds?	Is our town/village a tourist attraction? Why is the locality we are visiting a tourist locality?
What kinds of local/town shops do we have? Are they the same as those in place X we will visit soon?	Can we make up a barrier trail for our class friends to follow?
Are our nearest houses made from mainly natural or man-made materials?	Can we plan a tourist trail for our village?
	Can we make up a building materials trail for our village/area of town?
How will the by-pass/roundabout/road improvements change our village/town?	How have humans changed/influenced the course the stream takes?
How is a new road built and why is it being built?	How are many visitors to this beauty spot/site of special scientific interest, etc. affecting it?
Why is the new supermarket sited here?	

The content of geography

Traditionally geography has two themes: the physical environment and the human environment. Figure 1.5 suggests the way in which these two central elements interact with each other

The Teaching of Ideas in Geography, from the DES HMI 1978 series, Matters for Discussion, details the breakdown of the areas listed above for the specialist. Figure 1.6 indicates in straightforward terms the kind of content with which each theme might deal at primary geography level.

This is not the only way of describing the content of geography: there are many others. The geography Statutory Order represents a very specific way of describing content with an emphasis on places and themes.

Geographical skills

Mapwork is a major geographical skill. Indeed, to many people both inside and outside the world of education, mapwork *is* geography! However, this view is a very narrow and inaccurate one. The making, using and reading of maps is an essential

Figure 1.5

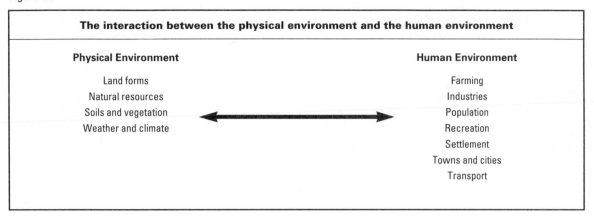

The interaction between the physical environment and the human environment

Physical Environment	Human Environment
Land forms	Farming
Natural resources	Industries
Soils and vegetation	Population
Weather and climate	Recreation
	Settlement
	Towns and cities
	Transport

and very important geographical skill, and one which is so wide that it can be broken down into many sub-skills (see Chapter 7). But mapwork is just one area of many geographical skills. These skills can be classified as primary and secondary skills, or direct and indirect skills.

Primary or direct skills involve children's first-hand experience or active learning either inside the classroom, or outside it (fieldwork) where the pupil is directly engaged in collecting data, be it information, evidence or samples. Indirect or secondary skills involve the pupil in collecting data second-hand, for example from information books, the teacher, educational television, radio or computer databases. Data and information collected via these skills then have to be handled, analysed and presented in some form which involves further skills, such as:

● Producing a map
● Producing a piece of writing
● Making a pie chart
● Constructing a line graph
● Making a flow chart
● Performing a role play.

The representation of geographical information in a non-written form, for example in charts, maps, diagrams or graphs, is referred to as graphicacy. The various groups of skills essential to good practice in primary geography will be examined in more detail in Chapters 7, 8 and 10 along with progression in the acquiring of these skills.

Geographical vocabulary

Each area of learning has a vocabulary which, although part of the English language as a whole, is also specific to its own area of learning. Geography has its own particular vocabulary which children begin learning unconsciously as soon as they speak. They become familiar with geographical words, build up their range of vocabulary and are able to use them in geographical contexts, for example 'this way', 'that way', 'map', 'signpost', 'shop', 'doctor', 'town', 'river', 'temperature', 'cloud', 'by-pass', 'country', 'equator', 'soil', 'desert', 'quarry', 'mountain'.

If you are aware that much of the vocabulary that you and your pupils use has a geographical context, then you will be able to encourage children's knowledge and use of it. Continuity and progression in

Figure 1.6

Content of physical environment at key stage 1 and 2	Content of human environment at key stage 1 and 2
Landforms Scenery, landscape (what makes the landscape) – hills, plains, rivers, mountains – and how they were formed; the rocks which form the landscape (igneous, sedimentary, metamorphic); the water cycle; outline explanation of weathering of rocks and building stone by rain, acid rain and the effect of wind; the erosion of rocks by sea, rivers, glaciers; the making of new land by the deposition of sediment / pebbles from the sea or rivers.	**Farming** Farming as an industry to provide us with food; types of farming (sheep, dairy, arable, etc.); the farm as a system with inputs (seed, animals, etc.) and outputs for sale (crops, milk, wool, animals, etc.); special types of farming and their location, e.g. pick-your-own fruit farms in heavily populated areas; how products travel to market; contrasting farming methods between UK and the developing world.
	Industry Primary industries (mining, fishing, quarrying), secondary industries (steel works, food processing), tertiary industries (service industries: transport companies, travel agencies); siting of industries.
Natural resources Understanding what natural resources are: water, rocks to be quarried, minerals, etc. to be mined, forests, woodland, indigenous animals, etc.; alteration of the landscape by extraction of natural resources, e.g. reservoirs, land fill, gravel pits, lakes; how we can preserve our resources; damage and pollution of our environment by using resources, e.g. rubbish tips, waste disposal, recycling.	**Population** People cluster together or space out to live according to the physical geography, lifestyle and employment opportunities; people migrate because of jobs, war, famine, etc.; too many people living in one place can strain resources.
	Recreation Leisure activities and facilities; holidays; environmental issues: increased recreation can cause pollution damage to landscape and wildlife.
Soils and vegetation Different types of soil (clay soil, sandy soil, etc.); variation in soil particle size (i.e. structure); how water drains through soil; different types of natural vegetation (rain forest, deciduous, coniferous); beginnings of knowledge of natural vegetation zones (desert, polar, tropical rainforest).	**Settlement** Reasons for siting of settlements (often rooted in local history): ease of communication, types of economic activities found in a place (function), the way the place has grown (form), how the place is linked to nearby places.
	Towns and cities The difference between town centre and suburb (i.e. zones), the kinds of economic activities found in centres; travelling in towns and cities; growth of towns and cities.
Weather and climate What weather is (sun, rain snow, etc.); measuring and recording weather (temperature, wind, sunshine rain, air pressure, cloud cover); the water cycle; microclimates – how temperature, sunshine, etc. can vary according to site, e.g one side of a building compared to another; change in weather over the seasons; satellite images in TV weather forecasts showing weather systems; beginnings of the idea that different climates exist in different parts of the world.	**Transport** Types of transport, systems or networks of routes linking places, why people travel, when they travel, the relationship between time and distance (a short distance can take a long time to travel), the effect of transport systems on our environment, barriers to communication, e.g. mountains, river channels, 'no go' areas in playground.

geographical vocabulary is part of good practice in primary geography. It is possible to identify chains of vocabulary which relate to the content of geography, for example home – house/farm – village – estate – suburb – town – city – capital city – settlement. A seven-year-old would happily use 'home', 'house', 'farm', and maybe 'town' or 'village', but it would only be reasonable to expect an older junior to use 'settlement' in context instead of 'lots of houses grouped together to make a town or village'.

The word chains suggested in Figure 1.7 give an idea of the range of words which primary children should be familiar with by the time they leave. It is possible to ask juniors to come up with their own word chains based on geographical vocabulary – it generates much discussion in groups! Such lists are illustrative, not exhaustive. Vocabulary in National Curriculum geography programmes of study will be referred to in Chapter 2 and in the Glossary at the end of this book.

Summary

What, then, is good practice in teaching and learning geography in the primary school all about?

It comprises:

- Teaching and learning through key questions to build up conceptual development
- An awareness of the general content of physical and human geography and how the two interrelate
- Developing geographical skills
- Using the enquiry approach
- Integrating fieldwork throughout primary children's work as a skill and through the enquiry process
- Developing children's knowledge and use of geographical vocabulary
- Dealing openly and sensitively with issues, attitudes and values.

Progression, coherence and continuity in all these elements of primary school geography

Figure 1.7

Physical environment word chains	
Scenery	bank – mound – mount – hill – foothills – mountains
Slopes	flat/level – plain – gentle – steep – cliff
Rock	clay – sand – silt – grit – pebbles – stones – boulders
Wind	calm – breeze – gale – storm – hurricane
Precipitation	mist – fog – drizzle – rain – downpour – hail – snow
Water	puddle – pool – pond – lake/reservoir – sea – ocean
Vegetation	tree – copse/coppice – wood – forest

Human environment word chains	
Place of worship	shrine – chapel – church – cathedral/synagogue/mosque/temple
Shopping/Retailing	market stall – shop – market – department store – supermarket – shopping centre – hypermarket
Recreation	garden – playground – playing field – recreation ground – park – theme park – countryside park – National Park
Population	few – sparse – spread out – scattered – clustered – concentrated
Environmental quality	polluted – spoilt – damaged – uncared for – well looked after – well conserved

are essential, whether the subject area is taught as an aspect of a broad topic or project, or as a specific subject in its own right. It also assumes that the teacher's management and organisation skills are good enough to enable teaching and learning to take place in a variety of styles – class, group, individual, teacher-directed, child-organised, and so on.

Geography is a way of studying the world and its people as they are today. With good teaching practices, the obvious relevance and usefulness of the subject to the children should make it one of the more fascinating and motivating curricular areas.

National Curriculum geography is helping many primary teachers towards the first essential step in good teaching and learning of primary geography – recognition of what the subject is about and how it can illuminate primary education. Nevertheless, National Curriculum geography should be seen as a part, not the whole, of good practice in teaching and learning geography in the primary school, since it does not emphasise the importance of the enquiry process, first hand experience and fieldwork as much as teachers who really understand the subject would like. This book seeks to highlight those areas within the framework of the Statutory Order.

2

GEOGRAPHY IN THE NATIONAL CURRICULUM

The background

In their report *Aspects of Primary Education, the teaching and learning of history and geography* (1989), HMI stated that:

> "*Although there was some good work, overall standards in geography were not satisfactory.*"

When geography was good it included:

- A curriculum coordinator in post
- Being part of topic work that achieved a balance across subjects
- A collegial approach to curriculum development
- Clear aims and objectives
- Good quality discussion and questioning in the classroom
- Use of the local environment.

However HMI also highlighted many problems in primary geography teaching:

- Lack of physical geography
- Children often repeating topics
- Not enough use of atlases and globes
- Limited work on other places in the UK
- Little work beyond the local area
- Geography used to practise skills in English and art
- Few schools with a teacher responsible for geography
- No clear rationale for the choice of topics

- Little effective planning
- Not enough time allocated to the subject
- Curriculum often television-led
- Barely adequate resources
- Too many case studies
- Lack of continuity and progression.

This list paints a very dismal picture of primary geography. The introduction of the National Curriculum provides an opportunity to put many of these things right. It offers you a framework to build a curriculum for your school that gives geography its full status as a foundation subject within the total primary curriculum. This framework is designed to be flexible so that you can develop your own schemes of work, integrating geography, if applicable, with other subjects.

In the terms of reference given by the Secretary of State for Education to the National Curriculum Geography Working Group, it was stated that the following should be addressed:

- Skills, knowledge and understanding
- Developing a sense of place
- Understanding the relationship between places.

What the Order covers

The geography Order is divided into five attainment targets, each being divided into

11

ten levels of achievement in line with the National Curriculum documents. The attainment targets are:

Gg 1 Geographical skills

Gg 2 Knowledge and understanding of places

Gg 3 Physical geography

Gg 4 Human geography

Gg 5 Environmental geography.

Gg 3–5 are the 'theme' attainment targets.

In common with other National Curriculum subjects, you need to plan from and teach

Figure 2.1

An overview of National Curriculum coverage

KS1	KS2
Gg1: Skills • Enquiry, direct experience, local exploration, questions • Geographical vocabulary • Directional activities • Using maps and globes • Early map making • Picture interpretation, aerial photographs • Weather recording	**Gg1: Skills** • Fieldwork investigations • Enquiry based classroom investigations • Features of map drawing and interpretation • Air photographs, oblique and vertical • Collect and present field data • Use a wide range of instruments • Extract information from secondary sources • Plan small scale environments • Measure and record weather
Gg2: Places • School's locality – as a resource in its own right, as a contrast to other localities • Contrasting UK locality • Locality beyond UK • State where they live, name of home country, name UK countries • Locate home locality and name features on UK and world maps	**Gg2: Places** • Local area, levels 2, 3 and 4 • Home region, levels 4 and 5 • Contrasting locality in the UK, levels 2, 3 and 4 • Locality in an economically developing country, levels 2–5 • Locality in a European Community country, level 5 • Name features on maps A B C D, then E and F
Gg3: Physical geography • Rocks and soils • Seasonal weather patterns • World weather • Water in the environment, rain and run-off • Landscape features	**Gg3: Physical geography** • World weather and climate • Site conditions, effect on temperatures, wind and plant growth • Soil type • Simple landforms • Erosion, transportation, deposition and weathering • Earthquakes and volcanoes • Water run-off and river systems • Floods and flood control
Gg4: Human geography • Function of buildings • Diversity of settlement size • Function and origin of settlements • Moving home • Journeys, how and why • Types of transport • Variety of work • Local goods and services • Land use, small and large sites	**Gg4: Human geography** • Migration • Population density • Origin of settlements • Transport, links and terminals • Location of work • Land use, intensive/extensive • Conflicts over land use
Gg5: Environmental geography • Natural materials, how they are obtained • Effects of extraction • Personal likes and dislikes • Environmental change – describe an environmental improvement • Improving their own environment	**Gg5: Environmental geography** • Extraction of resources • Renewable and non-renewable resources • Water supply and pollution • Moral attitudes to exploitation • Likes and dislikes • Restoration and protection of environments • Participation in environmental improvements

the programmes of study (PoS) and assess the pupils against the attainment targets. Figure 2.1, drawn from the PoS, provides an overview of the areas of work covered by the geography Order and Figure 2.2 the geographical language used in the PoS. As you can see, the majority of these words are in common usage in the primary classroom, which illustrates the fact that geography is alive in many primary classrooms without being recognised as such. The list is not a complete one. There are other geographical words teachers and pupils will need to use beyond those in the PoS.

The Working Group intended that work on skills, places and themes should be integrated into units of work. When teaching about a specific location, for example, a range of skills should be used whilst dealing with an environmental issue in the area.

Gg 1: Geographical skills

"Pupils should demonstrate their ability to use skills to support work for the other attainment targets in geography and in particular: i) the use of maps; and ii) fieldwork techniques."

Geography in the National Curriculum, DES HMSO, 1991

Figure 2.2

Physical features	Climate and weather	Settlement	Transport	Economic activity	Locational words
Key stage 1 hill stream slope river lake sea waves land soil rock pond steep gentle beach valley mountain wood forest	**Key stage 1** season desert wind rain cloud frost ice storm weather spring summer autumn winter	**Key stage 1** house shop park settlement village town city building	**Key stage 1** road car pedestrian canal railway journey transport bridge tunnel	**Key stage 1** shops work jobs farm factory service quarry mine	**Key stage 1** map plan country area place position north south east west near/far left/right up/down
Key stage 2 source tributary mouth erosion weathering deposition floods environment moon tides vegetation relief landscape features volcano	**Key stage 2** temperature climate rainfall mist fog dew	**Key stage 2** population urban rural density port resort	**Key stage 2** routes barrier network system	**Key stage 2** industry manufacture raw material labour fuel/power energy market natural resources	**Key stage 2** latitude longitude grid reference distribution globe region

Geographical skills should not be taught in isolation but through attainment targets 2, 3, 4 and 5. In both key stage 1 and 2, the enquiry approach is emphasised, investigations both inside and outside the classroom, using primary and secondary sources. The skills are clearly set out in the programmes of study and non-statutory guidance.

Figure 2.3

Statements of attainment for Gg1: geographical skills organised into strands		
Attainment Levels		**The Use of Maps**
1	1(a)	follow directions
2	2(b)	make a representation of a real or imaginary place
	2(c)	follow a route using a plan
	2(e)	identify familiar features on photographs and pictures
3	3(a)	use letter/number coordinates to locate features on a map
	3(b)	use a large-scale map to locate their own position and features outside the classroom
	3(c)	make a map of a short route, showing features in the correct order
	3(d)	identify features on aerial photographs
4	4(a)	use four-figure coordinates to locate features on a map
	4(b)	measure the straight-line distance between two points on a plan
	4(c)	identify features on both a large-scale map and on a vertical air photograph of the same place
	4(e)	Use the index and content pages to find information in an atlas
	4(f)	draw a sketch map using symbols and a key
5	5(a)	use six-figure grid references to locate features on Ordnance Survey maps
	5(b)	interpret relief maps
	5(c)	follow a route on a 1:50 000 or 1:25 000 Ordnance Survey map and describe the features which would be seen
	5(d)	extract information from thematic maps which show distribution patterns
	5(e)	demonstrate an awareness that the globe can be represented as a flat surface
		Fieldwork Techniques
1	1(a)	follow directions
2	2(c)	follow a route using a plan
	2(d)	record weather observations made over a short period
3	3(b)	use a large-scale map to locate their own position and features outside the classroom
	3(c)	make a map of a short route showing features in the correct order
4	4(d)	measure and record weather using direct observation and simple equipment
5		(No statement)

The statements of attainment are shown in Figure 2.3.

Gg 2: Knowledge and understanding of places

"Pupils should demonstrate their increasing knowledge and understanding of places in the local, regional, national, international and global contexts, particularly:
i) a knowledge of places;
ii) an understanding of the distinctive features that give a place its identity;
iii) an understanding of the similarities and differences between places; and
iv) an understanding of the relationship between themes and issues in particular locations."

ibid.

The requirements for coverage are set out in Figures 2.4 and 2.5.

Figure 2.4

Localities, regions and countries to be covered in key stage 1 and 2					
Level	1	2	3	4	5
Localities:					
Local area	•	•Δ	•Δ	Δ	
Contrasting UK locality	•	•Δ	•Δ	Δ	
Locality beyond the UK	•	•	•		
Locality in an economically developing country		Δ	Δ	Δ	Δ
Locality in an European Community country outside the UK					Δ
Region:					
Home region				Δ	Δ

key stage 1 = •   key stage 2 = Δ

14

Figure 2.5

Coverage of Gg2: places	
key stage 1	**key stage 2**

key stage 1

Places
- Local area
- Contrasting locality in UK
- Locality beyond the UK
- Place knowledge maps A and C   *L 3*

Local area
- Identify familiar features, buildings and places
- Investigate places for work, leisure and services
- Know home address, countries of the UK

Other localities
- Identify similarities and differences with local area
- Investigate features, buildings, people and lifestyles

Level 3
- More precise descriptions of localities and explanations of the features, activities and lifestyles
- Patterns observed within and between localities

These locations should be used as the setting for teaching geographical skills, and the geographical themes of physical, human and environmental geography. Geographical study units should be designed using the key question approach and often deal with issues.

key stage 2

Places
- Local area   *L 2, 3, 4*
- Contrasting locality in UK   *L 2, 3, 4*
- Locality in an economically developing country *L 2, 3, 4, 5*
- Locality in an European community country outside UK *L 5*
- Home region   *L 4, 5*
- Place knowledge on maps A B C and D   *L 2, 3, 4*
- Place knowledge on maps E and F   *L 5*

Local area
- Land uses, buildings, features, economic and leisure activities
- Identify, describe and explain locations of the above

Home region
- Understand how locality links to region
- Main features – physical, settlements, occupation and routes

Level 5
- Add links between above features

Other localities
- Investigate and compare features, occupation and lifetsyles with the home locality
- Examine impact of landscape, weather and wealth on lifestyles
- Investigate recent and proposed changes resulting from human actions

Level 5
- Relate occupations, land use and settlement patterns to the area's environment and location.

Gg 3: Physical geography

"Pupils should demonstrate their increasing knowledge and understanding of:
i) weather and climate;
ii) rivers, river basins, seas and oceans
iii) landforms;
iv) animals, plants and soils."

ibid.

There are three strands to the physical geography attainment target. Figure 2.6 shows the elements within these strands.

Gg 4: Human geography

"Pupils should demonstrate their increasing knowledge and understanding of:
i) population;
ii) settlement;
iii) communications and movement; and
iv) economic activity – primary, secondary and tertiary."

ibid.

There are four strands to the human geography attainment target. Figure 2.7 shows the elements within these strands.

Figure 2.6

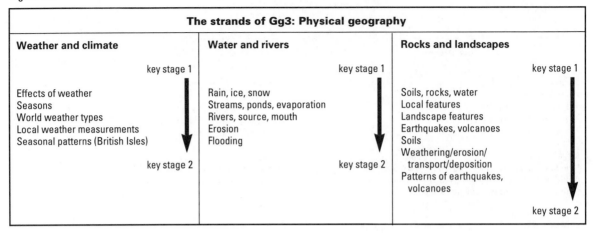

The strands of Gg3: Physical geography

Weather and climate	Water and rivers	Rocks and landscapes
key stage 1	key stage 1	key stage 1

Effects of weather
Seasons
World weather types
Local weather measurements
Seasonal patterns (British Isles)
	Rain, ice, snow
	Streams, ponds, evaporation
	Rivers, source, mouth
	Erosion
	Flooding
		Soils, rocks, water
		Local features
		Landscape features
		Earthquakes, volcanoes
		Soils
		Weathering/erosion/
		   transport/deposition
		Patterns of earthquakes,
		   volcanoes

key stage 2	key stage 2	key stage 2

Figure 2.7

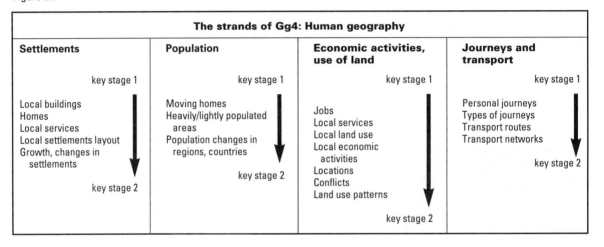

The strands of Gg4: Human geography

Settlements	Population	Economic activities, use of land	Journeys and transport
key stage 1	key stage 1	key stage 1	key stage 1

Local buildings
Homes
Local services
Local settlements layout
Growth, changes in
  settlements
	Moving homes
	Heavily/lightly populated
	  areas
	Population changes in
	  regions, countries
		Jobs
		Local services
		Local land use
		Local economic
		  activities
		Locations
		Conflicts
		Land use patterns
			Personal journeys
			Types of journeys
			Transport routes
			Transport networks

key stage 2	key stage 2	key stage 2	key stage 2

Gg 5: Environmental geography

"Pupils should demonstrate their increasing knowledge and understanding of:
i) the use and misuse of natural resources;
ii) the quality and vulnerability of different environments; and
iii) the possibilities for protecting and managing environments."

ibid.

There are two strands to the environmental geography attainment target: Figure 2.8 shows the elements that make up these strands.

Figure 2.8

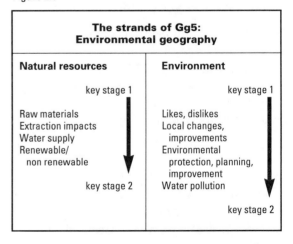

The strands of Gg5:
Environmental geography

Natural resources	Environment
key stage 1	key stage 1

Raw materials
Extraction impacts
Water supply
Renewable/
  non renewable
	Likes, dislikes
	Local changes,
	  improvements
	Environmental
	  protection, planning,
	  improvement
	Water pollution

key stage 2	key stage 2

3

PUTTING THE NATIONAL CURRICULUM INTO PRACTICE

Where to start

Even those primary teachers whom HMI might describe as good practitioners have been have been taken aback by the planning issues raised by the geography Statutory Order. Its framework is largely content-led. This makes the planning of geography quite restrictive, unlike other more process-led subjects such as English or technology. There is a continuum in the Orders for the attainment targets of particular National Curriculum subjects that looks like the one given in Figure 3.1.

The programmes of study and attainment targets for geography specify knowledge, skills and understanding, with a heavy emphasis on knowledge. For this reason, we stressed in Chapter 1 the need for a broader view of geography rather than the narrow view implicit in the Statutory Order.

Figure 3.1

```
National Curriculum subjects: the process-
                content continuum

Process  ━━━━━━━━━━━━━━➤ Content

English ATs                      geography ATs
technology ATs               science ATs
                         maths ATs
                    history ATs
```

Reassessing topic work

The introduction of the National Curriculum has already created a basic dilemma in primary school topic work, particularly with junior age pupils. The arrival of the geography and history Orders has compounded this. Worried teachers find themselves confronting a cluster of key questions:

'Is the National Curriculum telling us to teach subjects separately in a timetabled slot on a weekly basis?'

'How can we fit everything in?'

'Can geography and history fit in with my science topics already in place?'

'Do I have to teach all the statements of attainment in one year?'

'Can I focus on history, geography and science in successive terms of the school year?'

It is important to stress that, contrary to common belief, there is no legal requirement to deliver the National Curriculum in single subject units. However, it must be remembered that we are legally required to assess and report it on a subject-by-subject basis. There is a recommended time allocation for primary geography of 110 minutes per week. This can be regarded as an *aide-mémoire* when trying to balance topic planning, not as a requirement to timetable geography. Most teachers will want to continue topic work in some form because they are happy that pupils learn best in this way.

Nevertheless, we do have to plan topics with far greater rigour than previously, whether they are very broad ones which integrate many subjects or ones which have a single-subject focus. HMI has repeatedly argued for greater rigour in planning:

> *"The weakest work in primary schools occurs when too many aspects of different subjects are roped together within integrated themes or topic work … generally topic work is difficult to manage; frequently lacks coherence at the initial planning stage and consequently is a fragmented experience for the pupils. The most serious casualties of this practice are history and geography."*
>
> Standards in Education, 1988–9, Annual Report of the Chief HMI

Until the arrival of the science Statutory Order, the most common curriculum planning model was the topic web. The simplest type had a central starting point, which was brainstormed with unlimited choice, and therefore had unpredictable outcomes. More developed integrated topics had broad, umbrella titles such as 'Changes around us'.

Such models are ineffective for National Curriculum planning because:

- They cannot provide progression
- They cannot develop continuity across a key stage
- Incidental repetition is more likely over the years.

With the introduction of the science Statutory Order, attempts were made to keep and develop these models by relating existing planning to National Curriculum core subjects or attainment targets, often with science as the lead subject.

These interim models have functioned until the arrival of geography and history Statutory Orders but are no longer tenable because they cannot ensure progression in all subject areas, nor can they ensure full coverage of any one National Curriculum subject area. We are now seeing the development of two viable planning styles, especially for key stage 2:

1 Single-subject-focus topics which may have a broad, narrow or sharp focus
2 Multi-subject-focus topics.

Figure 3.2 explains these more fully.

Figure 3.2

Different ways of organising topic work at key stage 2

Single-subject focus
 	
Focuses on one National Curriculum subject only, e.g. geography
 	
Broad
   Based on a place, e.g. locality in an economically developing country, including physical, human and environmental strands
 	
Narrow (Running alongside other National Curriculum subject narrow themes)
   River system in a home region
 	
Sharp (Concentrated study of something for a short period of time)
   Designing a school trail for younger pupils to use
 	
Multi-subject focus
 	
Focuses on two or more National Curriculum subjects, e.g. geography/design technology or science/geography/ history
 	
Broad
   Topic which deals with water, drawing on PoS from science (water cycle), geography (water pollution, water supply, visit to a reservoir), English (role play about siting a reservoir), technology (designing a water wheel), maths (data handling of water usage figures)

Although it may appear simpler because more familiar, the multi-subject focus topic is difficult to work with. It has the same pitfalls as pre-National Curriculum integrated topic webs, even though there are now programmes of study and attainment targets to plan with. Deciding which of these are to be taught in which subjects becomes a major planning and record keeping task. The task becomes more manageable if the multi-subject topic is limited to two or three subjects.

The following points need to be addressed when planning all topics, whether or not they have a geographical focus:

- Programmes of study first and then attainment targets must be taken into account for most subjects
- Certain traditional topics will have to change
- Choice may be constrained
- Topic plans must become teaching tools and be adhered to in order to ensure full pupil entitlement
- Subject 'partners' in topics can change throughout the year
- Links between the statements of attainment of several subjects can be identified and taught through the same topic content, thus saving time, even though coverage must be separately recorded
- It is taken for granted that we can never totally isolate learning into one subject even in the single-subject focus approach; it is the rigour of focused planning that counts
- Provision must be made for continuity, progression and differentiation.

It is quite clear that total subject integration, if schools try to continue it, or multi-subject-focus topics, will be more manageable at key stage 1 than key stage 2, especially where geography and history are concerned. We are likely to have to limit the number of subjects we focus on in a topic as pupils become older. This is because of the constraining nature of the various subject Statutory Orders and the ways some programmes of study become more content-specific at key stage 2. Geography, in particular, becomes increasingly specific about the types of places to be studied at the higher levels (see Chapter 2, Figure 2.4). It seems that we can expect a pattern to emerge (see Figure 3.3), mixing and matching our approach to cover the whole National Curriculum across key stages 1 and 2.

Figure 3.3

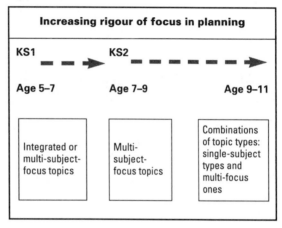

Planning needs to be equally rigorous at both key stages but the planning focus of both content and concepts of subjects will need to be more rigorous to ensure progression. Schools will need to consider topics of differing lengths. Two-, four- or six-week, half-term or even term-duration topics may be appropriate. In key stage 2 several topics may run alongside each other over the course of the year, depending on their focus, as shown in Figure 3.4 in a year's topic map.

Having reassessed topic work approaches, we next need to consider links with other learning areas.

Figure 3.4

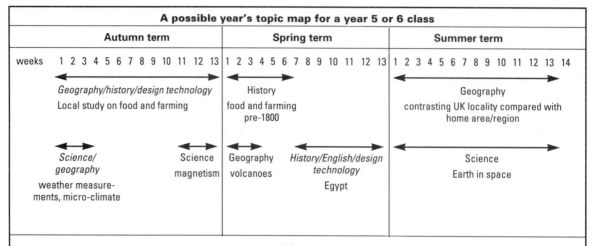

A possible year's topic map for a year 5 or 6 class		
Autumn term	**Spring term**	**Summer term**

It has been assumed that English, maths, art, PE, music and RE are also being considered within the topics or as discrete separate units.

Multi-subject-focus topic shown in italics

Working with other subjects

Geography is but one element of the whole curriculum. It would not be helpful for this book to imply that geography should be the centre of the curriculum. Instead, it seeks to explain the principles of geographical teaching and learning so that teachers can work with these and build geography into the whole curriculum. It is also recognised that there will be occasions when teachers may wish to deal solely with geographical work. The older the children, the more likely it is that this kind of focus will become sensible.

Before tackling the planning of key stages and breaking these down into units of study, we need first to understand exactly how geography links with other core and foundation subjects in order to make planning more manageable and learning more motivating. These links are outlined in the following section of this chapter. Links with cross-curricular themes can follow, and these are referred to in Chapter 11.

How can we work with science?

Geography is itself both a science and an arts subject, and is often described as the bridge between the two. Nevertheless, until the advent of the National Curriculum primary schools had tended not to exploit the strong links within this subject area. Much argument has ensued at secondary level about 'scientists hijacking physical geography', but fortunately at primary level we need only recognise the overlaps and capitalise on them. Non-statutory guidance for science recognises them in its advice on Earth Sciences in paragraph 3.6 and 4.0. These paragraphs should be read in conjunction with Gg3 and Gg5, Physical and Environmental Geography, and the related part of the programmes of study. This overlap is summarised in Figure 3.5 as applied to the new science ATs.

Both 'Weather' and 'Water' are frequently-studied primary topics. Using the focus of both geographical and scientific ideas and content, it is possible to plan high quality

Figure 3.5

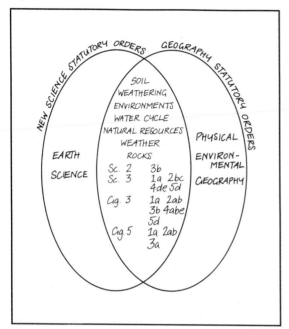

topics with these themes, as long as they are part of a key stage plan. One word of caution, however: as pointed out in Chapter 1, the content of geography relates to physical and human environments and the interaction between them. We must take care to emphasise the effect of humans on scientific processes in the environment, otherwise it is science that is being taught, not geography and science.

As well as key question overlap and content overlap between science and geography, the process of geographical enquiry is very similar to that of scientific investigation as required in Sc1. Thus active learning in both subjects is mutually reinforcing. It is important to recognise that the science/geography link is far stronger than the history/geography one!

Don't forget history partners!

Traditionally history has been the partner for geography. Links between the two have been very strong in the form of integrated humanities topics. However, sometimes the teacher's rationale for the history/geography link can be very tenuous and has resulted in a lack of clarity in the concepts which apply to the respective subject areas.

The history Order is more concept-led than the geography Order, although the history programmes of study specify content quite clearly. Because the history study units for key stage 2 and the contents of the geography order are both so prescribed, many primary schools no longer consider it realistic to link the two subjects at all. This is regrettable, as there are some areas where there are clear links which can produce excellent work so long as the concepts and skills relevant to the discrete programmes of study are recognised. Beware the incidental or spurious link: is a great deal of map drawing related to the history study unit on 'Invaders and Settlers' really the best context for developing mapwork and migration concepts for Gg1 and Gg4?

There is, however, one major area – local area work – where history and geography Statutory Orders do genuinely overlap, as Figure 3.6 illustrates.

Figure 3.6

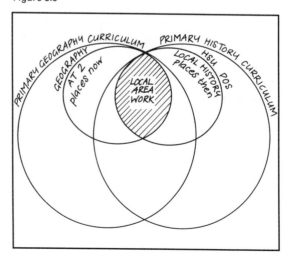

Figure 3.7

Key questions for geography local area and history supplementary study unit on local village/area of town/whole town	
Geography (now)	History (then)
Where is this place? What is it like now? Why is it like this? How is it changing? How can we find out about it now? What is it like to live there now?	Where is/was this place? What was it like in ...? Why was it like this? Why did it change? How can we find out what it was like then? What would it have been like to live there then?

Chapter 1 outlined the importance of the use of key questions in geography work. The same key questions can be asked in a different time context to motivate children to learn about the local area, present and past, as demonstrated by Figure 3.7.

It is important to notice the differing definitions of 'local' in the geography Order and the history Order. The 'local area' is defined as the immediate vicinity of the school or where the pupil lives; see p. 31 in *Geography in the National Curriculum*, DES HMSO, 1991. A local history study can also focus on 'a county or a region'. C25 paragraph 14.4 *History in the National Curriculum*, DES HMSO, 1991.

These key questions should naturally be applied to the model for the enquiry process noted in Chapter 1. The same process can be applied to investigations in history so that it is possible to collect data on past and present situations in the local area. This process enables the concepts of similarity and difference between now and then to be developed, as well as that of continuity and change in history.

Some of the core supplementary history study units in key stage 2 do lend themselves to a link with geography. Although there is a recommendation to teach the core study units in chronological order, this is not a requirement, so it is possible, on occasion, to relate the geography programmes of study at the required level to history unit work.

For example, a topic on Egypt could have a two-subject focus: 'Ancient Egypt' (Core Study Unit, history) and a locality study on modern Egypt (geography – an economically developing locality), which offers opportunities to identify similarities and differences and to compare past with present. 'Food and Farming' and 'Houses and Places of Worship' are Supplementary Study Units which also lend themselves especially well to a geographical link. The study of the theme over a long period of time as required by history may be stimulated by an investigation into current observation of farming and food production or an investigation of the type and use of local buildings. Design and technology can be made a third partner in such themes.

Other history Study Units such as 'Domestic life, families and childhood' and 'Writing and printing' are best kept quite separate from geographical learning. However, at key stage 1 it is easier to adopt a multi-subject-focus topic which can deal clearly with the history and geography Order requirements. For example, in a topic on 'Homes', pupils can start by talking about and drawing their homes today using geographical vocabulary, before they go on to ask questions such as, 'Is my house old or new?' or 'Have machines in my kitchen always been like this?' Similarly, an infant topic on transport may begin with how pupils travel to school, using graphs drawn from pupil data. Then pupils may draw a map of their mind's-eye route to school before going on to ask how their parents and grandparents travelled to school. This key question approach, endorsed by the Non-Statutory Guidance in history and geography is helpful at key stage 1, as well as key stage 2.

Mathematics and geography go hand in hand

Mathematics is indispensable to geography as a tool in the enquiry process. Good practice in both subjects enables pupils to work on their own, real-life data. Maths is essential in geography to:

- Collect data
- Record it
- Present it
- Interpret and analyse it.

The following examples relating to data collection in fieldwork and secondary source work should illustrate the point.

1 Fieldwork In order to meet the requirements of Gg1 level 4d, 'measure and record weather using direct observation and simple equipment', it is necessary to collect numerical data and represent it as a bar chart (rainfall) or a line graph (temperature). Pupils would then need to interpret the graphs to make judgements about the hottest part of the day or the wettest week of the period for which data was collected.

2 Secondary source work When using information in, for example, books, leaflets or posters on a locality in an economically developing country, an older pupil may need to sift through figures and statistics or a series of pie charts in order to answer the question 'How do people in this Indian village spend their day?' Having found such data, they then need to interpret it and present it in their own way, for example in percentage figures or as a summary in words.

The whole area of graphicacy skills in geography draws on maths. Indeed many of the examples in the mathematics Statutory Order used to illustrate the statements of attainment come straight from a geographical context, for example traffic surveys. Many concepts are shared by the two subjects at primary level:

- Distance
- Direction
- Area
- Links
- Networks (patterns)
- Shape
- Size
- Scale
- Time.

For older juniors, communicating facts about weather, climate, farming, industry and population through mathematical units and quantities lays the foundation for the description and analysis of these areas of content at the later secondary school level through the use of more complex statistics.

The maths ATs which need to be closely examined when planning geographical work are: Ma4, shape and space; Ma5, data handling; Ma1, using and applying mathematics.

HMI, in their report on the first year of National Curriculum mathematics, 1989–90, said that the AT concerned with using and applying maths received little attention. Geography can provide splendid opportunities to develop these maths skills. An analysis of maths schemes and textbooks will show a wealth of geographical maths exercises in isolation, as in the maths Statutory Order, for example traffic surveys, distance measuring, plan drawing, graph drawing. Sometimes it is appropriate to set pupils these isolated second-hand exercises for practice and reinforcement, but more often than not it can make sense to rationalise the maths scheme. Do this by omitting exercises which could be done in a geography enquiry context by using and applying maths within topic work. A common example is the over-used traffic survey. Pupils could predict the volume of traffic types they expect to pass the school within a certain period of time, then collect data in tally chart form, graph the results and compare their predictions. The geographical context for this exercise could be work on human geography and environmental issues in their local area.

As part of their school policy and in order to save time in an overloaded curriculum, maths and geography coordinators should:

- Analyse the school's maths scheme for geographical activities or exercises
- See how these might be better replaced or applied directly to first-hand data collection in geographical, scientific or historical work
- Take decisions about which exercises or activities to keep,omit or use as a reinforcement option

Figure 3.8

Direct maths/geography NC links	
Ma1,3c	Gg1, 2d
Ma1. 4b	Gg1, 3a
Ma2, 3e	Gg1, 4d
Ma4, 1b	Gg1, 1a
Ma4, 3c	KS1, PoS 3, Level 3
Ma4, 4b	Gg1, 4a
Ma5	All Ggs
Further examples of links between mathematics in the National Curriculum and geography may be found in the Appendix .	

- Take decisions about classroom management; for example, will some groups use the maths scheme activity rather than the real-life data in order to free the teacher to help the group working on their 'real' data?
- Make sure that pupils and parents are aware that important maths work is being done, even though it may not be 'in the maths book'.

Figure 3.8 indicates how many examples of maths work can be done in a geographical context, addressing statements of attainment in both subjects.

Geography as a medium for English

It is not possible to teach geography without using and improving central English skills. It would indeed be possible, although not desirable, to teach English at primary level solely in a geographical context using both language and literature. Listening, speaking, reading and writing are central to English and find a natural context in geography so long as we are aware of the requirements of both.

As with maths, a greater recognition of how we can develop English and geography simultaneously will save valuable teaching time and provide a more meaningful learning context for children. Figure 3.9 summarises how geographical activities help to develop work for the attainment targets in English.

Considerable emphasis will be placed on speaking and listening in geographical topics with infants, whereas it will tend to swing to reading and writing skills as the pupils grow older. Upper juniors should be dealing with higher order reading and writing skills using geographical texts. *Developing Tray* is a useful computer programme for developing English in a

Figure 3.9

Developing English through geography

En1 Speaking and listening

Speaking: describing photographs, describing postcards, talking about maps, using geographical vocabulary, giving instructions or directions, interviewing during fieldwork, role play to present an argument, answering geographical questions, asking/answering open-ended questions in a whole-class group, discussing in pairs or small groups, explaining geographical ideas.

Listening: teacher or peers reading a story based in a particular location or locations, factual information on television, radio programme, tape, etc. listening to a variety of speakers – peers, adults, in groupwork – listening to geographical ideas.

En2 Reading

Information from travel literature (advertisements, brochures, etc.), planning outlines, descriptions of places, descriptions of processes, descriptions of weather, encyclopedia and other classroom or library reference books, reading scheme books which are located in a particular place.

En3 Writing

Factual recall writing – descriptive, summarising, paraphrasing; creative writing – a story with a place base after studying a particular locality; analytical writing – explaining information gathered in fieldwork, note taking in fieldwork, note taking during television or radio programmes.

En4 Spelling

The use of geographical vocabulary where appropriate – focusing on the spelling and meaning of words currently being used connected with geography work, e.g. 'beach', 'cliff'.

En5 Handwriting

Geographical words and passages can be used to practise handwriting.

---

geographical context. Again, staff, parents and pupils need to be aware that English in a geography context is a valid medium for good practice in English teaching and can fulfil the English Statutory Order. Teachers can highlight this by:

- Explanation of the skills being developed
- Displays of work which pupils and/or teachers can label for subject-linked concepts and skills.

A word of warning about reading ages: most geographical textbooks and information books written prior to 1991 have a reading level suitable for literate, articulate juniors. This is a resource deficit and it is to be hoped that in the 1990s authors and publishers will address the reading-age issue, giving us texts suitable for infants and lower-reading-age juniors.

Geography and technology

Geography provides excellent opportunities for technology, particularly within the areas of artefacts, systems and environments.

Artefacts The weather aspects of Gg3 offer an ideal opportunity for children to design their own methods and equipment for recording weather measurements. Simple anemometers, weather vanes and barometers can be designed and used. Commercial ones can be used alongside or after these, or for evaluation purposes. We need to be aware of the criteria needed for such instruments to perform the task for which they are designed with reasonable accuracy. The variety of pupils' and teachers' books relating to the weather as well as the Geographical Association's *Geographical Work in Primary and Middle Schools* (ed. David Mills 1988) will help here.

Geography helps children apply what they are learning in design technology capability:

- Stressing the importance of technological developments in encouraging economic activity, explaining patterns in economic development
- Stressing that alternative technology is often more appropriate than grandiose solutions in developing localities; for example simple mechanical irrigation systems may damage the environment less and keep more villagers employed than a hydro-electric power scheme with an electronically controlled irrigation scheme.

Systems In explaining a process, geography uses the same concept as design technology capability. Processes can be broken down into systems with inputs and outputs. Input/output diagrams and flow charts can be studied and drawn by infants and juniors as an alternative way of showing information. For example, information about farming or factory processes which children may have studied at first hand through visits

or through secondary sources can be represented with inputs or outputs (Figure 3.10).

Environments Many geographical enquiries are directly transferable to technology, and statements of attainment from both Orders can be addressed simultaneously.

Many of the enquiry questions and focused statements in Chapter 1, Figure 1.2, could be developed to satisfy concepts of both subject areas, for example 'How can we improve our school grounds?' and 'Where is the best place to site the new flower beds we are going to design in our school grounds?'

It is, however, important to recognise that sometimes where links seem likely, the learning objectives need to be made explicit if the two sets of National Curriculum subject requirements are to be fulfilled simultaneously. In the example in Figure 3.11 from Technology Non-Statutory Guidance, the actual topic and its starting point activity sound as though they will aid work on several statements of attainment from Gg2, the local area, as well as some human and

Figure 3.10

The inputs and outputs of rum manufacture on the island of Martinique – an economically developing locality in the Caribbean

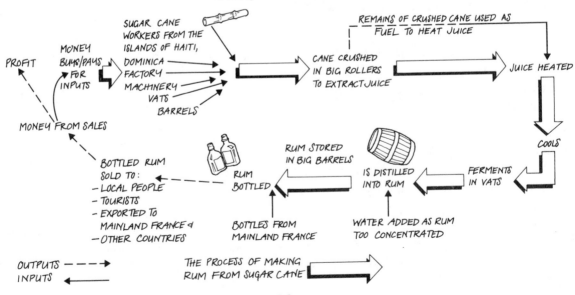

Figure 3.11

Example of topic linking geography and technology

Key stage 2

ENVIRONMENT THEME

Topic	Pupils in year 6 investigate the local environment
Activity	Groups of pupils visit a local harbour. They talk with people who work there, and investigate the activities which take place.
IT capability	Group 1 investigates the problems of craft manoeuvring in a congested port. Pupils learn about lighthouses and design and build a working model, controlled by computer. They find out about the sequences of flashing lights used by lighthouses, and use control LOGO to produce different sequences on their model.
	Group 2 considers safety. Pupils devise and make a computer-controlled swing bridge, with a siren to sound a warning.

Non-Statuory Guidance, Technology in the National Curriculum

environmental themes from Gg4 and Gg5. The suggested follow-up activities are largely unrelated to geographical work and focus very much on technology. It would be a wasted opportunity not to record and analyse the layout, work patterns and geographical issues relating to the local harbour visit as well as developing the technology aspect as stated.

Perhaps the most important link between geography and technology is the application of information technology as a tool throughout primary geography.

IT – the perfect tool

The information technology AT is different from any other AT because it does not deal with a body of knowledge, skills or a process but with the development of learning how to use information technology as a tool in other areas of the curriculum. It encourages the development of the problem-solving or enquiry approach to learning which is pertinent to geographical enquiry. It enables children to explore abstract ideas and test theories. It encourages group work and collaboration between pupils. IT can also help in the presentation of children's work leaving them to concentrate on the content. As with all skills, IT skills should not be practised in isolation but in concrete situations. Geography provides a perfect curriculum area to work in.

There are five strands of IT capability in Te5:

- Communicating information
- Handling information
- Modelling
- Measurement and control
- Evaluating applications and effects.

Communicating information This can be done in the form of pictures, words and numbers. It can be used to develop or revise ideas. It enables pupils to communicate with a wide range of audiences. This strand uses word processing packages, desktop publishing, electronic mail systems and graphic packages. All of these types of programs can be used within geography work.

Handling information This deals with storage retrieval, modification and presentation of data. It examines patterns and relationships in infomation and teaches pupils to access information from a variety of sources.

It uses database packages, spread sheets and remote databases. Geographical enquiry provides relevant data for the pupils to work with, making this type of work relevant to the pupils' curriculum, enabling them to store and manipulate information they have collected themselves. If IT is used to process, display and sort information collected by the pupils, more time will be available to question the data and test hypotheses.

Modelling Software is used to create real and imaginary situations for children to investigate. It uses simulations, adventure programs, spreadsheet and programming languages such as *Logo*. These can be used to investigate environments that cannot be investigated at first hand. Using map adventure programs and directional languages develops spatial awareness, mapping and directional work.

Measurement and control This involves using computers and electronic devices to collect data and control the environment. It uses data-logging devices, programmable toys and control software. Programmable toys help children to develop spatial awareness and practise their skills. Sensors can be used to collect data, for example soil temperatures, humidity or length of sunshine for analyis. Computers can be used to sense and record changes in the environment.

Evaluating applications and effects This encourages children to reflect on the role of IT and develop a balanced approach. By using IT for storing and retrieving information children will become aware of the implications for electronically stored data. They can look at IT around them to see the advantages and disadvantages and, within human geography, look at the effect of technology on employment patterns and everyday life.

Auditing current practice

Once you have a clear idea of the demands of National Curriculum geography and its links with other subjects, you can begin to plan how to deliver it in your school. In order to do this effectively you need to audit the current state of geography teaching and learning in school.

Decide first who will carry out the planning for the key stages. It could be:

- The headteacher and/or deputy
- The whole staff (especially in rural schools)
- A team of teachers
- A subject coordinator
- A coordinator and advisory teacher together.

Here it will be assumed that the planner is the geography coordinator.

Auditing involves the coordinator, head teacher and staff taking stock of:

- What geography is currently being done in which years (even though it may not be being taught under a geography label)
- Which geography skills are covered in which years
- What resources for geography already exist in school
- What methods of recording and assessment exist.

It has been said, quite rightly, that primary teachers are 'sick to death of auditing'. Yet it remains a useful activity which will enable you professionally to:

- Assess current practice
- Provide a way forward in the planning process
- Actually save time in the long run.

Auditing part of the current curriculum is rather like taking on a new class. A good teacher will want and expect to know what pupils have done before and what they should do next, so that continuity and progression can be maintained. In order to promote continuity and progression in learning geography, the same applies.

Guidelines for auditing

1 Use the photocopiable statements of attainment grid (see Figure A1, Appendix) as an audit of what geographical learning is already taking place. The grid can be used in two ways:

   a) Pass the grid to each member of staff in turn and ask them to examine their year's topics for geography or their year's specific geography teaching. They should tick off statements that they have worked towards with their pupils/groups of pupils. (In vertically grouped classes the teacher may prefer a separate grid for each age group.) Each member of staff should use a different colour or symbol to record. Alternatively copy the grid onto overhead projector transparencies and give one to each member of staff to tick as appropriate. Then overlay them and project to get an idea of strengths and weaknesses in any particular attainment targets and at any particular level. Yawning gaps will show up, as will areas of constant repetition and lack of progression. This exercise can then act as a guide to planning: the visual summary provided by the grid will indicate to staff and coordinators where they need to reassess and plan very carefully.

   b) The same process can be undertaken by individual teachers on a single topic they have taught, to establish how its content fulfils the Statutory Order at their pupils' relevant levels. The completed grid can then be used as a prompt to establish which parts of the programme of study and, therefore, statements of attainment, need to be planned for if the topic or unit of work is repeated.

2 Ask all staff to list current geography resources against the checklist in Appendix A2, compiled from the Statutory Orders, programmes of study and attainment targets. Decide which are lacking, prioritise them in order of need, balanced against budget availability.

3 Audit current record keeping and assessment systems for geographical work. (According to HMI and LEA inspectors, it is not unusual to find that they do not exist!) In order to ensure continuity and progression as well as to comply with legal teacher assessment requirements, they will need to be designed (see Chapter 6) if they do not already exist.

4 Examine sensitively with staff how much the key questions and the enquiry process are being used in geographical work to date. The answer could be 'not at all' – so bear them in mind during in-service work and when planning units of work (see Chapter 5).

5 Decide on the types of topic approach through which geography will be taught.

Having undertaken this exercise, you are now in a position to plan to meet the needs of National Curriculum geography.

4

PLANNING A KEY STAGE

Why plan key stages?

As there is a lot to be covered and a limited time in which to do it, the coverage of National Curriculum geography must be planned to avoid repetition and aid progression and continuity in the children's geographical experience. The Order for geography contains 93 statements of attainment to be covered in the primary key stages, 49 in key stage 1, levels 1 to 3 and 80 in key stage 2, levels 2 to 5. Some children may reach levels beyond those for their key stage, increasing the overall number of statements. So there is a correspondingly large programme of study to be covered. The five attainment targets and the programme of study are divided between the themes of physical, human and environmental geography, geographical skills and the knowledge of places. The formal assessment of National Curriculum geography will take the form of teacher assessment (SATs will be optional), so all the statements must be covered within the key stage plan at the correct levels. To work properly, teacher assessment will have to be ongoing throughout the key stages, with the appropriate record being kept and passed on (see Chapter 6).

Although content-led, the geography document was intended to give schools flexibility when planning their curriculum. You should be able to tailor-make a curriculum that fits your own school, building on current practice and any particular strengths you or your colleagues have.

There is no ruling on how long a unit of work must be, and a flexible approach to this helps to balance the topic or project element of the 'whole primary curriculum'. Schools must decide this for themselves. Obviously an in-depth study of the home region would take a term, but a look at the transport networks in the home region could be covered in four weeks, and the other elements of the home region taught at another time. In all the planning the authors have done themselves, a mixture of unit lengths has been found to work best. Consider units of any length between two and twelve weeks. Also, a mixed approach where subjects are taught separately and in an integrated way seems to produce the best results. A balanced approach to all the National Curriculum subjects is needed to give pupils their full entitlement curriculum. Flexibility helps to create a broad, balanced primary curriculum.

The attainment targets were not designed to be taught in isolation, from levels 1 to 5. Work at similar levels from different ATs should be drawn together when planning units of work. Figure 4.1 based on the cube – from the Interim Report – illustrates this.

Figure 4.1

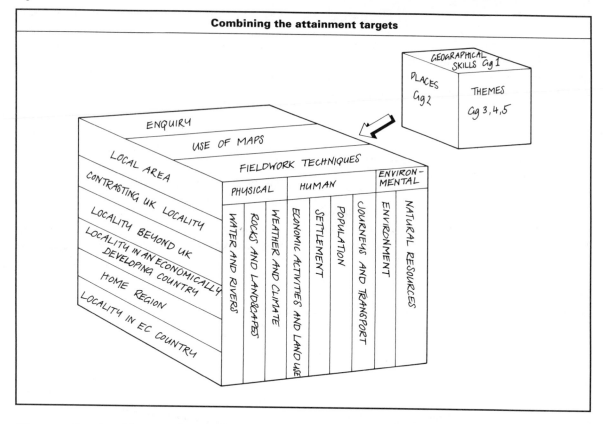

These units should provide a balance and breadth of geographical experience to the children, while allowing for progression, differentiation, different teaching and learning styles, school situations and pupil experiences, difficult as that might be! So physical and environmental geography can be taught together, or a unit may contain some elements of human, physical and environmental themes. These units can be set in the context of different places in Gg2, knowledge of places, to include those PoS which relate to the knowledge of places. Gg1 – skills – will be planned for all units.

Key stage planning helps schools to address these major issues :

Curricular issues
- Progression within the key stage
- Links with other subjects
- Balance of place, theme and issues within and between years
- Cross-curricular themes, dimensions and skills
- Opportunities for fieldwork
- Resources
- Continuity between KS1, KS2 and KS3
- Enquiry process.

School Issues
- Time allocation
- Subject-focused topics – broad, narrow or sharp
- Multi- subject-focused topics
- Pupil groupings, horizontal or vertical
- Staff expertise and commitments
- Policy for planning, long term and short term
- Subject budget
- Cross-phase liaison.

How to start

Planning a key stage is a logical process (see Figure 4.2). Having established aims and objectives and audited current practice, parts of the PoS can be clustered together and the units they make arranged across a key stage matrix.

When planning a key stage it does not matter whether you start with a theme, an issue or a place. The theme approach uses concepts to link the areas of the geography curriculum, for example Transport networks from Gg4 – human geography – includes the concepts of pattern, spatial awareness and location. Issues usually involve economic, social, environmental or political dimensions, with the children studying both sides of the issue. A places approach uses areas or regions as the focus for the study of geographical themes.

The enquiry process should be used within the units in whichever approach is used in the planning stage. These approaches combine to make a coherent curriculum.

There are various constraints that have to be considered when you start to plan the primary key stages. Key stage 1 spans two

Figure 4.2

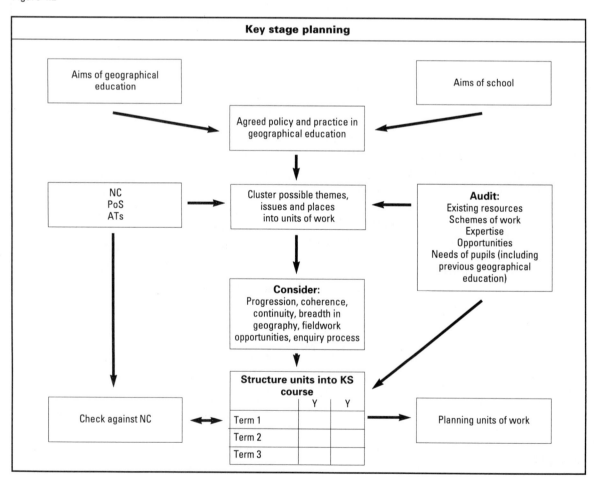

Figure 4.3

Key stage planning			
	key stage 1	key stage 2	
	R Y1–Y2	Y3–Y4	Y5–Y6
Gg2 The places fall into these stages of the key stage plan	Local area Contrasting locality in UK Locality beyond UK	Local area Contrasting UK locality Locality in economically developing country	Local area Home region Contrasting UK locality Locality in economically developing country Locality in EC country
The strands of **Gg1,3,4** and **5** are to be taught at all levels across both key stages	**Gg1** Use of maps: fieldwork techniques **Gg3** Water and rivers; rocks and landscapes; weather **Gg4** Economic activity; settlement; population; journeys and transport **Gg5** Environment; natural resources Vertically grouped classes will have to pay particular attention to Gg2		

years and key stage 2 four. It is easier for the purposes of planning to treat the six primary phase years as three blocks of two years each, Y1 and Y2, Y3 and Y4, Y5 and Y6 (see Figure 4.3).

This helps to balance the themes and places across the plan. Balance, breadth and places to be covered can be checked in the two-year blocks and it enables planners to fit everything in. This does not mean there are no geographical experiences for the children in their reception years; these should be ongoing (see Planning for key stage 1, below). Attainment target 2 defines certain areas or places to be studied at different levels (see Figure 2.4, Chapter 2). These constraints have to be taken into account when planning the key stage. They fit the two-year planning model (Figure 4.3). All the strands of attainment targets 3, 4 and 5 (see Figures 2.6, 2.7 and 2.8, Chapter 2) are taught at all levels across the two key stages. It is not necessary

to teach all of them at the same time. They should be taught across the key stage with a balance within each two-year section, for example the strand of water and rivers, Gg3:

Y1 and Y2   water in the environment
Y3 and Y4   local river study
Y5 and Y6   study River Thames, including erosion and deposition.

If your school has vertically grouped classes, this planning model can be adapted by planning a two-year rolling cycle. For example, in a vertically grouped infant department there could be an 'A' year plan and a 'B' year plan. All the classes would teach plan 'A' in the first year and plan 'B' in the second year. In a vertically grouped junior school it would be best to have two rolling plans, one for the lower juniors and one for the upper juniors.

If a school is organised with some vertical and some horizontal groupings, a strategy is

Figure 4.4

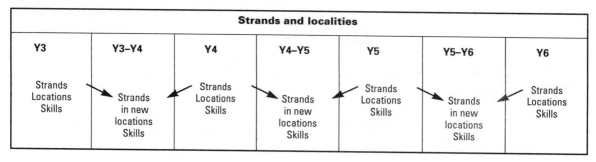

Strands and localities						
Y3	**Y3–Y4**	**Y4**	**Y4–Y5**	**Y5**	**Y5–Y6**	**Y6**
Strands Locations Skills	Strands in new locations Skills	Strands Locations Skills	Strands in new locations Skills	Strands Locations Skills	Strands in new locations Skills	Strands Locations Skills

to design a key stage plan on the two-year model (Figure 4.3) and add extra year plans for the vertically grouped classes. As your plans are mixtures of strands taught in locations, using skills, you can take the strands from the appropriate horizontally grouped classes and set them in a new locality (see Figure 4.4).

Planning for key stage 1

- Read the Planning check-list (Fig. 4.5).
- Make a set of cards and a matrix (see Figures 4.6, 4.7 and 4.8 for examples).
- Fill in any already agreed curriculum.
- Cut up the cards.
- Experiment in grouping them into units of work.
- Arrange the units over the matrix.
- Check for balance and breadth of geographical experience:
  — progression and continuity
  — fit within the whole primary curriculum
  — full coverage of the PoS.
- Cross reference with the PoS.
- Discuss with staff.
- Build in evaluation and review.

Before starting, refer to the key stage planning check list (Figure 4.5). This list raises 12 points of which planners should be aware and these points should also be referred to at the end of the process. For each key stage,

make a set of planning cards and a blank matrix to start planning on (see Figures 4.6, 4.7 and 4.8). It is easier if the matrix is enlarged to A3 size before starting. There are two versions of the matrix for key stage 1, one with a continuous experience for the

Figure 4.5

Key stage planning checklist

1 Agree the school aims, policies and practices for the teaching and learning of geography

2 Audit the established curriculum, existing resources, teaching expertise, fieldwork opportunities and pupil needs.

3 Make sure teachers have and understand the National Curriculum documents.

4 Plan the key stages with the aid of the planning cards, clustering themes, issues and places into possible units of work.

5 Build up units of work from the programmes of study.

6 Remember to balance human, physical and environmental geography.

7 Remember the principles of progression, continuity, coherence and breadth of geographical experience when planning.

8 Be aware of the time constraints on the primary curriculum.

9 Look for links with existing school practice, other subjects and cross-curricular themes.

10 Ensure that the key stage plan will support individual lesson plans.

11 Check the plan against the National Curriculum requirements to make sure of full coverage.

12 Within the school's development plan build in a time to evaluate and review the geography key stage plans.

Figure 4.6

Key stage 1 programme of study summary cards			
Local Area 'Classroom' Gg2	*Local area 'Local area' Gg2*	*Contrasting locality in UK Gg2*	*Locality beyond UK Gg2*
Local area 'Classroom' Gg2	*Local area 'Local area' Gg2*	*Contrasting locality in UK Gg2*	*Locality beyond UK Gg2*
Local area 'School grounds' Gg2	*Local area 'school' Gg2*	*Local area 'School grounds' Gg2*	*Local area 'School' Gg2*
Plans and maps Gg1	Plans and maps Gg1	Directional work Gg1	Directional work Gg1
Buildings Gg4	Settlement Gg4	Weather Gg3	Natural resources Gg5
Buildings Gg4	Settlement Gg4	Weather Gg3	Natural resources Gg5
Buildings Gg4	Settlement Gg4	Weather Gg3	Natural resources Gg5
Rocks & landscape features Gg3	Journeys Gg4	Goods, services , amenities Gg4	Changes in environment Gg5
Rocks & landscape features Gg3	Journeys Gg4	Goods, services, amenities Gg4	Changes in environment Gg5
Rocks & landscape features Gg3	Journeys Gg4	Goods, services, amenities Gg4	Changes in environment Gg5
NB Place cards in italics, remaining cards are theme cards			

Figure 4.7

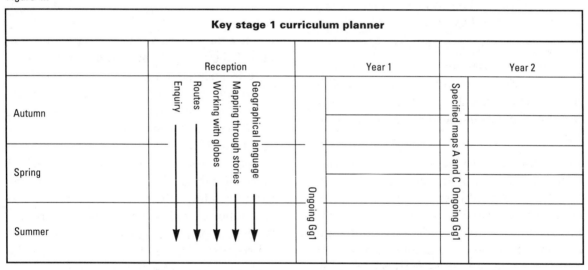

reception year and one to give the reception year units of study as in Y1 and Y2. If science is already in place as topics or units of work starting in the summer term for the reception year, then geography should do the same, with the continuous experience moving up into the autumn and summer terms only. As with all curriculum planning, do what suits your school best. An explanation of the continuous experience ideas can be found at the end of this section.

The theme cards have been drawn up from the appropriate programme of study and then cross-referenced back to the ATs for easy reference. The fact that there are three cards saying 'Weather', 'Journeys', and so on, does not mean that these strands have to be taught three times, but that they may well

Figure 4.8

Key stage 1 curriculum planner					
	Reception	Ongoing Gg1	Year 1	Specified maps A and C Ongoing Gg1	Year 2
Autumn					
Spring					
Summer					

occur more than once in a well-balanced plan. Cut up the boxes. Do not worry if you have some over when you have finished, but *a minimum of one of each must be used.*

The locality of the school has been split for planning purposes into four areas. Infants should work on the classroom, school buildings, school grounds and the surrounding locality. Planning is clearer if these are split up.

In pencil, write into the bottom of each half-term block on the matrix any agreed school curriculum content in either science or history. These may have to be modified slightly, but it is easier to take their position into account when you begin planning. Also, add any fixtures in the three-year cycle such as harvest work, Y2 seaside visit, Festival of Lights linked to a science project. Then cluster the places and themes on the matrix. As you combine them, remember you will look at more than one theme in a place, for example: school building – amenities and services – journeys.

One of the best ways of doing this is to use Blu-Tack® to position the cards on to the matrix. This means they can easily be moved as the plan develops, but will not accidentally be knocked off seconds before you finish. Check the key stage plan for balance of themes and breadth of locations; read it back against the PoS to see if any have been left out. If they have, change the emphasis of a unit to include them. The next step is to write out on a fresh matrix an outline of the unit for the teacher; the easiest way of doing this is to state the area to be studied and the PoS to be included in that half or full term. This gives teachers flexibility of approach in delivering the PoS to their classes, and they need to refer only to the appropriate PoS when they plan their units. The PoS can easily be annotated to make this task a lot simpler (see Figure 4.9). At this stage the draft plan should be discussed with the staff. These planned units of work will develop into a resource for the school (see Chapter 5).

No mention as yet has been made of the third dimension of the cube: skills (see Figure 4.1) in key stage planning. Geographical skills are on-going and taught progressively throughout the key stage. Once the context of Themes and Places has been selected, then the teacher can explore the appropriate skills for pupils to develop

Figure 4.9

according to level, from the PoS of Gg1. Mapwork, fieldwork and other essential skills are dealt with in Chapters 7, 8 and 10.

How to annotate programmes of study for key stages 1 and 2

Home region
10 Pupils should be taught:
(a) that their own locality can be considered as part of a region;
(b) the geographical features of the home region.
11 Pupils working towards level 5 should be taught:
(a) how the main features of the home region are inter-related.

Other localities
12 Pupils should study a contrasting locality in the UK and a locality in an economically developing country. They should be taught:
(a) to investigate features of other localities, for example, through looking at holiday postcards and photographs, and how these features might affect people's lives;
(b) to describe the features and occupations of the other localities studied and compare them with those of the local area;
(c) to identify and describe similarities and differences between their local area and other localities;
(d) how the localities studied have changed as a result of human actions;
(e) to investigate recent/proposed changes in a locality;
(f) to examine the impact of landscape, weather and wealth on the lives of people in a locality in an economically developing country.
13 Pupils working towards level 5 should be taught:
(a) how the occupations, land-use and settlement patterns of both a locality in an economically developing country and a locality in an EC country outside the UK are related to the areas' environment and location.

Physical geography
14 Pupils should be taught:
(a) to identify and describe landscape features, for example, a river, hill, valley, lake, beach, with which they are familiar;
(b) how site conditions can influence surface temperatures and affect wind speed and direction, and the effect of different surfaces and slopes on rainwater when it reaches the ground;
(c) the nature and effects of earthquakes and volcanic eruptions, and how the latter produce craters, cones and lava flows;
(d) to identify water in different forms;
(e) that rivers have sources, channels, tributaries, and mouths, that they receive water from a wide area, and that most eventually flow into a lake or the sea;
(f) that rivers, waves, winds and glaciers erode, transport and deposit materials;
(g) to recognise seasonal weather patterns;
(h) about weather conditions in different parts of the world, for example, in polar, temperate, tropical desert and tropical forest regions;
(i) to investigate and compare the colour, texture and organic content of different types of soil

Geography in the National Curriculum, DES HMSO, 1991

The continuous experience for the reception year

As children sometimes start in the reception class at different times, the work is very often arranged as a continuous experience rather than a set topic or as units of work . This approach builds on current infant practice and can continue on in a modified form into Y1 and Y2 alongside planned units of work, or as part of those units.

Geographical language Good infant practice includes a lot of vocabulary work, extending and clarifying children's use of words. There is no reason why a proportion of the words should not be geographical. Words such as 'right', 'left', 'up', 'over', 'road', 'path', 'sea', 'cloud', 'town', 'hill', 'river', 'map', 'shop' and 'factory' are all relevant geographical vocabulary and should be explained and used. If in a story, words such as 'forest' or 'cliffs' appear, it should be checked that the children know what the words mean. This check may be reinforced with the use of pictures of different forests and beaches. Classifying and sequencing are familiar reception activities. There is no reason why sorting cannot involve sorting geographical pictures, hot and cold countries, countryside and towns, hills and flat land, farms and shops. Postcards or pictures from magazines and travel brochures can be used. Large pictures of landscapes can be put up with three or four features clearly labelled. These become some of the words to be emphasised with the pupils that week. Sequencing from the largest to the smallest can be done with pictures, for example of a tree to a wood to a forest, or gravel to stones to rocks.

Mapping through stories This involves illustrating a story with a large map and the pupils moving the characters around the map as the story is told. Many infant books are suitable for this, for example:

- *Rosie's Walk*, by Pat Hutchins
- *Gerry's Seaside Journey*, by Michelle Cartlidge
- *Dino the Dinosaur and the Volcano*, Longman's Easystart Reader
- *Winnie the Pooh*, by A.A. Milne
- *Thomas the Tank Engine*, by Revd W. Awdry
- *The Great Round The World Balloon Race*, by Sue Scullard.

A large-scale map, if possible covered with tacky-backed plastic and mounted on card, can be beside the teacher; pictures of the characters, either drawn or coloured by the children or teacher, can be moved around the map as the story progresses. In primary schools a good design project for Y6 children is to read various suitable books and, in groups, design and draw the relevant maps and characters for the reception class to use. This is a good way of assessing Year 6 pupils' spatial awareness and map skills.

Working with globes Young children are fascinated by globes, and there are lots of activities they can do with them – Which colours are sea and land? Where are the hot countries? Where are the cold areas of the world? The new inflatable globes are very good for this age group, and a variety of sizes helps to begin the idea of scale. Children of this age group are used to playing with models such as cars, houses and trains, so why not the world? It provides a basis for the development of geographical language.

Routes An essential activity in the reception class is finding your way around your new environment – the classroom and the school and playground. Routes to various places can be talked through, walked in groups, in pairs with or without adults until the children are familiar with their surroundings. An extension of this is to have an old black or white board and paint on it a simple outline plan of the school. Whenever the class comes back from the library or hall, draw the route they have used on the plan, talking it through. This can be extended to a situation where a child comes back from taking a message and tries to draw the route on the plan.

Enquiry process Reception pupils are by nature very inquisitive, and this can be channelled into the enquiry process. The beginnings of this approach can be laid by developing simple activities, talking about:

- their likes and dislikes in the classroom
- what they think it would be like to live in a hot or cold country
- whether they live in a house or flat
- can they describe their home?

An example of a key stage plan

This plan (Figure 4.10) was developed using these materials; after the PoS had been checked for coverage the AT numbers were added for teacher reference. The plan was developed by the geography coordinator of Danson Primary School, Bexley. Some units will be taught in an integrated way, others as geography-focused units.

Planning for key stage 2

- Read the Planning check list.
- Look at the relevant key stage 1 plan.
- Make a set of cards and a matrix.
- Fill in any already agreed curriculum.
- Cut up the cards.
- Experiment in grouping them into units of work.

Figure 4.10

CURRICULUM PLANNER

Key Stage 1

	Reception	Year 1	Year 2
Autumn	Geographical Language →	**Locality of the School** Pos 15b GgS level 1/2. Routes, plans, pathways around the classroom and school. Sensory walk around school and grounds. Likes and dislikes of the school environment.	**Local Area: Buildings** Pos 9abc GgS2 level 1/2. Pos 13a 13e GgS4 level 1/2. Types and variety of buildings, shops, garages, churches, library. Uses of different buildings. Jobs related to buildings, work as in a library? etc.
	Mapping through stories →	**Locality outside the UK.** Pos 9c GgS2 level 1/2. Globe/map work linked to Christmas - cold waters in other lands. Lifestyle and weather of a particular locality, how they spend Christmas.	**Plan drawing + Environment** Pos 15c GgS5 level 1/2. Plan drawings of dolls house + furniture. Use overhead projector. Likes and dislikes of school and environment. Draw a plan of how they would change their playground, toilets etc.
	Working with globes →	**Locality of School; Weather** Pos 3h GgS1 level 2. Pos 11b d GgS3 level 1/2. Weather observations and recording. Water in different forms.	**Local Area: Journeys** Pos 13b d GgS4 level 1/2. Types of journeys you make and the different vehicles you use. How does food and goods get to the shops.
Spring	Routes →	**Locality of School; School community** Pos 13de GgS4 level 1/2. Services and amenities of school. Pupils who help us - dinner ladies, caretaker, secretary, nurse, teachers, parents, etc. Go round the school, look at amenities and put on a map.	Assess Places Pos 6abc GgS6 level 1/2. **Locality outside UK.** Pos 9de GgS2 level 1/2. Pos 12c GgS3 level 3. Pos 13c GgS4 level 1/2. Weather related to hot and cold regions of the world. Locating shade in Polar or desert region. How climate affects life style and settlements.
Summer	Enquiry →	**Contrasting UK Locality** Pos 11ac GgS3 level 1/2. Pos 15a GgS5 level 1/2. Pos 9c GgS2 level 1/2. Farm Visit - rural locality compared with the local area. Prepare what on a farm? Look at the animals. Farmers diary - what they are. Lifestyle of work and life style. Look at landscape features. Raw materials, rocks and soils etc. Wool, timber, etc.	**Contrasting UK Locality** Pos 9de GgS2 level 1/2. Pos 10c GgS2 level 3. Pos 12a GgS3 level 3. Field trip to seaside, rocks and landscape features. Compare and contrast homes and names with local area. eg. Caravans and chalets etc.
		Ongoing ATT	Specified Maps A & C / Ongoing ATT

39

Figure 4.11

Key stage 2 programme of study cards				
Local area L2 L3 L4	*Contrasting UK locality L2 L3 L4*	*Local area L2 L3 L4*	*Locality in an economically developing country L2 L3 L4 L5*	*Locality in an EC country (not UK) L5*
Gg3 Weather: L2 Recording effects on seasons L3 Comparison of weather types L4 Weather measurement L5 Weather/Climate British Isles **Gg3 Weather**	**Contrasting UK locality L2 L3 L4** **Gg3 Erosion/Transport/ Deposition** L4 by water, wind and ice	**Gg3 Volcanoes and earthquakes:** L4 Formation and effect L5 Global pattern	*Locality in an economically developing country L2 L3 L4 L5* **Gg4 Goods and services** L2 Provision	*L4 L5* **Home region** **Gg3 Soils** L4 Investigate/compare
Gg3 Landscape L3 Landform recognition	**Gg3 Rivers** L3 Identification rain on slopes/surfaces L4 Features of a river L5 Flooding **Gg3 Rivers**	**Gg4 Settlement** L2 Size L3 Function, origin and features L4 Form, function and change L5 Location and growth **Gg4 Settlement**	**Gg4 Journeys and transport** L2 Journeys of different length L3 Types of transport L4 Different routes L5 Networks and changes **Gg4 Journey and transport**	**Gg3 Weathering and erosion** L5 Effects of weathering and erosion, differences between weathering and erosion
Gg4 Population L3 Reasons for moving home L4 Reason for different population sizes L5 Population changes, region/countries **Gg4 Population**	**Gg4 Land use** L2 Describe local area L3 Different types L4 Location and conflict L5 Explanations **Gg4 land use**	**Gg5 Environment** L2 Identify change L3 Local improvements L4 Restoration **Gg5 Environment**	**Gg5 Natural resources** L2 Extraction L3 Results of extraction definitions of resource L5 Renewable/non-renewable **Gg5 Natural resources**	**Gg5 Water as a resource** L4 Fresh water supply L5 Pollution

NB Place cards in italics, remaining cards are theme cards

- Arrange the units over the matrix.
- Check for balance and breadth of geographical experience:
  - progression and continuity
  - fit within the whole primary curriculum
  - full coverage of the PoS.
- Cross-reference with the PoS.
- Discuss with staff.
- Build in evaluation and review.

If possible, look at the key stage 1 plan to find what the children will have previously experienced. In junior schools with a wide catchment area this may not be possible, but some contact between postholders, subject coordinators or heads helps to aid continuity and stop repetition. Make a set of planning cards and an A3-sized blank matrix on which to start planning (see Figures 4.11 and 4.12). Cut out the cards. The cards show a summary of the PoS and the levels at which they have to be taught. They are cross-referenced to the ATs and the strands. Some of the cards are referenced at the top and the bottom, so they can be cut in half. This is

Figure 4.12

Key Stage 2 curriculum planner							
	Year 3		Year 4		Year 5		Year 6
Autumn	Gg1 skills ongoing		Gg1 skills ongoing		Gg1 skills ongoing		Gg1 skills ongoing
Spring							
Summer							

because they cover a wide range of levels and it is best to plan the work so that levels 2 and 3 can be taught in the two-year block of Y3 and Y4 (see Figure 4.3) and levels 3, 4 and 5 in Y5 and Y6. When planning the units of work, this grouping of levels will aid differentiation in classroom teaching. Fill in any already agreed curriculum at the bottom of the half-termly or termly boxes as an *aide-mémoire*. Changes might have to be made, but the fewer the better. The aim must be to create a balanced whole primary curriculum. Experiment with clustering the places, themes and issues into units of work. Remember the links with other subjects, fieldwork opportunities, resources, cross curricular issues and themes. It's a lot to cope with, but well worth it!

To plan for full coverage of National Curriculum geography, every statement in every box needs to be used; to enable planning to revisit ATs at different levels and in different combinations, you might need an extra copy of some boxes. Build up the key stage plan, checking each two-year block for a broad, balanced curriculum, making sure that the correct places from Gg2 have been covered (see Figure 4.3). In the Orders there is an emphasis on physical geography at levels 4 and 5. Allowance will have to be made for this when planning for Y5 and Y6. When the plan is completed check the proposed units against the PoS to ensure full coverage. If the document is cross-referenced when teachers come to plan their units, they will know exactly what the planners meant them to cover. At this stage it is good management to discuss the plan with the staff. It is best to clear up now any feature that has been overlooked, or a section that is not clear.

Geographical skills are on-going and taught progressively throughout the key stage. Once the context of Themes and Places has been selected the teacher can then explore the appropriate skills for pupils to develop according to level, from the PoS of Gg1.

Figure 4.13

Mrs G. Hunt
Darison Primary School

Curriculum Planner

Key Stage 2

		Year 3	Year 4	Year 5	Year 6
AUTUMN	ONGOING SKILLS AT1	Schools locality Land use Pos 16e Gg4 L2 Environment Identify change Pos 18d Gg5 L2b Local improvements Gg55 L2c Local Area: Natural Resources Locality Pos 9ab Gg5 2 L2a b 3e Extraction of resources Pos 18 ab d Gg5 L2a 3ab	Locality in Economically Developing Country: India Locality study: Chembakolli; Compare and contrast local needs and life styles. Pos 12a c e f Gg 2 Weather – how it affects people living effects of seasons Pos 14g Gg32a Comparison types Pos 14h Gg3&3a landscape features of India landform Meaghalaya Pos 14a Gg3&3c Rivers Pos 14 b d Gg3 L2b 3b	Schools locality: Weather Atlas work graphs + charts Pos 14b measurement Gg3 L4a Pos 15e weather Gg3 L5a Pos 15d British Isles Gg3 L5b Locality in E.C.: Holland Lifestyle and link with land school Pos 12 a b c d e f 13c land reclamation Gg 2 L4b occupations/land use settlement related to environment and location Gg2 L5c	Locality in Economically Developing Country – Brazil family life Pos 12 a b d f Gg5 2 L4 Population Pos 17a c 13a Gg54 L5a landuse Pos 16h Gg4 L4d location/conflict – Maximiza growth L5c Environment – Brazil Protection of rainforests Pos 18e 19ab protection of environments Gg55 L4b Motivation 4c 5a 5b pollution Renewable/non renewable resources
SPRING	ONGOING SKILLS AT1	Mapping Skills Plan drawings, mapping skills co-ordinates using a compass Transport, island maps, Atlas skills, Aerial photographs. IT Lego – Maq venue Sound and movement maps noise pollution maps Pos 3a b c d e f g h j Gg1 2b c e 3a b c d Assessment of maps A and C levels 1 and 2	Locality of school: Landuse Field work, map landuse, housing industrial, recreational and commercial. Pos 16h Gg4 L 3d 4e Shaping in the local area Pos 16g h + Economic + Industrial understanding Different types of shops why do we need local shops? Hierarchy of shops	Thames Study: Home region Pos 14e features of a river Gg3 L4c Gg3 L5c river flooding Gg3 L4b visit to Thames Barrier Water Fresh water supply in the region Pos 18c Gg5 L4e Assessment maps B/b topic assessment L3	Settlement: Whole of GB. Look at settlement patterns of GB mapping skills/place names for origin Pos 16a c 17c form function + change Gg54 3a 4ab location and growth Gg4 5b Volcanoes Global Pos 14 c 15b Volcanoes and earthquakes formation + effect Gg3 L4 Global pattern Gg3 5e Asset Assessment L3h Maps Atlas L5
SUMMER	ONGOING SKILLS AT1	Schools Locality Field work in local area using large scale maps Physical features in relation to man-made features Pos 9ac Gg3 2 3c 3f Transport Journeys of different lengths Gg4 L2b Types of transport Gg4 L3c Graph + map l want journeys of children.	Contrasting UK locality: Lake District Locality study Pos 12 b cde Gg2 Landscape features Settlement Pos 16e f Gg4 L2a 3b Transport links Pos 16d Gg 4 Environmental issues – protection planning and land use Pos 16h	Home Region: Physical Own locality as part of a region, main geographical features. Pos 10a b Gg2 L5b Pos 11a Gg4 L4d Home Region: Transport different routes Pos 16d Gg54 L4d networks + change Pos 17b Gg54 L5a Region Landuse patterns Pos 17a c Gg4 L5e	Contrasting UK locality: Isle of Wight field trip. Locality study Pos 12 abc Gg2 Compare and contrast Erosion, transport + deposition Pos 14f Weathering and erosion Pos 15a Gg3 5d 4b Gg3 4e Soil types Pos 14i Gg3 4e

The units of work can then be planned: a method for doing this is explained in Chapter 5. They do not all have to be planned at once, but as needed throughout the year. A review and evaluation of the key stage plan needs to be built in to the school development plan, so that amendments can be made where necessary. The units should be evaluated on completion and any changes noted. Revised units can be tried in the next year. The key stage plan should be evaluated at the end of a two-year cycle and amended as necessary.

For an example of a key stage 2 plan developed using this method, see Figure 4.13.

From plan to units of work

The next step is to turn the key stage plan into units of work, which can be called topics, projects, study units or whatever term the school uses. This is the move from long-term planning into medium-term planning, producing the units the teachers will actually teach at a given time. If, as was suggested earlier, the key stage plan has been checked against the programme of study to ensure full coverage and the references noted, this task is easier for the teacher. They will know which programmes of study they have to include in each unit. They can read the appropriate ones, look for links within the whole primary curriculum and turn these into a unit of work to suit their class and their own teaching style (see Chapter 5, Planning Units of Work).

Key stage planning check-list

1   Agree the school aims, policies and practices for the teaching and learning of geography.
2   Audit the established curriculum, existing resources, teaching expertise, fieldwork opportunities and pupils' needs.
3   Make sure teachers have and understand the National Curriculum documents.
4   Plan the key stages with the aid of the planning cards, clustering themes, issues and places into possible units of work.
5   Build up units of work from the programmes of study.
6   Remember to balance human, physical and environmental geography.
7   Remember the principles of progression, continuity, coherence and breadth of geographical experience when planning for geography.
8   Be aware of the time constraints on the primary curriculum.
9   Look for links with existing school practice, other subjects and cross-curricular themes.
10 Ensure that the key stage plan will support individual lesson plans.
11 Check the plan against the National Curriculum requirements to make sure of full coverage.
12 Within the school development plan, build in a time to evaluate and review the geography key stage plans.

5

PLANNING UNITS OF WORK

Introduction

Every school should teach geography within a framework which ensures clear progression. Whether you call the geographical element of work a topic, project, study unit or integrated studies, it has to be planned. For the purposes of this chapter, we will use the term 'unit of work'. The length of a unit is best defined for official requirements in terms of hours taken, but this must not become a constraint. The same results can be achieved by a class working for one morning and three afternoons a week for two weeks, as by a class working one afternoon a week for eight weeks. A flexible approach to which subjects should, or could, be taught with geography should be considered when planning units (see Chapter 3).

The medium-term planning of units of work is the next step. You will have been given various PoS to be covered in a term, half-term or year, and it is up to you to decide how best to turn those PoS into units of work which suit your class and your own personal teaching style. Look at the whole primary curriculum for the term or half-term and decide how much integration with other subjects is desirable or possible. Remember to think about the cross curricular themes of environmental education, health education, economic and industrial understanding,

citizenship and careers education as well (see Chapter 11). The amount of integration will vary over the year depending on the structure of the science, history and technology key stage plans. To a lesser or greater degree the links with maths and English will always be there. It is worth stressing that variety in the duration and depth of units of work and the integration of geography with different subjects at different times should lead to a broad, balanced primary curriculum. You may wish to teach:

- Termly units
- Half term units
- Short focused units of a few weeks
- A broad unit of work incorporating all subjects
- A technology and history unit alongside a science and geography one
- An integrated history and geography unit with a science unit running parallel
- Three separate units running parallel or in succession.
- Any other combination that fits with your circumstances.

Your decision must be guided by school policy and the fact that different teachers work best in different ways. The nature of your class and the school's long-term plans will also lead to work being developed in different ways. The focus-planning approach described here can be used for individual subjects or for integrated planning. It provides the head, coordinator or school with a copy of the medium-term planning related to the National Curriculum and assessment. It also provides the teacher with a working document to use throughout the unit of work as a lesson planner and, at the end of the unit, it can be used to evaluate – thus saving everybody's time. This focus-planning approach can be used equally well for history, science or technology. It is often easier for teachers if the same planning format is used for all these subjects within a school.

Beware if you have just been given a list of topic or unit titles to cover over the year. It is possible to teach familiar titles such as 'My Home', 'Houses', 'Underground', and so on, without teaching the PoS required by National Curriculum geography. It is very comfortable to see favourite topic names and you could be excused for feeling that it is alright to carry on teaching them in the way you always have. But, if you do it is likely you will teach without covering any of the PoS or SoA. So, when you have to assess the pupils' work for teacher assessment, you will be unable to record any achievement. A lot of work will have been done by both pupil and teacher, but it will not be relevant to the National Curriculum or geography itself. It is only through working from the PoS and identifying clear learning objectives that National Curriculum geography can be delivered. Titles can be reused, but the content of the unit must be directly linked to the PoS and, through them, to National Curriculum assessment.

Planning the achievable

Time is the most precious commodity in the primary classroom; by planning only that which you can achieve, you save time. The 'topic web' approach to planning, which was based on brain storming around a title or theme, generated lots of work and activity in many areas of the curriculum which was integrated to a greater or lesser degree. You then taught as much of this as you were capable of in the time available. This often led to a sense of frustration 'I never got round to …', or 'I wish I had time to do …', or 'How can I fit geography in to this?' The web-planning approach often involved the preparation of a list of content or general approaches with no reference to concepts, skills and knowledge. Topics were often unfocused and the potential was there for them to become more complex as more National Curriculum subjects came on line. Within the National Curriculum we have to be much clearer in our thinking as to what we need to teach, when, and the skills the pupils will require to be able to do it (see Figure 5.1).

Your starting point is the PoS you have been asked to deliver. Read them through and see how you think they will best fit together to make a coherent unit of work. Then try to focus the main ideas from the PoS into questions. By using the enquiry approach you

Figure 5.1

Sequence for planning units of work	
PoS	Read the PoS required to be taught.
Questions	Formulate focus questions targeted to PoS.
Tasks	Devise pupil tasks to encourage and produce evidence of pupil understanding.
Resources	Make a note of the resources you have and any you need to collect.
ATs and PoS	Cross-reference the unit to ATs and PoS for easier record keeping.
Links	Add any cross-curricular links and any link to the cross-curricular themes.

will raise questions which will lead the learning process. The children's completed tasks will produce evidence to show you whether they understand the concepts and knowledge and have mastered the skills necessary. This means that the children's completed units of work can be used for assessment purposes; assessment does not have to be tacked on to the end of every unit (see Chapter 6). Figure 5.2 gives some examples of focus questions for various key stage 1 and 2 units of work. These are by no means the only questions you could use for these units. Remember to plan only what you can achieve in the time you have: you may only be able to cover four to six questions in half a term or six to ten questions in a full term. Make allowances for a short calendar term or for Christmas taking time from the term. With experience you will get to know the amount of work and time needed: it could take a couple of weeks' work to answer one question, whereas another could be answered in half an hour.

Think about the tasks you will ask the pupils to do:

- Will they be working in groups, alone or as a class?
- What do you expect the outcomes to be?
- How will you teach?

Figure 5.2

Focus questions for grid planning

People who help us KS1

Who works in our school?
Where do they work?
Can you list what they do for us?
How many people visit the school as part of their work?
How often do they come?

Seaside KS1

How is the seaside different from your own local area?
What is the land shaped like at the seaside?
Do you know any special words to describe the land at the seaside?
What buildings do you see at the seaside?
Can you design a coastal landscape?
Do people damage the seaside?

Our area KS2

What is the land used for in our area?
How can we map the land use?
Is it mainly residential, commercial, recreational or industrial?
Can you see a pattern in the land use?
When did the settlement in our area develop?
What type of settlement is it?
Is there a pattern to the settlement?

Chembakolli (India) KS2

Where is India and how big is it?
Do all parts of India have the same weather?
What are the main landscape features of India?
Where is Chembakolli?
What do the photos tell us about life in Chembakolli?
What happens during one day in Chembakolli village?
What might happen during one day in our local area?
What is the weather like in Chembakolli?
How does the weather affect peoples' life in Chembakolli?
How does Chembakolli compare with our local area?
What ten things would you send to Chembakolli to tell them about our area?

What transport links does our area have? KS2

How many different types of transport are there in the area?
Who or what uses different types of transport?
Where do the transport networks go and why?
Is there a pattern to the networks?
Are the transport networks changing?

River Thames KS2

Where does the River Thames start and finish?
What are the Thames' vital statistics?
As you travel along the Thames from W to E what changes would you see?
How can the River Thames affect people's lives?
Do people have an effect on the river Thames?
How and where can you get to the other side?

Journeys KS1

What is a journey?
Where do we make journeys to?
How do we make journeys?
How many journeys do we make in a week?
What long journeys have you made?

- What resources do you need/do you have?
- How will you differentiate – by task, teacher intervention or outcome?
- How will you deal with children who have special needs?

Remember, as you decide what tasks the children will do, to build in assessment. There is no time in the primary curriculum to assess the children at the end of a topic. They need to be assessed on the work they do during the unit (see Chapter 6). If the tasks are targeted towards the programme of study and through them towards the statements of attainment, then evidence of achievement will be available for you to use for teacher assessment. It is possible when using a whole unit of work to achieve differentiated assessment, with one pupil activity showing achievement at two or three levels (see Chapter 6).

Fill in the resources column on the unit plan, listing both what you know is available and what you will need. You will not need to assess all the tasks for key stage assessment, so state in the assessment column those you

need to assess and how you will assess them(see Chapter 6). Cross reference the unit by putting the PoS, ATs and levels in the correct columns: this makes record-keeping at the end of the unit a lot quicker.

Note any cross-curricular links in the appropriate column, unless you are designing an integrated unit, when they will be shown. Also make reference here to any links with the cross-curricular themes of environmental education, health education, economic and industrial understanding, citizenship, careers and work education.

Unit planning grids

Two examples of blank planning grids are shown in Figures 5.3 and 5.4. These grid plans will help you to focus your planning and develop classroom tasks that are targeted towards the National Curriculum. There are many forms of these grids, but the annotated one (Figure 5.5) is the one the authors have found most useful for unit planning in key stages 1 and 2.

Figure 5.3

Unit planner						
Theme .... Key idea .... Class						
Focus questions	Tasks	Resources	Assessment	PoS	AT	Cross-curricular links

Figure 5.4

Unit planner					
Title of unit .... Year .... Length					
Cross curricular elements					
Key questions	**Learning objectives** Concepts Skills Content including differentiation	**Pos and ATs**	**Pupil activities**	**Assessment objectives and tasks**	**Resources**

Some examples of completed grids are shown in Figures 5.6 and 5.7. The completed grids show examples of planned units of work for both key stages. They are not the only way of tackling these units, just one way, using an enquiry-based approach.

Differentiation

Differentiation is central to the process of learning and assessment. It should be built into the units when you are planning the children's tasks. It may be by task or outcome. All children learn at different rates, in different ways and to different levels of achievement. The fact that they need to be given equal opportunities to achieve must, however, be kept in mind when planning their tasks. We need to offer the children tasks where they can demonstrate their progress. When planning units of work the relationship between the task and the focus question is important because that targets the children's work directly to the National

Curriculum. The levels and types of differentiation are equally important for positive pupil achievement and equal access to learning experiences.

Differentiation by task is where pupils working on the same section of a unit of work are given different tasks. These tasks may require different levels of support and resources. This type of differentiation can also involve a series of structured or stepped tasks; these are usually open-ended and children can progress through them.

Differentiation by outcome is where pupils are involved in the same task; the work they produce indicates their level of achievement.

This example shows differentiation by task and outcome in a local area study, looking at the form and function of the settlement. This unit included work from Gg1, 2, and 4. The mixed-age-group class of seven- to nine-year-olds was going to a local viewpoint, a hill in their rural locality. The class worked in three ability groups.

Figure 5.5

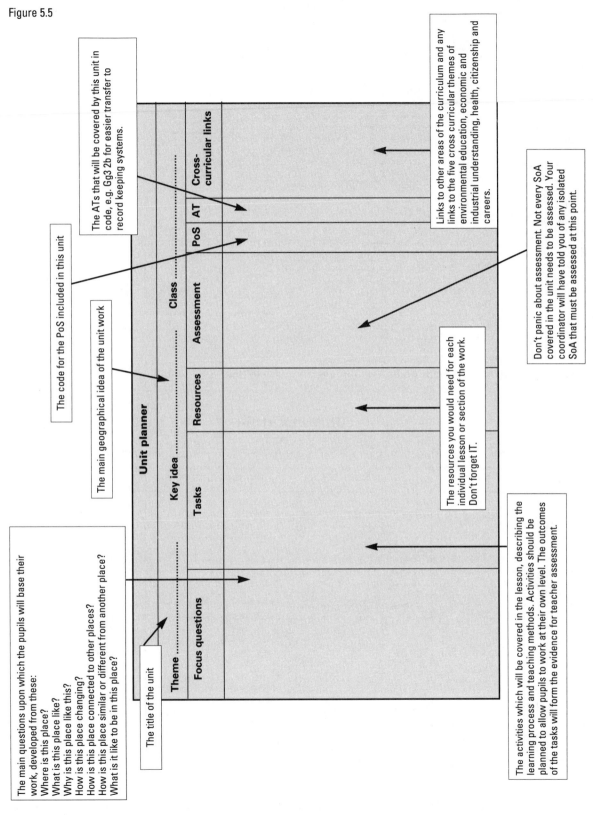

The main questions upon which the pupils will base their work, developed from these:
Where is this place?
What is this place like?
Why is this place like this?
How is this place changing?
How is this place connected to other places?
How is this place similar or different from another place?
What is it like to be in this place?

The title of the unit

The code for the PoS included in this unit

The main geographical idea of the unit work

The ATs that will be covered by this unit in code, e.g. Gg3 2b for easier transfer to record keeping systems.

Links to other areas of the curriculum and any links to the five cross curricular themes of environmental education, economic and industrial understanding, health, citizenship and careers.

Don't panic about assessment. Not every SoA covered in the unit needs to be assessed. Your coordinator will have told you of any isolated SoA that must be assessed at this point.

The resources you would need for each individual lesson or section of the work. Don't forget IT.

The activities which will be covered in the lesson, describing the learning process and teaching methods. Activities should be planned to allow pupils to work at their own level. The outcomes of the tasks will form the evidence for teacher assessment.

Unit planner

Theme ....   Key idea ....   Class ....

Focus questions	Tasks	Resources	Assessment	PoS	AT	Cross-curricular links

49

Figure 5.6

UNIT PLANNER

Key Stage 2

THEME: Brazil   E.D.C.

KEY IDEA: Differences between Brazil and local area.

FOCUS QUESTIONS	TASKS	RESOURCES	ASSESSMENT #	PoS	AT	CROSS CURRICULAR LINKS
Where is Brazil and how would you get there?	Use maps, globes and atlases. Introduction to Map C. Flight timetables.	Atlases blank maps	T. observation	6c	AT1 4e 5a	Economic and Industrial understanding
Where is the Tropical rainforest?	Locate rainforest, map work, size in relation to G. Britain, South America		Maps and descriptions		AT1 4f	Environmental education.
What makes the Tropical rainforest different from other vegetation zones?	Watch video, look at weather statistics, plants. Annotated diagrams. Vegetation zones on concept key board.	Books Video pictures Touch explorer plus.	Diagrams	12ab	AT2 5c AT3 3a	IT.
How do human actions affect the rainforest?	What comes out of the rainforest. Database of answers to key questions on the rainforest compiled by pupils	Child of the Rain forest Pack. Cross Database	Data base Questions and answers.	12d	AT2 4bd AT4 4e AT5 3a 5b	IT
How can we protect the rainforest?	Write to Greenpeace, friends of the Earth, etc and debate issue	Simon Le Bon + Sting material.		12e 18e 19a	AT5 4bc	
What would life be like in the rainforest and a Brazilian town?	Compare different life styles in two areas in Brazil, present the data in a chart format.	Video and photos	Charts ; compare and contrast	12bf 14 ac	AT4 5ab	
How is that life style different from life in ....?	Posters showing the differences in life styles working in small groups	Pictures here and there, large coloured sugar paper.		12c	AT2 3d	

Figure 5.7

UNIT PLANNER

Key Stage 1

THEME: Buildings

KEY IDEA: Use of buildings and types of work

FOCUS QUESTIONS	TASKS	RESOURCES	ASSESSMENT #	PoS	AT	CROSS CURRICULAR LINKS
How many types of buildings do we know?	Class brainstorm	Pictures		2b	AT1 2b AT4 1a	
What are the buildings in our local area called?	Identification of local buildings – walk round and investigate			8a 9ab	AT1 2e 3b AT2 1a 2b	
Can you find them / put them on a map?	Making a class map / individual maps locating buildings.	blank map of buildings	Map evidence verbal explanations	9ab	AT1 2b 3a AT4 1a	
What are the buildings used for?	Classifying building by use – finding out what happens in them.			13a	AT2 1b	
Who works in the building?	Identify the types of jobs that go on in different buildings. Card game – draw pictures linking jobs to buildings	Packs of job/ building cards	picture evidence linking jobs to buildings	13e	AT4 1c	EIU.
Who works in the school building?	On a school plan indicate where different people work.	School plan				

50

Task

Group A

Pupils are given a prepared sheet showing two boxes, one in which to draw their home and one in which to draw their school. They have to join the boxes showing their route to school and put in three landmarks along the way.

On a second sheet two boxes showing the school and the viewpoint must be connected by drawing the route and three landmarks whilst in the field.

Group B

Pupils predict the route and check it in the field. They mark, on a photocopied O.S. 1:2500 map, the route they expect to take to get to the viewpoint, and indicate certain features the teacher asks for. En route to the viewpoint they check and amend their maps.

Group C

As for group B, then colour code the buildings along the way according to use and type, for example, farm, shop, detached house.

Outcome   All groups were asked to do a landscape sketch from the viewpoint, naming as many features as they could. This work was then differentiated by outcome as shown in the pupils' work. It could also be differentiated by the resources offered to the pupils or by teacher intervention through constructive questioning.

Conclusion

Remember to keep things simple when you are planning units of work. Only plan that which you think you can achieve in the time provided. Start from the PoS and integrate where possible. If there is any extra time, build in other good geography activities or use it for extension tasks and reinforcement.

6

ASSESSMENT: NOT THE BOLT-ON EXTRA

Assessment in geography

Teacher assessment is not a new task; we have always assessed children informally to be able to plan the next steps in their learning. Whether we knew it or not we were using the skills of diagnostic, formative or summative assessment in ordinary classroom practice. We observed pupils, asked open-ended questions, listened to children, looked at their work, and used the knowledge gained to judge where the children were in their development and what the next step was for each pupil.

In 1988 the Task Group For Assessment and Testing (TGAT) said:

"Assessment is at the heart of the process of promoting children's learning. It can provide a framework in which educational objectives may be set and pupils' progress charted and expressed. It can yield a basis for planning the next educational steps in response to children's needs. By facilitating dialogue between teachers, it can enhance professional skills and help the school as a whole to strengthen learning across the curriculum and throughout its age range."

Figure 6.1

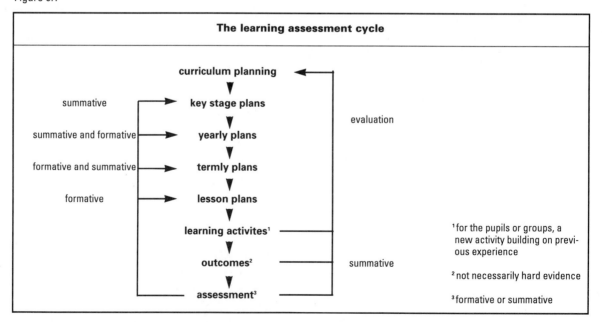

The learning assessment cycle

	curriculum planning	
summative	key stage plans	
summative and formative	yearly plans	evaluation
formative and summative	termly plans	
formative	lesson plans	
	learning activites[1]	
	outcomes[2]	summative
	assessment[3]	

[1] for the pupils or groups, a new activity building on previous experience

[2] not necessarily hard evidence

[3] formative or summative

52

This idea of assessment as a framework means that assessment cannot be the bolt-on extra, but has to be built into the structure of the geography curriculum. The link between the learning process and assessment should follow the steps shown in figure 6.1.

You need to assess in order to know that a pupil has learnt. The next step in the learning process cannot be planned if you have not informally assessed where the pupil is now, after the latest input. So assessment should not be viewed as some separate formal activity, but as an integral part of your teaching.

These are the general principles of assessment that a primary school should consider in planning its assessment policy:

- Assessment must be an integral part of teaching
- Assessment must provide all pupils with the opportunity to demonstrate achievement
- A variety of techniques should be employed so that the assessment is appropriate
- Assessment strategies and standards should be agreed by all teachers involved in the assessment
- The opportunity should be available to assess when ready and reassess if necessary
- Assessment should involve the pupil
- Assessment should be enjoyable.

There may be a need to rethink the approach to National Curriculum assessment. It is not a matter of 'What and how can we assess?' but rather of 'Why are we assessing?' The purpose is to help in children's development and/or give factual information about progress. We need to create positive opportunities for pupils to demonstrate what they know, understand and can do, not erect assessment hurdles for them.

Planning for assessment

There are six stages in NC assessment:

- Defining the area to be assessed
- Organising the learning
- Measuring performance
- Keeping a record
- Making a report
- Informing further planning.

These well-defined steps have to be kept in mind when planning for geographical assessment. To help teachers, a school needs to have a coherent policy and planned approach to assessment. As a starting point, the school should consider the following points and questions. The answers will form the basis for a school assessment policy.

- What are the learning objectives?
- How will they be taught in the classroom?
- What are the assessment objectives?
- What are criteria for assessment?
- Who will make the asessment?
- How will individual pieces of work be assessed?
- What evidence of achievement will be needed?
- Will pupils be involved in assessment and recording?
- How can uniform marking techniques and standards be ensured ?
- How will achievement be recorded?
- How will moderation between classes, schools and LEAs occur?
- How will evaluation be carried out?
- How will assessment be used to inform further planning?

The method of National Curriculum assessment in geography will be teacher assessment at key stage 1 with optional SATs in support. These SATs can be used at any time in the key stage as support material. There may be no SATs at key stage 2, so we are looking at planning and providing opportunities for teacher assessment. In key stages 1 and 2 there are 93 Statements of Attainment in the Orders for National Curriculum geography. To be able to cover such a vast assessment load, the delivery of the geographical content of the curriculum must be structured (see Chapter 4), with teachers being responsible for assessing certain SoAs during the key stage. National curriculum assessment is an on-going integrated process, building on the good practice of teacher assessment. If it is included at the unit planning stage (see Chapter 5) the classroom task will provide the evidence of children's achievement. The unit plan is cross referenced with the PoS and ATs, so the record-keeping becomes an easier task at the end of every unit.

Creating opportunities for teacher assessment

'Good assessment' requires a range of techniques, tasks and learning strategies to enable teachers to judge a child's achievement in the different areas of factual knowledge, geographical concepts and skills. These three areas are all part of the wider geographical process of enquiry which is not formally assessed, but is equally important. Pupil tasks should be targeted on learning objectives which will make the outcomes or evidence valid, meaningful and easier to assess. The types of evidence that can be used to show pupils' achievement can be split into teacher and pupil evidence. The types of pupil evidence are shown in Figure 6.2.

Apart from photographs, teacher evidence is mainly in the form of:

● Observations recorded in notes, records or annotation slips

Figure 6.2

Pupil evidence	
Written evidence	**Graphical evidence**
reports	maps
notes	drawings
diaries	diagrams
questionnaires	graphs
stories	print-out
essays	labelled photographs
newspaper articles	landscape sketches
short-answer questions	
multiple choice questions	
cloze procedure	
Products	**Oral evidence**
models	questioning
artefacts	discussion
	interviews
	sequencing
	explanation
	hypothesising
	describing
	evaluating
	role play
	pupil presentations
	tapes
	video recordings
	debates

● Pupil records
● Class records
● Notes in notebook.

It is best to develop a range of teaching and learning strategies; this will give the pupils a variety of ways in which to demonstrate their achievement. Some children will achieve at a higher level if asked to present their evidence in a certain way; for example a child with poor coordination might perform better verbally than graphically. The chart 'Creating opportunities for teacher assessment in primary geography' (Figure 6.3) contains some ideas of children's activities that can be built into units of work and used for assessment purposes. This is by no means a definitive list but can be used as a starting point to develop your own ideas. Figure 6.4 is an assessment check grid. It

Figure 6.3

Opportunities for teacher assessment in primary geography		
Type of activity		**Geographical context**
OS map	Using and interpreting maps	Story to include features you can see from a given grid reference; Postcards: stand at point X and draw what you can see. Swap cards with other pupils – where was your postcard written? Give a detailed account of a journey from points A to B by car or foot; signpost maps from given grid references.
Atlas	Make your own postcard	Postcards to show which country you are in. Give at least three clues in your picture and writing.
Map and plan	Giving directions to other children	Can they follow instructions? Where did they end up? Construct maps for younger children. Do they need a key? How much information to put in?
	Listen to instructions	Draw a map of X's route to school.
	Types of maps	What sort of map would you need to ...? Who would use ... type of map?
Factual recall	Normal classroom writing	Write two pieces of work, one before and one after about a place/issue; make up a crossword, word search to include some clues and facts on a given topic. Devise a test for your friends and construct an answer sheet.
Vocabulary	Explanations of vocabulary and concepts	Write a sentence/paragraph/draw a picture to illustrate x; geographical cloze procedure with or without words. Use the following geographical terms correctly, e.g. hill, reservoir.
Drama	Role play and/or assemblies	If possible these should be written by the children, e.g. a day in the life of a family in India.
Tape	Tape recording of discussion or explanation	Explaining settlement types from pictures.
Artwork	'Before and after' pictures	Drawings in different mediums, e.g. mountains and rock strata or deserts.
Treasure trails	Directional competitions	Design a trail. Follow a trail.
	Orienteering	Collect letters to make up a word.
Playground games	Directional games	Bouncing ball on a large map of unnamed countries. Move to N, S, E, etc.
Board games	Designed by the children	Cross-curricular games (geography, technology, maths, English): routes, treasure islands, collecting sets of different shop types, etc.
Computer	Directional activities Data bases	Logo for spatial awareness. Roamers and Turtles can all be used to check direction and routes. Use atlas, book to fill gaps in a data base. Add climate statistics or place names.
Technology	Project briefs	Can be made to include geography, grid references taught previously, e.g. playground, park or room plans.
Poems	Write a poem	Following a route on a map or draw a map to go with a written poem.
Video	Video discussion	For teacher moderation and consideration: pupils make video about an issue, e.g. siting a new local pub, supermarket or park.
Photographs	Take or use them	Where were these taken on the trail? Can you map them, identify them or take them at given points? Spot trails are adaptable to age levels, etc. Sort and locate photographic evidence.

enables you to check how many different types of evidence you use now or have planned into your geography units of work. This will help you to maintain a balance of different tasks over the key stage.

Criterion-referenced assessment

When you plan units of work, there are always intended outcomes and objectives which are either explicit or implicit. This does not mean there will be no unintended outcomes. During a unit you will make professional judgements to assess children's progress against your objectives. The National Curriculum with its format of attainment targets, statements of attainment and ten levels of achievement is a criterion-referenced model of assessment. This is when a child is assessed or measured against

externally set targets. The Order sets the criteria against which we have to assess our pupils for the purposes of summative assessment. There are 93 SoA in the primary key stages, so unless we incorporate assessment at the planning stage the tendency will be to assess anything and everything in case it fits a SoA. If you have used the unit planning approach, pupil tasks will already be targeted on National Curriculum objectives through the PoS. These can be checked back with reference to SoA to ensure that only valid and meaningful assessment occurs.

Moderation

Although teacher assessment is something we are familar with, particularly in the fields of maths and language, assessing geographical primary work is a new task to most of us. Talking to other teachers will help decide

Figure 6.4

Assessment evidence check grid											
Year............										Key stage.........	
Evidence / Unit	oral	models/ artefacts	graphics	notes	essays	role plays	video/audio presentations	factual recall	observation	photographs	other

what constitutes evidence for each level of attainment. Moderation can be done within the school, across schools, in cluster groups and LEAs. Agreement trials common to those which some key stage 1 teachers held before the SATs can be very helpful in clarifying your ideas on different pieces of work. A good strategy is to start to collect pieces of assessed and moderated work for your school. These examples will help you to maintain a moderated standard and lead to a shared understanding across the school.

It is highly likely that in geographical work there will be evidence of achievement in more than one attainment target in any piece of work. In a river study it is possible for a piece of work to show achievement in Gg1, 3 and 5 (skills, physical and environmental geography). An explanation of the water supply in a village in India could show outcomes in Gg2, 3 and 5 (place, physical and environmental geography). You will find it easier to consider the evidence in context and to look at the complete study unit when assessing achievement. This is because some SoAs are made up of many parts and can only be awarded when work from different tasks is combined. Remember to be clear in your own mind as to whether you are assessing skills, concepts, knowledge, attitudes and values, or a mixture of these.

The in-service materials in Figure 6.5, which deals with the strand of settlement, may be useful if as a staff you want to try to moderate some work. As the children were aged between nine and twelve, the examples have been typed out to stop any assumptions being made and the assessment becoming age-related. Although it is difficult to assess work out of context, the aim is to see for which SoA, or part of SoA, the work shows evidence. The pieces would be part of a wider set of outcomes from a unit of work

and more evidence would be available before deciding on a level. But it is still a good starting point to begin to share decisions on what particular outcomes show us about a child's National Curriculum achievement – a very useful exercise which helps you to think about outcomes when planning pupils' tasks in other units of work.

Record keeping

When considering record keeping these questions spring to mind:

- Who is it for?
- What do I really need to record?
- Who is it to be done by?
- When do I do it?
- How much time will it take?
- What do I record it on?
- How do I use the records to inform my teaching?

Who is it for?

Most formative assessment is done by you for yourself and for the pupil. Summative assessment has a wider audience – the head, governors, LEAs, DES, parents and the next teacher. It is useful for the pupils to be involved in setting some of the learning objectives and recording their achievements.

What do I really need to record?

The amount of formative assessment that is recorded will vary from teacher to teacher and is a matter for individual preference, but it is usual to record major steps made by the pupils. At the time of writing the latest news from SEAC is that every child will have to be assessed for a level in all five attainment targets, but they will not need to have a level for every SoA. We do not know whether an overall geography level will have to be

Figure 6.5

National Curriculum, settlement strand

Gg4 human geography, SoA 1a, 2a, 3b, 4b, 4c, 5b

Example A

People can live in different places, like houses, towns and big cities. I live in a town it has shops and houses and a park. There are things like hospitals, a swimming pool and a police station. If I lived in a village these things would not be there.

Does this work cover any of these SoA adequately or partially?

Example B

The centre had a pedestrian shopping precinct with many new small shops and some department stores. See chart. Round the edge of this there were older smaller shops, some of these had shut or looked as if they were closing, houses were mixed in with shops here. On the map you can see the houses spreading out from shopping centre there are smaller groups of shops in the houses, sometimes just one shop. By the railway station there are shops (see chart), different types of shops, a florist, paper shop, off-licence and a dry cleaner especially for commuters.

Example C

Shops are built in different places, in the middle of towns or in between the houses. There are many different types of shops some sell things like food, furniture, clothes, records or shoes but others do things like solicitors, banks, dry cleaners and travel agents.

Example D

The centre, crowded and dirty,
Noisy, machines and workmen everywhere,
Cross traffic, diversions.
Where's the car park?
Can't cross here,
pedestrians 'this way',
When will they finish?

Example E

Once there were all sorts of shops in the centre of the town. Before the new centre was built we could go to all the little shops. Each one sold one sort of thing, clothes, shoes or food. In the new centre there are more big shops which sell all sorts of things so you can get shoes and clothes in one shop.

---

worked out. They say it is up to a teacher's professional judgement as to how many SoA need to be assessed to establish a level. So if you have a pupil who has achieved three out of the level 4 SoA in Gg3 then you could say they are at level 4. But if they have achieved two level 4 SoA and two level 3 SoA, then you will need to assess another piece of their work before you can say whether they are at level 4 or level 3.

Who is it to be done by?

As formative assessment is integral to the learning process it will be done by the teacher delivering the lesson. It is usual for the classroom teacher to update the summative records for their pupils.

When do I do it?

The nature of the geography Order means that some SoA may be addressed only once

in a key stage, others twice and some, especially those in Gg1, frequently. So when the coordinator has worked out their main key stage plan, an assessment timetable should be drawn up. One way of doing this is to take a blank key stage timetable and from the plan note down which SoA will be covered when (see Figure 6.6). You can then identify any isolated SoA. It is likely you will be dealing with water pollution, volcanoes, Europe, leisure activities, etc. only once, so that is when you must assess them. Most plans include a locality study of an economically developing country twice, so these areas can be assessed twice in the lower and upper juniors. By looking objectively at the key stage it is possible to divide up the summative assessment so that each teacher is responsible for assessing three or four SoA every half-term towards the overall key stage assessment. This assessment timetable runs alongside the key stage plan, sharing

Figure 6.6

Key stage 2		
	Year 3	Year 4
Autumn	school locality settlement Gg4 2a 3b	locality in econ. developing country Gg2 2c 3d
	goods and services Gg4 2c	Gg3 2a 3a

the summative assessment through the key stage. Obviously classroom teachers will still be responsible for ongoing formative assessment.

How much time will it take ?

This does depend on you, but one of the quickest ways is to sit down at the end of a unit with your unit planner, showing the PoS and SoA for that unit. Check which SoA you need to assess summatively. Then look at each pupil's work on the unit. This will include many different types of evidence, including ephemeral evidence which you may have noted during the unit. The pupil outcomes should be looked at in the context of the unit, and there will be evidence of achievement in some SoA or parts of SoA which will need to be recorded for each pupil. Remember, you are using your professional judgement of what the pupil knows, understands or can do at that particular point in time. We recommend that you make your assessment at the end of a unit or during it but do not leave it till the end of the year. As you become more familiar with the SoA and assessing geographical work, the task will speed up.

What do I record it on?

There are many ways of recording achievement. Some schools have their own style of records for each subject, others have records of achievement for individual children. Figures 6.7, 6.8, and 6.9 are the Bexley geography records which have been offered to schools for them to use if they wish. The achievement sheet (Figure 6.7) is set out to cover levels 1 to 10 to aid continuity and progression across the four key stages and cut out the need for transferring records from previous schools. There is room for a comment at the end of every key stage; a yearly comment should be made on the pupil's report and it is unnecessary to copy it on to the record sheet. The boxes should be dated, not ticked, so it is possible to trace the achievement back to a unit of work if necessary. Figures 6.8 and 6.9 are coverage records of the places and themes taught to a pupil during the key stage.

The major assessment dilemma is trying to balance the three issues of manageability, reliability and validity. Any assessment activity must be manageable in the classroom, usually by non-specialist teachers. It must be reliable in ensuring children's progress and development, and it must have validity for the audiences it seeks to inform. We hope that this balancing act will become easier as you become more familiar with planning and assessing geographical work within the National Curriculum.

Our priority as teachers is to:

● Plan
● Organise
● Facilitate pupils' learning.

Many teachers feel that recently three other priorities have been added to the list:

● To assess
● To keep records
● To retain evidence.

We must not let these concerns take over from our main aim of helping pupils to learn. The formative assessment that feeds back into the learning process or cycle is very important; we have to take care that it is not swamped by summative assessment. Summative assessment summarises what the pupil knows, understands and can do at a given moment in time. Its audiences of parents, LEA, governors, government and next teacher are different from those of formative assessment audiences: the pupils and teachers. Formative assessment should have the priority over summative assessment. One way of doing this is to ensure that the summative assessment is built into the planning at all levels and not just 'bolted on at the end'.

Figure 6.7

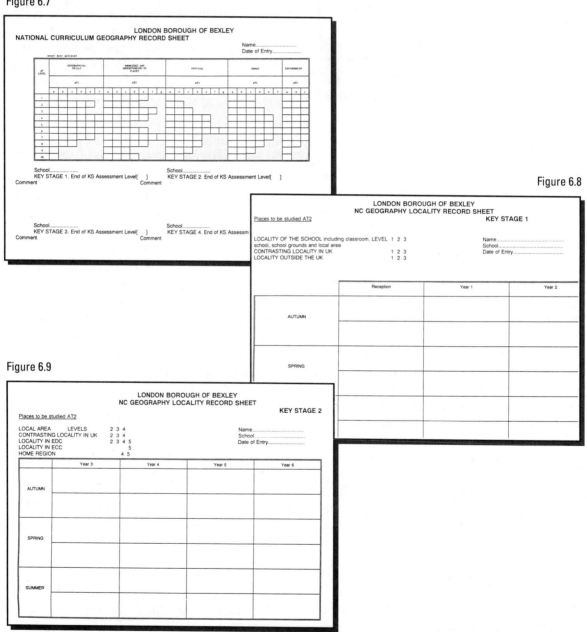

Figure 6.8

Figure 6.9

7

MAPWORK

Geographical skills

Enquiry, mapwork, fieldwork and other more general skills essential to geography are crucial to good primary geography work.

In National Curriculum geography, skills provide the third dimension of the places/themes/skills cube (Chapter 4, Figure 4.1). Once places and themes have been planned for, learning objectives which incorporate skills can be developed through key questions in units of work. It is not possible to teach geography without planning pupil activities which develop skills. However, we need to ensure that we develop all four types of skills, and that we do so with due care and attention to continuity and progression.

The importance of the enquiry process and its skills is stressed throughout this book. Although it appears in the Statutory Order programmes of study, it is not fully explained or given priority. Continuity and progression in mapwork and fieldwork skills are built in via the assessment objectives in the Order's statements of attainment (see Chapter 2, Figure 2.2a), but a bare skeleton of skills is sequenced.

Chapters 7, 8 and 10 attempt to explain the various skills and techniques which need to be planned into pupil activities as the third dimension of the work.

Tackling mapwork

Considering that for many people geography means mapwork, it is a cause for concern that HMI were not able to be positive about the teaching and learning of mapwork in the sample of schools studied:

"Pupils achieved satisfactory or better standards in mapwork including the use of atlases and globes in only one quarter of the schools."

The Teaching and Learning of History and Geography, 1989

The reason for this could be that primary teachers have not had much help in identifying the sequence of skills and experiences children need to cope with maps. Most children have a natural curiosity about maps in spite of their abstract nature. With an awareness of the continuity and progression needed to build up these map skills and experiences we should be able to direct this curiosity towards improving their learning.

The Geography Working Group advised us in their Interim Report in 1989 that, 'In mapwork, maps may be created, used, compared, or analysed either in the classroom or field.' In other words, pupils need to make, use and read maps in the classroom and in fieldwork. Ideally, children should develop their mapwork in a context relating to a specific place or theme – not as a mapwork topic or lesson. They should be making, using or reading a map because the need to do so has been generated by a wider activity relating to place and theme.

With these issues in mind this chapter offers an analysis of the detailed skills and issues of mapwork in the primary years. Children at primary level need to be introduced to a wide range of different types of map making, as follows.

Making maps from first-hand observation

Freehand or sketch maps When we draw freehand or sketch maps we are trying to fit some real, larger area which we see around us – be it desk top, flowerbed or recreation ground – on to a small sheet of paper. Both children and adults can be fearful of this activity because they feel they have to get it right; but they do not have to. Because it is a sketch map not a scale map, it can only ever show relative position – where the tree is in relation to the fence and the classroom. A way of introducing this activity could be to give each child a paper with the title and one important feature of the map already in place. This gives some security for the child. Later work can start with a blank page.

Mental or cognitive maps We carry the information we need to sketch this kind of map in our heads as we cannot see the whole area to be mapped. Children may make a mental map of a route around school or of their route to school from home. When we direct a stranger to a place, we put a mental map into words, or sometimes we draw it on paper to show the way.

Imaginative maps Such maps may only exist in the drawer's mind or in descriptions in fiction, for example, children may draw:

- A map of their treasure island, and locate hidden treasure on it
- A map of Red Riding Hood's walk

- A map of a place described in a story written by themselves.

Scaled maps There is a close connection with maths here. Distances on the map may be represented in exact proportion to their real-life dimensions. It is easier for children to use a scale map from which to measure size and distance than to draw a sketch map to scale for themselves. Both activities need considerable practice, and opportunities to achieve this must be built into units of work.

Making maps from second-hand sources

Maps made from aerial photographs Tracing maps by overlaying an aerial photograph with an overhead transparency acetate or good quality tracing paper, helps develop recognition and understanding of plan form. This activity highlights the need for labelling, or for a key, because buildings and outlines so easily recognised in the photograph will become meaningless lines or shapes on the map unless appropriately annotated.

Copying maps from maps This is usually to be avoided unless there is a very good reason for it. Practice in hand-eye coordination is about the only justification, along with copying a base map or outline to create a map for a new purpose. It is better for pupils to fill in information on a blank map prepared by the teacher than to spend time free-drawing or tracing an outline.

Working with partially completed maps This activity can only come after early free-hand map-making experiences as it assumes some understanding/recognition in the children that what they are being asked to deal with is a map. Using a partially completed map assumes that children have:

- Some idea of plan form and symbols
- Some idea of relative scale

- Some ability to turn the map to the right position relative to surroundings
- Some ability to follow simple instructions to complete the map.

Remember to train your pupils to include on every map they make:

- A title
- A north arrow
- A scale, approximate or accurate.

Infants should manage a title as a minimum requirement; the other elements will be included according to a child's age, ability and experience. By the end of key stage 2, it should be possible to incorporate all of these for most maps.

Using maps

It is essential that children have the opportunity to use maps in the field (see Glossary). They should be able to use on site as appropriate:

- Their own maps
- Maps produced by their teacher
- Their peers' maps
- Maps made by older children
- Commercially produced maps, including play maps and plastic floor maps.

Using maps on site and in the classroom develops map-reading skills. A map communicates information to its reader via signs and symbols. Pupils may need to read just one or two sets of information from a map – the number and location of telephone boxes or the height of the land. Older juniors may be able to begin to describe the kind of landscape they will expect to see when they visit a place on an OS 1:50 000 scale map they are looking at. The key question 'What will the area look like when we visit it?' will prompt them to use their map-reading skills. They will be able to confirm or deny their predictions when they make their visit.

Types of maps for the primary school

Ordnance Survey maps and plans The Statutory Order has made these essential for geographical work. Large-scale maps of the local area are of paramount importance. The checklist for skills and equipment in the geography Statutory Orders (see Figure 7.1) shows this, as does the resources audit check list included in the Appendix.

Many LEAs have OS copyright licence certificates which allow schools to obtain relevant sections of OS maps for school use as long as the photocopier in an educational establishment is used. Local authority planning offices can often provide sections of maps or a single photocopy on the same basis. Some LEA teachers' centres or subject resource centres hold copies of OS maps for loan or limited photocopy.

If a school cannot access OS map copies in this way, then good local bookshops stock the OS 1:50000 and Pathfinder 1:25000 series. The larger-scale maps have to be obtained from specialist suppliers. Some of them will supply parchment-quality maps, others digitally produced ones which are like high-quality photocopies on thinner paper – cheaper but less robust. Multiple-copy sets of OS 1:50 000 map extracts are held by secondary schools because of each year's GCSE exams. You could try asking the geography departments of your local secondary schools for some unwanted sets. They are unlikely to be of the local area. Colour copying of OS 1:50 000 map extracts borrowed from secondary schools is possible, but cost is an issue if multiple copies are required. Borrowing the large-scale OS maps mentioned on page 65 from a secondary school geography department in order to take a photocopy is a further possibility. Remember to check that your LEA does hold a licence for copying in school.

Figure 7.1

Checklist for skills and equipment listed and implied in Statutory Orders

	Mapwork – making, reading and using maps		Fieldwork	
	Skills	**Equipment**	**Skills**	**Equipment**
Key stage 1 Enquiry process — ongoing →	Identification of features on photographs and pictures	Photos, pictures, postcards - ground level and oblique aerial	Observation, follow directions, follow a route using a plan. Record weather observations. Data collection	**Equipment** Plans – teacher-made or pupil-made. Notepad or micro tape-recorder
	Draw round 3D objects	Maths shapes, models, wooden tracks and toy buildings		
Vocabulary development practice	Using large scale maps, make plans and maps	OS 1:1250 or 1:2500 maps - photocopied extracts blown up. Teacher drawn maps. Computer and software	Make a map of a short route experienced	Notepad
	Use letter and number coordinates			
Levels 1–3 included	Identify land and sea on globes	Globe	Use eight compass points and follow directions	Direction compass
Key stage 2 Enquiry process — ongoing →	Use letter and number coordinates to locate features on a map. Identify features on aerial photographs	Aerial photographs	Data collection for weather measurement	**Equipment** Pupil-made, parent-made or commercial rain gauge, thermometers, wind vane. Maximum–minimum thermometers, barometer, anemometer (wind speed gauge)
	Making maps	OS 1:50 000 maps or any other suitable map		
	Use four-figure coordinates		Record evidence: questionnaire making, listening, note taking	Notepad or micro tape-recorder. Clipboard
	Measure straight line distances on maps. Identify features on related map and relate map and aerial photographs	Cotton, ruler, 100 cm tapes. e.g. OS 1:10000 map and 1:10000 scale aerial photograph	Taking photographs, sketching and labelling sketches. Height measurement. Distance measurement. Space mapping (quadrats). Profile or transect drawing	Camera. Clinometer. Surveyor's tape, trundle wheel, metre rules, hoops, quadrat frames. Canes or poles, surveyor's tape, trundle wheel or metre rules
	Use index and contents page in an atlas. Use latitude and longitude	Atlases		
	Make a key. Devise own symbols. Use symbols and a key. Draw sketch maps			
Vocabulary development practice	Orientate a map on site using landmarks and/or a direction compass. Use six-figure grid references. Interpret relief maps. Follow a route on OS maps. Describe routes on maps. Use thematic maps	Directional compass. 1:50000 maps or map extracts. Atlas maps. OS 1:25000 maps. OS 1:50000 maps. Atlas maps showing rainfall, population, etc.	Measure width/girth, e.g. of trees. Measure rate of flow, e.g. of a stream	Callipers. Stop watch
Levels 2–5 included →	Show that a globe can be drawn flat	Orange peel!		

Acquire the largest-scale maps first, as they are the least easy to get hold of and the most useful. Provided the LEA holds a licence, small sections can be blown up on a photocopier for practical use. Parts can be blanked out for children to fill in on site. Finally, once safely covered with clear, tacky-backed plastic, children can trace their own sections on transparent overlay with overhead projector pens. The following OS maps will be useful:

1:1250, 1 cm to 12.5 m (old 50" to a mile) Each map sheet covers an area 500 m by 500 m and so measures 40 cm by 40 cm. These maps are available for urban areas. All building numbers or names of houses and roads are shown.

1:2500, 1 cm to 25 m (old 25" to a mile) One sheet covers an area of 1 km² and measures 40 cm by 40 cm. Often double sheets are produced – useful if your school is on the edge of two single sheets! Each double sheet covers 2 km from east to west and 1 km from north to south, measuring 80 cm by 40 cm. Individual buildings, some names of roads and large buildings, along with boundaries, field acreages, spot heights and bench-marks are shown. Rural schools will find these are the largest-scale maps available to them.

1:10 000, 1 cm to 100 m (old 6" to a mile) One sheet covers an area 5 km by 5 km and so measures 50 cm by 50 cm. Roads, buildings or building blocks and boundaries are shown. Contour lines are shown in brown.

1:25 000, 4 cm to 1 km (old 2½" to a mile), Pathfinder series Each map covers an area 20 km from east to west by 10 km from north to south, measuring 80 cm by 40 cm. Colour begins to be used extensively on these maps: roads in orange, contours as fine orange lines, woodland in green and streams and lakes and sea in blue. A key accompanies the map. Children sometimes have these maps at home, especially if their parents walk.

1:50 000, 2 cm to 1 km (old 1" to a mile), Landranger series Each map covers an area 40 km by 40 km and so measures 80 cm by 80 cm. Colour is very extensively used. Children are most likely to have these maps in their homes. Although these maps are the most abstract for children, they seem to enjoy using them.

1:50 000, 2 cm to 1 km, Tourist maps Some examples of these are of Snowdonia and the North Yorkshire Moors. They can be useful for local area, home region or contrasting locality work, depending on the school's location.

Issues relating to commercial maps Teachers are often concerned that maps, however recent, are out of date and that maps are now in metric measures, yet our road distances are quoted in miles on signs and by the general public.

It is not necessary to worry that a map has inaccuracies which show it is out of date; children need to know that the landscape is constantly being altered by people. Updating the map from their observations as they go along is part of the process of using maps, and is a constructive activity for children to do.

Commercial map scales need not concern pupils until the upper junior stage, unless a pupil is especially bright and needs to understand scales earlier. The strange British practice of using metric measurements on maps and miles in travel does need to be dealt with. Children need simply to accept that we use the two different systems and begin to relate to them. Remember the useful 5 miles = 8 km relationship. The multiples of this can also be helpful: 50 miles = 80 km and 500 miles = 800 km.

In practical terms, the best way to get children to understand the issue is to ask them to think of a local distance that they are familiar with and preferably have just walked. If this distance is about a kilometre, then a mile can be related to this. One mile equals one and three-fifths of a kilometre or one kilometre and just over half as much again. If pupils in a class have travelled abroad, for example in mainland Europe or Canada, then the teacher can remind them how kilometres are used on road signs there.

Other commercial maps Pupils should have access to and be allowed to become familiar with the wide variety of other maps available – AA and RAC motoring maps, town plans, A–Z town maps, tourist trail maps and diagrammatic maps such as the London Underground ones. These may be used in locality studies or in relation to the theme of transport and transport patterns. Foreign maps – with kilometre distances, of course – may be used in the context of a locality in an EC country at level 5. Pupils will often have maps at home that they will be allowed to bring into school.

The elements of mapwork

Understanding maps is a very complex process. Many elements built up and brought together lead us to be able to make or read a map effectively. Practice of all kinds of preparatory concepts is needed before maps can be made. These skills are:

- Location
- Direction
- Representation
- Perspective
- Distance.

Figure 7.2 shows what each element is about in terms of mapping concepts and skills. Within each element is a progression of learning in which children need practice.

Figure 7.2

Key elements of mapwork	
Location is about *Grid references*	Where? 'personal'▶'relative'▶'absolute'
Direction is about *Compass directions*	Which way? 'personal'▶'relative'▶'absolute'
Representation involves *Key*	How do I show it? 'pictorial' symbols and shapes
Perspective involves *Plan view*	Which relationships am I showing? 'pictorial/personal'▶ spatial/abstract
Distance involves *Scale measurement*	How far? How big? Size? 'personal'▶'relative'▶'absolute'

Location

There are three clear stages in location work:

1 Pupils first need to be able to locate their position or the position of a particular feature on a map.
2 They must learn to locate their position relative to another feature or person when making a map or to locate the position of, say, a seat in the playground relative to that of a flowerbed.
3 Finally they must understand that absolute position uses an abstract grid to relate one object's position to another's, as in maths coordinates. This is referred to in geography as grid references. An age-old way of remembering which co-ordinates to take first is 'along the corridor and up the stairs'.

When dealing with grids, the progression is as shown in Figure 7.3.

Traditionally grid references or coordinates form part of paper and pencil or crayon

Figure 7.3

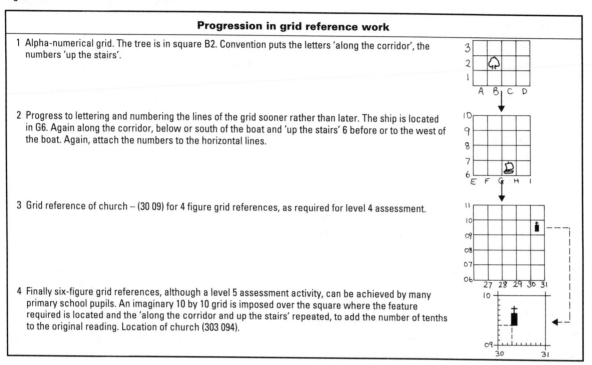

Progression in grid reference work

1 Alpha-numerical grid. The tree is in square B2. Convention puts the letters 'along the corridor', the numbers 'up the stairs'.

2 Progress to lettering and numbering the lines of the grid sooner rather than later. The ship is located in G6. Again along the corridor, below or south of the boat and 'up the stairs' 6 before or to the west of the boat. Again, attach the numbers to the horizontal lines.

3 Grid reference of church – (30 09) for 4 figure grid references, as required for level 4 assessment.

4 Finally six-figure grid references, although a level 5 assessment activity, can be achieved by many primary school pupils. An imaginary 10 by 10 grid is imposed over the square where the feature required is located and the 'along the corridor and up the stairs' repeated, to add the number of tenths to the original reading. Location of church (303 094).

exercises – often in maths books. More recently Information Technology (IT) has introduced another motivating way of dealing with practising grid locations through software like *Map Adventure* and *Adventure Island* (see Chapter 12).

There are also many 'concrete', fun activities which infants and lower juniors can do to become familiar with grid references. They can overlay three-dimensional models and maps they have made themselves with a grid and then locate features or objects.

Model people, animals, streams and trees can be stood on card. String, coloured paper or even rulers can be used to make a simple grid. This can be lettered and numbered as appropriate.

A three-dimensional model of, say, the route Little Red Riding Hood took to get to Grandma's house or a magic island may need to be given side supports before a grid

can be made across the top for children to look down on the model to locate features. Similarly, a shoe box with models in it could have a very simple grid, two squares by three, pegged over it for children to 'read' the location of objects in the model.

A large-scale map of the local area, which the children have helped to draw, laid out at their height on a low table, can have a string grid made over it in order to locate the absolute position of features. If the children understand where the grid comes from in the first place by having a hand in making it, they are far more likely to be able to read off positions.

Often the pond in the school grounds offers the opportunity to reinforce grid reference work with juniors. Some ponds are in paved areas – the paving lines offer a ready-made grid to be 'extended' across the pond with bamboo canes or metre sticks so that pupils can locate a clump of weeds or surface weed when they 'map' the pond. A variety of methods can be used to 'label' the grid – paper held down with stone, for example. The pupils will no doubt invent their own.

For a small pond surrounded by grass or tarmac, a bamboo or string grid can safely be made over it. Some ponds even have permanent metal safety grids over the top - a ready-made geographical aid!

A good self-assessment task using coordinates is for the pupils to design a ship or a house on squared paper, then swop coordinates with a friend and draw from their instructions. Do the two pictures match?

Direction

A great deal of practice in using directional vocabulary and following directions is needed before direction work can be related to maps. The concept is a difficult one, but active learning in the classroom and in fieldwork brings success. Points 1–16 suggest stages in the progression for direction work.

1 Infants need to discuss direction using simple terms – 'this way', 'that way', 'over here', 'over there', 'up', 'down', 'beneath', 'above', 'turn left', 'turn right', 'carry straight on'.
2 They need to play directional games in PE and in the playground to become practised at simple direction finding and telling.
3 Games involving turns – such as quarter, half and three-quarter turns – can also be introduced and used throughout the infant and junior school years to reinforce directional concept and compass directions.
4 Then introduce shadow sticks and the link with the sun. The Statutory Order for science has now made the use of shadow sticks standard in key stage 1. An

extension of this is to introduce compass points showing that the sun rises in an approximately eastern direction, is due south at midday Greenwich Mean Time in winter and 1:00 p.m. in British Summer Time. The sun sets roughly in the west. It is not possible to be more accurate than this in the UK – but this is sufficient. North can then be located and a direction compass repeatedly used in the school grounds. Try checking for yourself that you know where east, south, west and north are in different locations – as long as the sun is out! Then it is easier to be more confident when helping pupils.

5 Children can chalk their own compass rose on the playground if the school does not have one already marked (see Figure 7.4).
6 Now further route-finding games can be played along the lines of 'Walk five paces north, three paces east', and so on, with peers and teacher calling instructions.
7 Infants can try mapping this direction game on 2 cm square grid paper from a friend's instructions (see Figure 7.5).

All sorts of permutations on directional games of this kind, played in groups,

Figure 7.4

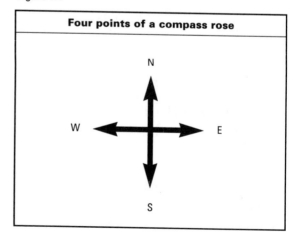

Four points of a compass rose

N

W   E

S

Figure 7.5

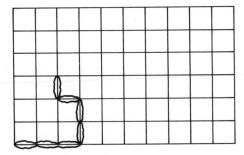

The snail trail leads:

3 paces east;   2 paces north;

1 pace west;   1 pace north.

pairs or as a whole class, reinforce the concept.

8 Control technology toys such as *Roamer* and *Turtle* are excellent for direction work where schools are lucky enough to afford them. It is possible to draw a map or a picture on an acetate and stick this over the monitor screen. Then the pupil can move the turtle from place to place on the map.

9 A giant paper compass rose can be attached to the classroom ceiling if it is reasonably low; you can also mark one on the floor or on a surface which is low enough for infants to see and reach. The children should be involved in the correct orientation of the rose by using the direction compass to find north.

10 Every available opportunity should be taken to find north – first of all in the school grounds, then in the local area and further afield – otherwise children tend to think that 'north' only exists in the classroom. Every time the class goes out, as many direction compasses as possible should go with them, preferably one for every two or three pupils. A compass is as indispensable to geography as a pencil is to English, but it is rare for it to be used as a matter of course. It only takes a few minutes to find north and do some direction-pointing activities, whether in the school grounds with infants or on a residential field trip with older juniors. We need to remind children that magnetic compasses will be deflected from the north reading if near metal – for example a car, a metal bulldog clip on a clipboard, or a metal bar under a table.

11 Pupils should now relate plans and maps that they are using to their relative positions in the landscape. They need to orientate the plan or map – that is turn it the right way around so that the position of features on the plan or map match up with the direction in which they will be found in the landscape, be that landscape the school field or a view from the top of a castle in another part of the UK. The easiest way to do this is to locate a feature in the landscape, for example the wall of a building – find it on the map, then locate two or three more features, for example a tree or steps – work out their relative position on the map and turn the map around to match up with the general direction of the features.

12 North can be marked on the plan or map using the direction compass to find it once it has been orientated.

13 Similarly, if pupils have been given a plan with a north arrow marked on it, they can use the direction compass to relate its position accurately to the real landscape by making sure that the north arrow of the map and the compass north arrow are parallel, or that the map north arrow is lined up underneath the direction compass arrow (see Figure 7.6).

14 Once pupils can orientate large-scale maps outside the classroom, they need repeated and progressive practice in this technique, too. They should have the opportunity, every time they go out, to

Figure 7.6

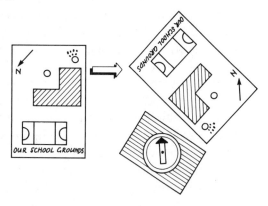

OUR SCHOOL GROUNDS

orientate a map on site. The progression is to start with large-scale maps and plans and to work with increasingly smaller-scale map extracts. Plenty of practice in matching up features and then checking orientation with the compass is needed.

15 What about all the different kinds of north? Many teachers who have not specialised in geography, unless they have pursued orienteering or serious walking, do not realise that there are three types of north, as shown in the key area of the 1:50 000 scale OS maps. Magnetic north is the compass needle north, actually found to the west of polar or true north, due to magnetic influences. Magnetic north is always a variable number of degrees west of polar or true north. It changes every year, but is really not enough to worry about with junior children. Grid north is just 'paper' north, or the north we impose on a piece of paper when we put a grid overlay on it so that north to south is parallel to the side edges of the paper. True north or polar north is to be found at the literal 'North Pole' as on the globe.

16 'Signpost' mapping. This activity can be used in context and in progression with primary children of all ages and is very useful for reinforcing directional work. Ideally, start signpost mapping with infants. Show them a real signpost in a photo or drawing and give them the concrete experience of adopting a fixed position in the classroom with a signpost pointing to other children (see Figure 7.7). You can combine this activity with developing representational skills. How do you want children to show the location of what they are signposting

- With words?
- With pictures?
- With symbols?
- With symbols and a key?

You can also develop distance and scale measurement work. Do you want:

- Proportional length arrows or 'signposts' (that is short arrows)?
- Distances paced out and the pacings recorded along the 'signpost' line?
- The map drawing to scale?

Build in more precise directional work as you signpost map. Have pupils use the compass on site as they record their signposts and approximate directions. Alternatively, for pupils who are only able to use the four cardinal points, choose locations to signpost which represent these. 'Signpost' mapping offers many opportunities for differentiation by both task and outcome (see Figure 7.8).

Representation

As soon as the children make their own maps, they begin to explore representing life-size information on paper in their own way. They may draw pictures which they intend to replicate the feature, use the word for the feature or use a sign or symbol to show it. Infants will probably draw pictures. Side-view pictures will prevail for a long time. Children will often use word pictures and symbols side by side for years, occasionally including words, too. This is normal and

Figure 7.7

A progression in signpost mapping

Progress to graphical representation of this by getting pupils to record on paper where they are sitting in relation to pupils on their table.

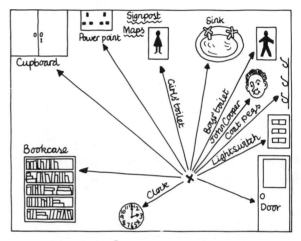

Extend this to objects in the room.

Do the activity in the school grounds, first within a limited space, e.g. the playground. Always get children to point first, then record, if they are very young.

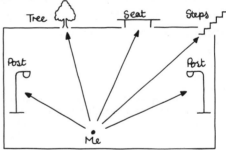

Extend the limits of the space.
Signpost map in the local area on a field visit.
Do the same activity in a contrasting area.

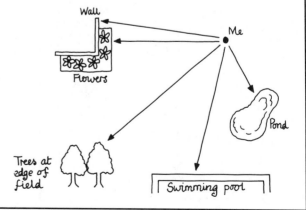

Figure 7.8

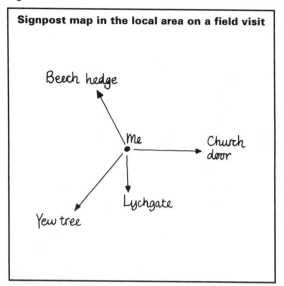

Signpost map in the local area on a field visit

Beech hedge

Me

Church door

Yew tree

Lychgate

acceptable child development in mapping. Figure 7.9 shows the general pattern of development in representing symbols.

Our objective is to guide children gradually towards seeing the need for a common code of symbols and a key to unlock or explain these symbols to others.

Figure 7.9

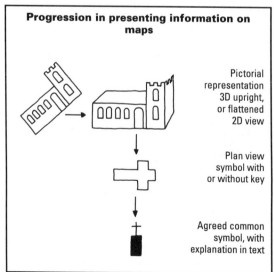

Progression in presenting information on maps

Pictorial representation 3D upright, or flattened 2D view

Plan view symbol with or without key

Agreed common symbol, with explanation in text

Children should have plenty of opportunity to use their own signs and symbols and talk about them to their classmates. They should not be made to feel that there is a right or wrong way of representing features on maps while they are infants or young juniors. Their development experience in plan view will encourage them to experiment with symbols, as will exposure to maps produced by teachers and commerce.

Eventually, we should lead children towards seeing the need for a commonly understood key such as Ordnance Survey maps use. Mapping in context, where the whole class has to map the same area, can be one opportunity to discuss this. When children have drawn their map, ask them to show each other their maps and get their partner to read their symbols. If their maps were to be published and sold, would thirty-six maps with thirty-six different sets of symbols and keys be helpful? How would map publishers get around this problem?

Once they understand the need for common keys and can decipher them to some extent on commercial maps, they should still have the freedom to have fun with their own symbols. Many computer programs will reinforce work on representation at different levels.

Perspective

The concept of perspective, which in mapwork is all about bringing children to an understanding of plan view, is a very difficult one. However, the basic activities which can be practised with infants to develop an understanding of plan view are numerous and fun. Many of them involve using traditional, standard classroom materials, but with a geographical awareness. Many of the materials are standard 'maths' equipment – for example 3D shapes or 'play materials':

sand, play mats, train tracks. Many materials traditionally used for art can aid the development of perspective.

Here is a range of activities which infants and older children with special educational needs will benefit from, with the objective of developing the concept of perspective.

Using maths shapes Maths shapes have **a** variety of uses in a geographical context.

1 Classroom standard regular 3D maths shapes can be drawn around, creating the first map the child has ever produced. Young children may need to work in pairs, with one holding the shape and the other drawing the outline if their motor control is poor.

2 After plenty of practice with standard regular shapes, pupils can draw around more difficult and irregular shapes, for example pyramids and cones.

3 The teacher or adult helper can use the overhead projector and screen to help illustrate plan view. Help the children identify the object and sketch it, if appropriate, first from the side view or elevation. Then ensure that they look down from above to predict what they expect to see on the screen. Next project the plan view silhouette of the object onto the screen and ask the children to record and label the plan view. Beware of translucent or transparent objects such as plastic beakers, as you will get an outer and an inner silhouette for top and base – but this is in itself a discussion point.

Using everyday objects A surprising number of everyday objects can be used to support geographical activity.

1 The same activities can be done with everyday classroom and household objects, with or without the overhead projector (see Figure 7.10).

2 Using doll's house furniture with an

Figure 7.10

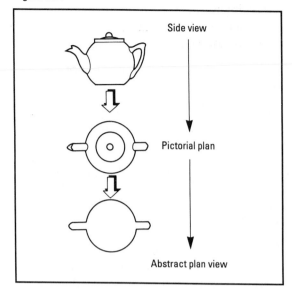

overhead projector is a useful activity. Let the children arrange the furniture to their choice in an imaginary room shape on the overhead projector, then let them talk out and match up the projected plan with their model room shapes.

Figure 7.11

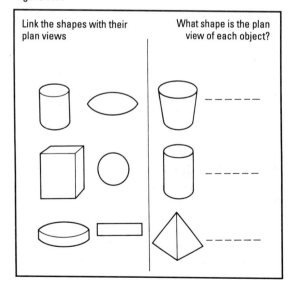

73

A more complex range of activities can also be developed with these everyday objects. Footprints and handprints can provide a useful starting point.

Ask children to classify a range of objects by height related to the plan view shape.

Ask children to sort the objects by function, colour or shape, and then draw around them.

Can children classify the objects by shape and then map their plan view? Is there a connection between shape and plan view? (See Figure 7.11.)

Can pupils add imaginary routes around their object maps? How could they record the route a snail might take around the map?

Printing in art can also be used to draw attention to plan view. Printing with 3D shapes will produce a plan view. Printing with flat shapes can also produce a type of map: a leaf will print a vein map if the reverse side is used to print.

Make rubbings in the local environment, for example of a manhole cover, as part of work on services is recording evidence by plan view.

Using the sand tray After free-play experience, the sand tray is ideal for developing geographical work.

Ask the children to 'print' in the damp sand with their shapes. Ask them to talk about, compare and name the plan views seen.

Encourage them to finger trace routes around 'mapped' shapes. Can they copy their sand picture on paper? Sometimes some sand in a book storage tray is more manageable than the vast expanse in the whole sand tray.

Ask pupils who have some geographical vocabulary to make hills and valleys in the

sand tray, to place shapes for houses, and so on. They are then creating a landscape which can be talked about and mapped at their level – with picture and plan view.

Set criteria for the landscape after free practice – a landscape with two hills, a river, a lake, a road and a small village. Can they design the map on paper first and then create it in sand?

Using play mats Play mats *are* plan views – of roads, fields, parks, railways – although sometimes their buildings are shown pictorially rather than in plan view.

After the children have had some free-play experience with the play mat, listen to their talk when using it. Can you interject and make them aware of the appropriate vocabulary – park, playground, and so on? Can they imagine that they are an inhabitant of their playtown flying over their play mat in a helicopter? What can they see?

Using model tracks and model building blocks There are more everyday materials that can help develop plan view.

Why not ask children to link their train tracks, road pieces, etc. on large pieces of paper as a base? How could they turn their model into a map? Once they have drawn around the tracks, can they ask some friends to recreate the model on the map base? Brio® track is excellent for this.

Add imaginary 'buildings' alongside the tracks or roads, using cardboard boxes or Bauplay® blocks. Children will turn the blocks into homes, shops, buildings, and other buildings. They can be drawn around, removed and given a colour key.

Using children's own models If groups of children have made their own model village or model landscape, why not get them to draw around the model houses, bridges, etc. and then remove them to show plan view?

They can then add road lines and stream lines and think how to show the plan view of a tree to complete their map of the landscape.

Placing small modelled objects in a shoe box and then mapping their plan view and location is another good activity to develop the concept of perspective .

Distance

Distance is the most difficult concept of mapwork. Although pupils do relative scale drawing every time they make a map as they are reducing real life to smaller proportions, absolute scale drawing is a difficult activity in both maths and geography. The mathematics Statutory Order requires accurate scale work for level 5. The geography Statutory Order refers specifically to scale at level 4. Gg1 level 4b requires that children 'measure the straight line distance between two points on a plan'. For both subject areas, progression in relative and comparative scale work is necessary throughout the junior school before actual scale measurement can be grasped. You will know when individual pupils in your class are ready to address accurate scale drawing.

Here is some tried and tested advice on starting scale work.

Making scale drawings Try starting with a large, regular 3-dimensional feature. How can you fit a mobile classroom shape onto paper? What about the school or local swimming pool?

How can we turn that into a diagram on paper? This can be a more stimulating alternative to the 'draw a plan of the classroom'. A simple 1 cm to 1 m scale – 1:100 – is the easiest to manage.

Fieldwork activities indicated later – such as trying to find the height of a tree or cliff – involve ground measurement and scale recording at a 1:100 scale.

Use 1 cm or 2 cm graph paper to start scale work. Either can be used on a 'one unit on the paper equals one unit on the ground' basis, or by relating the actual distance on the paper to the ground measurement.

Reading measurement scales Remember that without a scale bar or scale explanation, a scale map is meaningless.

When using large-scale OS maps or their extracts, introduce meaningful scales at some point. OS 1:1250 means that 1 cm on the map equals 12.5 m on ground while OS 1:25 000 means 1 cm on the map equals 25 m on the ground. To help develop the concept of map scale, make sure children have concrete experience of what 12.5 m and 25 m feel like to walk and of what they look like.

One activity for starting scale drawing is scaling down a ruler or small box to half size, or 1:2 scale, followed by drawing a scale plan of the desk. This is, however, an isolated skill practice activity unrelated to a geographical context such as place or theme.

An enquiry activity could be used to start scale work. Faced with the question 'Can we improve the layout of our classroom?' children will need to scale map the classroom and its main features. The main features may be approximated to full metre or half metre lengths for ease, and the class grouped to produce scale plan cut-outs of the classroom, table groupings, etc. They can then move the cut-outs around on the classroom plan, think about the space between their arrangements, translating scale distance into real distance, and decide on the best layout before any classroom reorganisation. Perhaps they will discover that the current organisation is the best one!

Figure 7.12

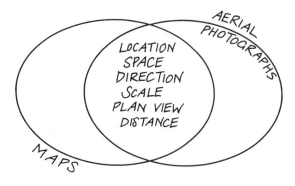

Photographs and satellite images

There is an important link between mapwork and the use of photographs, especially oblique and aerial photographs. Both types of material can help pupils to develop the concepts of location, direction, plan view and distance as shown in the overlap diagram (Figure 7.12).

The use of photographs to develop geographical concepts and skills is new to many primary teachers. Some teachers find it useful to have the difference between maps and aerial photographs defined. An aerial photograph is an actual snapshot in time of the landscape, taken from a plane or a balloon. If it is oblique, it was taken looking down towards the ground at an angle from the plane. It is a vertical photograph if taken from directly above the scene. A map is an abstract representation of the landscape and usually includes a limited range of information, whereas an aerial photograph includes everything visible.

The geography Order programme of study for key stage 1 requires children to use oblique aerial photographs by level 3. The use of vertical aerial photographs is required in key stage 2.

Progression in the use of photographs

There is a progression in familiarising children with the use of aerial photographs so that they can identify features on them and match them to a map by the end of key stage 2. This progression is in Figure 7.13.

This progression goes hand in hand with the progression in viewing objects which develops plan view or perspective as already discussed (see Figure 7.14).

Here are some suggestions to encourage the use of photographs in geography. The use of geographical vocabulary will be developed at the same time .

Take photos around your school buildings and grounds – side view, oblique view and plan view. This need only be done once. Have them mounted for young infants to

Figure 7.13

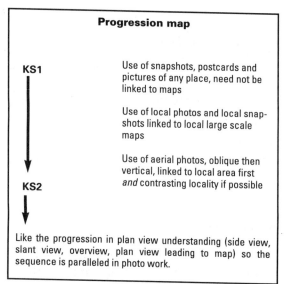

Figure 7.14

Viewing objects	
Actual objects	**Photos of scenes**
Side view 2D or 3D ▼ Slant view 3D ▼ Overhead view 2D ▼ Plan view 2D 'Map' of object	Side view photo ▼ Oblique view photo ▼ Vertical aerial photo ▼ Plan view photo – the more abstract, the smaller the scale

talk about and identify. Recognising familiar objects from unfamiliar angles – brick bonding, manhole covers, corners of buildings, the pond, seats – helps develop the idea of oblique and plan view.

Build up a collection of postcards. Some of them will often show oblique coastal views, oblique views taken from towers or high view-points. Children can discuss and identify geographical features freely or with your guided questions. Picture views from old calendars, etc. often have oblique views, as do illustrations from books. Local newspapers can often supply oblique and vertical aerial views, but they are usually in black and white.

Finally progress to vertical aerial photograph use. The children can use magnifying glasses to help them identify features if they want.

Figure 7.15 shows a range of activities which can be undertaken using vertical aerial photographs.

Currently the cost and availability of aerial photographs are issues for schools. A set of about six identical photographs is the most that is necessary. The class should be organised into groups, one of which can use the photographs individually or in twos. A

Figure 7.15

Using a vertical aerial photograph	
For ease of use the photo should be laminated! Otherwise use overhead transparency acetate overlays. Wipe-off pens essential.	**Overlay it with an alpha-numerical grid to locate features** *Key question: Where is our school?*
Use with familiar oblique or side view photos to link photo to location on aerial photo *Key question: Can you locate roughly where this photo was taken?*	**Practise compass directions** *Key question: Which way do you travel to get to ...?*
Use with corresponding OS map to match up features *Key question: Is this building really a church?*	**Measure distance** **a Direct distance as the crow flies** **b Distance along a road, river, canal or railway** *Key question: How far is it from our school to the leisure centre? Measure in 'ruler' distance or use scale according to maths ability.*
Draw a map Freehand (or same scale) by using an overlay – select out certain information according to map purpose. *Key question: Can you show why the town grew up here?*	**Plan a route** *Key question: How do we get from our school to the leisure centre?*
Identify changes on photo from personal experience *Key question: This photo was taken in 1989. Was the supermarket built then?*	**Map the land-use** Linear land use – road, rail networks *Key question: Is this place easy to get to?*
Talk about features *Key question: What is this?*	Spatial land use – housing areas, fields, woods *Key question: Is there more settlement than green space in our environment?*

minimum requirement is to have a set of vertical aerial photographs showing the pupils' school and its environs. If your school is twinned with a school elsewhere in the UK you may be able to acquire aerial photographs of the twin school and its locality. If the children are investigating this twin school by distance learning, then an aerial photograph is a useful information source. If they are able to visit this distant locality, then the photographs can be used before, during and after the visit as an aid to to predicting what pupils expect to see and to check up on what was actually identified.

Satellite imagery

The Statutory Order does not require primary children to use satellite images – images of the earth's surface taken from special satellites many miles above the surface of the earth. The satellite image represents, in a way, an extreme of the camera 'zoom lens' image. The images are taken at a very great distance away from the earth and show large areas of land. Technically satellite images are not photographs. They are responses recorded according to the amount of heat emitted by land, sea and man-made features. Scientifically-minded children may benefit from knowing this, but it is not essential at primary level. Nevertheless, the primary teacher who did not make use of the children's awareness of satellite images would be unwise, as primary children are constantly exposed to them in both home and school life.

In school life, the newest atlases often contain satellite images of the UK, Europe and the world as alternatives to actual maps. In home life, television presents children with satellite images of north-western Europe and the UK on the weather forecast. These satellite images help bring a better,

easier understanding of the globe and of weather and climate processes, and we help children by referring to them. The complex matter of false colour interpretation and technical details is for secondary school work. The connection with atlas, globe and weather work is all that we need to deal with at primary level.

Atlas and globe work

Atlas and globe work is often seen as an activity quite unrelated to mapwork. Atlas and globe work is, however, the smallest-scale work at the end of the chain of geographical vocabulary referring to maps (see Figure 7.16).

The smallest-scale representations of landscape and sea are to be found in atlases and on the globe. Children will not necessarily make the connection between large-scale maps and atlases and globes without your help.

Figure 7.16

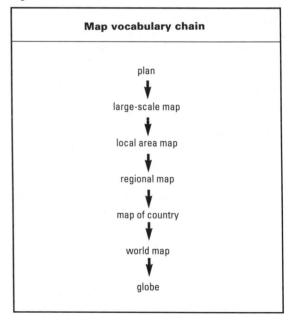

The large-scale map of the local area can be likened to what the camera zoom lens might see if it zoomed in on a particular spot on the globe or world atlas map. Older juniors are surprised to learn that an OS 1:50 000 map they may be using covers a measurable portion of the atlas map of the UK.

Children of all ages are usually fascinated by atlas maps and the globe, even though fascination does not equal understanding. Traditionally, the use of the globe and atlas, where it occurred, took place in upper junior classes. A more comprehensive building up of understanding is likely if the globe is used constantly throughout the primary years. Each classroom needs its own. This is now a financial possibility with the introduction of inflatable globes (see Chapter 12).

Some atlas work is necessary in top infant classes and in lower juniors, too. A variety of large-format, clearly presented atlases, appropriate to this age range, is now coming onto the market.

The Statutory Order now requires us to address globe and atlas use in very specific terms. The programme of study for key stage 1 requires pupils to do work which enables them to:

- Identify land and sea on maps and globes
  (PoS, paragraph 3)
- Name where they live
- Name the country in which they live
- Know that their own country is part of the United Kingdom, which is made up of England, Wales Scotland and Northern Ireland. *(PoS, paragraph 6)*

Pupils working towards level 3 should be taught to:

- Identify on globes or maps the points of reference specified on Maps A and C at the end of the programmes of study (i.e. maps of the UK and the world)

- Locate on a map the constituent countries of the United Kingdom
- Mark on a map of the British Isles approximately where they live.
  (PoS, paragraph 7)

In the key stage 2 programme of study relating to level 4, pupils need to:

- Find information in an atlas using the index and contents pages.

Pupils working towards level 5 should be taught to:

- Use latitude and longitude to locate places on atlas maps
- Recognise that a globe can be represented as a flat surface
- Interpret relief maps
- Extract information from distribution patterns shown on maps.
  (PoS, paragraph 4)

Pupils should learn to identify, on globes and maps, local places, places that are frequently in the news, and places they are studying. They should be taught to:

- Identify on globes and maps points of reference specified on Maps A and C and on Maps B and D at the end of the programmes of study (i.e. both maps of the UK and maps of the world)
- Name and locate on a map the constituent countries of the United Kingdom and mark on a map of the British Isles approximately where they live.
  (PoS, paragraph 6)

Pupils working towards level 5 should be taught to:

- Identify on globes or maps the points of reference specified on Maps E and F at the end of the programmes of study (i.e. the simpler and more complex maps of Europe). *(PoS, paragraph 7)*

Some suggestions for starting globe work

1 Recall for the children the satellite images of the world that they often see on television, for example at the beginning of the weather forecast or on the news.
2 Talk about what the men who travelled to the moon saw when they looked back towards the Earth.
3 Have pictures of the Earth in space in the classroom.
4 Talk about how things get smaller when you go up away from the ground in an aeroplane. Maybe, if any have flown, one of your pupils had a window seat and did look down.
5 Use every opportunity, planned and spontaneous, to point out, or let children point out, first land and sea, and then countries and places on the globe.
6 Let children handle the globe, talk about it, and point out places to each other.
7 Sometimes rolling a flat atlas map into a tube can help pupils make the connection between globe, world map and atlas (atlas being a book of maps).

As the globe becomes an integral and often-used classroom resource, introduce the atlas use alongside it.

Suggestions for starting atlas work

1 Let the pupils enjoy looking at and talking about the atlas.
2 Relate places pupils have mentioned on the globe to their location on the atlas map. Pupils can reinforce this new knowledge by place-name stickers on globes, plastic floor maps and wall maps, or by writing directly on to special washable-surface floor and wall maps.
3 Always have available a large wall atlas map showing countries or relief on which to point out locations.

4 Let the children talk about and point to locations on these large wall maps.
5 Use the maps with the children to make displays. Mount pictures, postcards, drawings, cut-outs of products, and so on around the map, linked by strings to the locations of their origin. Refer to the display after it has been finished. Don't just let it merge into the 'wallscape'.
6 Get children to write about their holiday in the 'shape' of the island or country to which they travelled (see Figure 7.17).
   They can then trace the shape with the help of a friend, or the teacher could trace it for them, building a photocopy outline bank of Spain, France, the UK, Crete, Australia, and so on.
7 Refer to places identified on the large wall maps in the children's atlases – on world and continent maps, etc. – so that the children recognise that the same shape represents the same county or continent, even at different sizes.
8 Use every opportunity, spontaneous and planned, to point out, or let children point out, places mentioned in classwork, in the news, or by their friends.

What about the atlas knowledge required in the programmes of study?

There is a great danger that rote learning may prevail with atlas work in the primary school as a result of the Statutory Order. Apparently, the easiest way to deal with the place knowledge required for the various maps at the end of the programmes of study is to get the pupils to practise learning and drawing them, and to keep testing the memory outcome. Some schools have talked about 'sending the maps home for homework'.

Little understanding of the relationships between locations and spaces results from

Figure 7.17

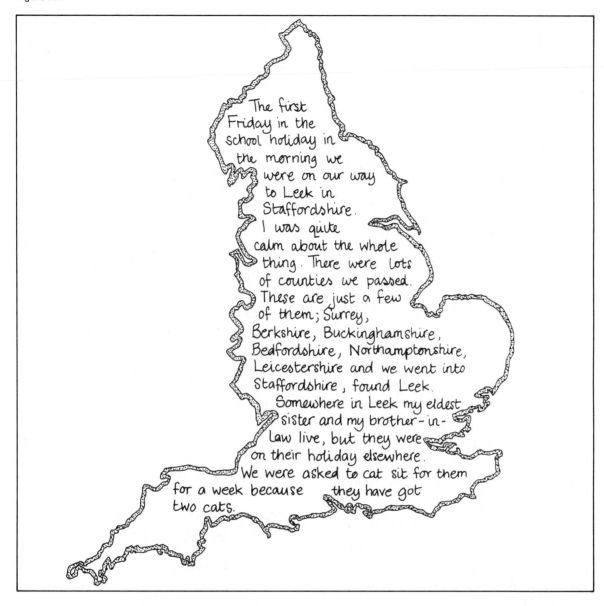

The first Friday in the school holiday in the morning we were on our way to Leek in Staffordshire. I was quite calm about the whole thing. There were lots of counties we passed. These are just a few of them; Surrey, Berkshire, Buckinghamshire, Bedfordshire, Northamptonshire, Leicestershire and we went into Staffordshire, found Leek. Somewhere in Leek my eldest sister and my brother-in-law live, but they were on their holiday elsewhere. We were asked to cat sit for them for a week because they have got two cats.

such learning. Take the real example of an eleven-year-old pupil who in a test located various places on a blank world map in the correct position relative to the edges of the paper, but with the world map upside down! Children have to build up an understanding of the relationship between world and country scale, space, and places within the space to grasp atlas work.

Although there may be a case for the occasional 'fill in these places on the map' assessment with older children, places and countries should always be referred to in context. That context does not always have to be in specific geography teaching. Every time a locality is referred to in geographical learning, it should be identified in the atlas, on a wall map or globe, as appropriate.

Upper juniors should have an atlas each or, at least, one between two. This ideal may well take time to achieve due to annual budgets and the need for a cycle of replacing worn stocks.

Atlases should be easily accessible to children as independent learners. Avoid locking them up or storing them in a central resource area. Avoid sharing atlases between classes. Children need to keep them in their trays, drawers or desks for quick, independent access. If the school budget has not yet permitted this critical provision, and central storage is necessary, there must be an atlas in the class library for quick reference in the interim.

A fun atlas quiz is a good occasional activity for the whole class to assess how children's knowledge is progressing.

If you are pointing out a place on a wall map or on an overhead transparency, or if a pupil is doing so, have the rest of the group locate it in their atlas, too.

- Who can do it first?
- Who can help their neighbour find the country shape and name?
- Who can show the shape and name to their neighbour?

Ask children to work in pairs or small groups, taking it in turns to quiz the others.

- On which page is the map of Europe?
- On which page is there a map of Australia?
- On which page is *just* Australia shown?
- On which map is the mouth of the Amazon shown most clearly?
- Find London on the map on page 20 and point it out to me.

Teach atlas skills; they do not get absorbed incidentally. The use of the contents list at the front and the index at the back has to be taught, in the same way that information reference book skills have to be taught. The learning and reinforcement of these study skills taught in this geographical context can develop the English curriculum and can be recorded as such. Practising these skills can be made fun for children by turning it into a whole-class speed game for ten minutes or so at periodic intervals during a term.

- Who can be first to tell me the page on which I can find a map of Europe?
- Who can find a map of England which shows how high the land is, using the contents page to start with?

Latitude and longitude also need to be taught and practised. Many atlases explain how the latitude/longitude grid is imposed on the globe and how to use the system, so familiarise yourself with it first. Latitude and longitude are in fact much more complex than OS map-type grid referencing. It is useful to make the link between the two systems, but tell the children that latitude and longitude always start from the Equator and use north/south references first, before east or west of Greenwich. 'Along the corridor and up the stairs' or two cardinal directions is no use for latitude and longitude!

Remember that in both globe and atlas work two different concepts are being developed – one relating to space or area, the other to specific locations or place. Land masses, sea and countries occupy SPACE. Settlements appear first as points on maps and therefore as points located – PLACE. Some linear features can also be recognised depending on scale – chiefly the larger rivers such as the Amazon or the Nile. Roads and railways may, of course, be shown on country scale maps.

Figure 7.18 summarises the development of map skills against levels as a check for your planning.

Figure 7.18

The development of map skills including all NC requirements

	Location	Representation	Distance	Perspective	Style	Drawing	Map use
Level 1	Follow directions: up and down, left and right.	Use own symbols on imaginary maps.	Use relative vocabulary: bigger/smaller, like/unlike, etc.	Model layouts. Draw round objects to make a plan.	Extract information and add to picture maps. Use globes.	Draw picture maps of imaginary places and from stories.	Talk about own picture maps.
Level 2	Follow directions: north, south, east and west.	Use class agreed symbols on simple maps.	Draw objects on a table to scale, using squared paper.	Look down on objects to make a plan.	Land/sea on globes. Teacher drawn base maps and large scale OS maps.	Make a representation of a real or imaginary place.	Follow a route using a plan.
Level 3	Use letter/number coordinates and eight compass points.	Introduce need for a key and standard symbols.	Simple scale drawing of classroom using 1 cm²: 1 m².	Draw sketch map from high viewpoint. Add slope and height.	Identify features on oblique aerial photographs.	Make a map of a short route with features in the correct order.	Use large scale map outside. Use maps of other localities.
Level 4	Use four figure coordinates to locate features on a map.	Draw a sketch map using symbols and a key.	Measure straight line distance on a plan.	Use models to introduce idea of contours. Submerge or slice.	Use index and contents page in atlases. Medium scale OS maps.	Draw a variety of thematic maps, based on own data.	Compare large scale map and vertical air photo. Select maps for a purpose.
Level 5	Use six figure grid references to locate features on OS map. Latitude and longitude on atlas maps.	Use OS standard symbols. Develop use of atlas symbols.	Scale reading and drawing. Comparison of map scales.	Interpret relief maps. Identify relief features.	Interpret distribution maps. Concept of globe as flat map.	Draw scale plans of increasing complexity.	Follow route on small scale OS map and describe features seen.

Based on the matrix in the GA book, *Geographical Work in Primary and Middle Schools*

8

GEOGRAPHICAL FIELDWORK

A philosophy of fieldwork

Fieldwork means active geographical learning outside the classroom. It has long been acknowledged by HMI and teachers with enthusiasm for primary geography as being a basic tool to foster sound learning and understanding. Fieldwork, like assessment, is not a bolt-on accessory; it must be an integral part of planning for National Curriculum geography. There are many opportunities which can be taken within any key stage plan to develop fieldwork skills. Well-planned and executed fieldwork enhances the children's learning. Some key questions and focus questions used in units of work will require fieldwork.

Our primary school pupils are entitled to continuity and progression in fieldwork for these reasons:

- Good practice in geographical topics requires it
- It helps develop process learning
- It is active learning
- It is motivating
- It is enjoyable
- It can be fun
- It can be exciting
- It helps develop a feeling for the environment
- It aids children's personal and social development

- It can aid cross-curricular learning
- Occasionally it can involve a small physical challenge.

What other area of the curriculum lends itself so easily to first-hand experience as geography? Geography is all around us *now* – a wonderful opportunity to be used as a teaching resource! Perhaps it is just because the landscape and the processes, natural and human, which operate upon it to produce patterns are always there, that both children and adults can take it for granted and ignore geography. Fieldwork is an essential skill to develop a child's sense of place and space, helping to answer the basic question 'Where am I?'

In the current climate, it is actually easier to choose not to take children beyond the confines of the classroom for active learning. Legal, financial and organisational considerations can overwhelm even the keenest teacher, so we need to be sure that our rationale for fieldwork is a strong one. We never need to convince our pupils that fieldwork is a good practice – they love it! But we may need to convince others that spending time *beyond* the school grounds is essential to good practice in primary geography, history and science. Head teachers, governors and parents will need to be convinced of the value of fieldwork, because of cost and safety issues.

Head teachers will have further concerns relating to supply cover costs to increase staff/pupil ratios, their own possible time involvement to lower these ratios, and general use of children's time through the whole curriculum. Other colleagues who have not necessarily been involved in fieldwork to date will need convincing, because they may feel it will involve yet more work on their part.

However, the geography Statutory Order does support good practice in fieldwork, because it would be impossible to deliver the programme of study and assess children's work without engaging in first-hand, enquiry-based fieldwork in, at the very least, the school grounds and the local area.

The programme of study for key stage 1 states quite clearly under Geographical Skills paragraph 1:

"Enquiry should form an important part of pupils' work in geography in key stage 1. Work should be linked to pupils' own interests, experience and capabilities and should lead to investigations based on both fieldwork and classroom activities. Much of pupils' learning in key stage 1 should be based on direct experience, practical activities and exploration of the local area."

and at key stage 2:

"Enquiry should form an important part of pupils' work in key stage 2. It should take account of pupils' interests, experience and capabilities, and lead to investigations based on fieldwork and classroom activities."

The programmes of study, like the attainment targets, are legally binding, so fieldwork is now made statutory. However, there is no stated time requirement for the fieldwork element of primary geography in the Statutory Order, as this would also be legally binding and put schools in an impossible position. But the National Curriculum *Geography for Ages 5–16 Final Report*, June 1990, suggested this as a minimum entitlement for work further afield:

"Every child in years 1 to 6 should experience at least one day visit per year to a location beyond walking distance from the school, so that the contrasting geography of another locality can be explored."

As a guide, the authors suggest that at least one fieldwork visit beyond the school gate every term is a realistic target. It is taken for granted that the duration of such fieldwork will vary according to the children's age and needs, and will include the demands of other subject fieldwork.

Both good practice in primary geography and the geography Statutory Order, reinforce the fact that fieldwork must be integrated into the geography curriculum. Like mapwork, it should not be done as a 'parcel' of learning, but should be a skill practised in the context of a place – Gg2, and one or more themes – Gg3, 4 and 5 – Physical, Human and Environmental Geography.

The integration of fieldwork skills means that they must be carefully planned for, carried out and followed up back in the classroom. Figure 7.1 indicated the minimum of fieldwork skills and equipment that need to be planned for in the primary school.

Continuity and progression in fieldwork

The key to achieving continuity and progression in fieldwork is setting learning objectives through key questions and the following criteria. Progression in fieldwork is achieved over key stages 1 and 2 by building up conceptual development through work in the following areas.

1 The precision and detail in collecting data.

2 Depth in the amount of follow-up analysis of data.

3 The scale of locality in which pupils do the fieldwork, moving from the familiar to the unfamiliar.

4 The complexity of ideas and techniques pupils use in fieldwork.

Here are some examples to clarify what is meant by this:

1 Increasing the precision and detail required in collecting, handling and recording data could involve:

- A key stage 1 pupil doing a building survey in the local area being required to observe front door numbers and colours and to ask the adult accompanying the group to record these on a large-scale map
- A key stage 2 pupil doing a similar survey being required to do their own recording and accompanying it with several sketches of complete houses, labelling all the house types (terraced, detached, etc.) and house features such as slate tiles, brick, weatherboarding, double-glazing.

2 Increasing depth in the amount of follow-up and analysis of data could be developed in, for example, weather work, which lends itself to such progression. Development can be observed in:

- Infants noting and displaying their weather observations in a class bar chart and writing a sentence to assess whether there are more rainy days than sunny days in one week
- Juniors inputting their observations made from accurate measurements into a computer database and examining the resulting computer graphs to see if a

pattern can be observed – the resulting pattern could be compared with the one from the previous year if statistics were kept for the same period.

3 Increasing the scale of the locality in which children do the fieldwork means moving from the familiar to the unfamiliar, involving:

- For the youngest children, fieldwork activities in the context of the school building and site – many studies can be made on a small scale in this safe and easily accessible location
- For children progressing through key stage 1, fieldwork in the locality around the school
- For children progressing through key stage 2, fieldwork in unfamiliar places away from the school, elsewhere in their home area, or much further away in the UK – some primary schools, particularly those located near the Channel ports, may even take a day trip to continental Europe or take a residential trip to a twin town or contrasting locality.

The length of time a field visit needs to take should, in theory, relate to the purpose of the fieldwork. Where costed transport is necessary, practice sometimes dictates that some geography-focused fieldwork needs to be included alongside some other activity such as historical or scientific fieldwork. In the past, the idea of fieldwork in the primary school developed from the post-war school outing to a well-known location a long way from the school, and we have inherited the feeling that a field trip needs to last for a school day.

The fieldwork activity needs to last as long as the teacher and pupils plan for it, although economics may distort best practice. It could be as short as one hour investigating their local shop. Progression is achieved by increasing the length of fieldwork experiences and moving to unknown, more distant, locations.

Figure 8.1 shows diagrammatically the progression and continuity of fieldwork experience which good practice in primary geography requires. The Statutory Order does not mention residential fieldwork because the charging issues following the Education Reform Act, 1986, would make it impossible to comply with them. Nevertheless, the requirement to study a contrasting locality in the UK will only be motivating for most children if they can visit such a distant place and study it at first hand.

4 Increasing the complexity of ideas and techniques can again be illustrated by weather work. The Statutory Order requires that:

Figure 8.1

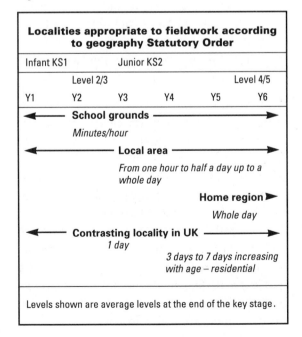

- Infants begin to notice the effects of rain-water on different surfaces such as soil and tarmac, and observe and experience daily weather patterns – both can be done in the school grounds

- Juniors at level 4 of key stage 2 study microclimate. Microclimate is a new concept for many teachers as well as pupils. It means studying the effect of site on weather measurements. Different temperature readings will be taken at different mini-sites in the school grounds. Those taken at the same time on a sunny site and in the shade of a building will vary. Those taken on a windy day in an exposed playground site in the sun will be lower than those recorded in a sheltered sunny site. Soil temperature readings will vary when taken under bushes and in a flowerbed. Such different readings will need to be collected and logged and their locations mapped as part of a wider investigation. The most sophisticated level of microclimate work for schools lucky enough to afford the technology (several hundred pounds in cost) is to use computer remote control sensors to log temperature, windspeed, etc. in the various mini-sites, but this progression should only be undertaken by pupils who have used and understood standard equipment for themselves first. This could be a sharp-focus enquiry on where to site some new playground seats or as part of a science/geography-focus weather topic.

Continuity in fieldwork goes hand in hand with progression. It is achieved by practising the same skills but at ever-increasing depth. The transference of skills learnt in one situation to another location is very important. The use of the compass in a fieldwork location, even though it may be used every time a class goes into the local area or school grounds, needs to be practised in a new and distant location. The child is often excited in an unfamiliar location and will need the confidence to repeat an activity already carried out in a secure environment by repeating it, and relating to it in a much wider context. Estimating north, checking this with the compass and pointing out landmarks and their direction relating to north, need to be applied at the top of that exciting castle, too, so that the children realise that the skill is transferable.

Continuity of location is also important. Fieldwork in the school grounds and local area will be ongoing throughout key stages 1 and 2, although new areas will be brought in with progress up through the junior school, as in Figure 8.1.

Greater depth and breadth of study in any continuous use of the same area is essential, reflecting the importance of whole-school planning and the passing on of records. A local stream examined as a geographical feature – its banks, meanders and direction of flow – in the lower junior years may be used with the upper juniors in the context of a pollution project to investigate pollution and conservation issues as part of a wider local area study.

Some examples of the kind of fieldwork activities which can be carried out in the local area in particular environments are given in Chapter 9.

Safety and organisational issues

Well-planned and effectively organised fieldwork will be one of the most satisfying professional experiences a teacher can have. It will prove extremely motivating and enjoyable for pupils by providing learning achievements and will win the admiration and respect of accompanying parents. On the other hand, fieldwork undertaken lightly will be a nightmare for all concerned.

Safety concerns and organisational issues are interlinked. For example, safety factors impinge on the organisation of pupils working in groups, which must be planned well in advance. The two areas will be dealt with together here, and they apply to all fieldwork whether it lasts an hour in the local area or a week in a contrasting locality.

Fieldwork will be a crucial part of the topic or theme the class is studying. It will most likely be part of an enquiry, so we shall need to plan:

- What key questions the pupils will be asking
- What tasks they will be doing on site
- What is to be done in the classroom before the visit
- Whether there will be one visit or several
- The time limits on each visit
- How the pupils will be organised on site – whether they will do every task, all collecting similar data, or whether each group will pursue a different activity to contribute to a whole study
- What follow up on the fieldwork will take place in school.

Additionally, your school should have a policy and guidelines on fieldwork which cover safety and organisational issues. A similar process needs to be gone through when organising every visit, so it will save time if teachers have a copy of the guidelines to act as a check-list. Moreover, some of us are naturally expert at hazard perception – seeing where the dangers could lie on a visit – whereas others amongst us may not have had a great deal of experience. It is hoped that the following may prove helpful for primary geographical fieldwork.

The essential formalities

1 Think through the aims, objectives and broad learning outcomes of the field-work.
2 Check that you are familiar with any school or LEA documents regarding pupil – teacher ratios, costing, insurance, etc.
3 Ensure that you understand charging legalities and your own school's charging policy; obtain costings.
4 Seek permission from the head teacher and governors to take pupils off site for fieldwork.
5 Arrange dates and times.
6 Consult any colleagues who need to know.
6 Arrange for extra adult help.
7 Obtain parental consent on a standardised form. *These forms must be carried off-site by the party leader on any occasion, whether local or residential.* Many schools have two types of consent form: those which are filled in once a year to give blanket consent for local visits over the year; and those which are filled in specifically for residential visits or those of longer duration. The DES book mentioned at the end of this fieldwork section provides examples of such forms. Remember that consent forms for residential trips need to include any notes on:

- consent for surgery if action is considered to be urgently needed
- religious limitations on surgery
- details of contact numbers of parents or guardians.

Prepare yourself

1 For your own peace of mind, make yourself aware of pupils' up-to-date medical and dietary details. This is essential for residential work, but good practice also for day fieldwork visits. Bee-sting allergies can be as dangerous 15 minutes away from school as 100 miles, as can diabetes and asthma! Religious beliefs may forbid pupils to eat certain meats such as beef or pork, or any food in which beef and pork products are ingredients.
2 Make a visit to the fieldwork site. *This is essential preparation.* For residential fieldwork at least the party leader should have made a visit in advance.
3 Collect any relevant materials on your pre-visit. List and assess potential hazards and organisational details.

- Where can the coach drop off and pick up safely?
- Do you know where the nearest toilets for pupils are?
- Which site will be suitable for lunch?
- Is there a telephone box nearby in case help is suddenly needed?
- Are there any points which will present difficulties for special needs pupils?
- What alternatives or modifications can you make to your plan if the weather is bad?
- What equipment might you need to bring?

4 Sort out costing and insurance procedures with the head teacher.

Prepare your helpers

1 Take the time to explain the purpose and expected outcomes to other colleagues or, more likely, parent helpers. *They cannot be effective if they are not fully aware and involved.* Work outside the school site is

Figure 8.2

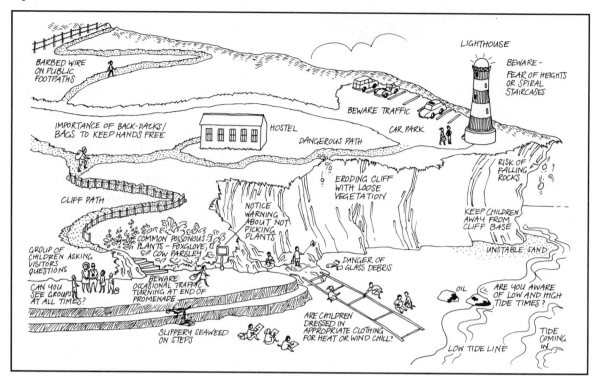

Figure 8.3

not a holiday for helpers; make them aware of this!

2 Ensure that they know what to do in the event of an accident and who has final responsibility for decisions on the trip.

3 Ensure that they know what your discipline standards are and what their role is regarding them.

Prepare the parents

1 Inform the parents in writing of the field trip location, date, time and nature of cost, voluntary or compulsory, and method of optional payment.

2 For residential trips, arrange a parents' meeting to explain supervision arrangements, clothing and footwear needs, spending money arrangements and expected behaviour standards. Allow parents to air any concerns. Face-to-face communication is usually far more beneficial for everyone, but provide a written checklist for parents at the meeting, too, and see that any absent parents receive it.

Prepare your pupils

1 Carry out the work you have planned to do in the classroom before you go.

2 Practise any necessary fieldwork skills in the school grounds before you go according to your knowledge of the children's experience.

3 Ensure that the children understand why they are going to do fieldwork.

4 Ensure that children know what their tasks are to be on the visit. Make them aware that you have prepared parent helpers. If any child's behaviour threatens the safety of the party, you are entitled not to take them off site. You must enlist your head teacher's support. Due discussion with parents in advance about expected standards of behaviour, is

reasonable. If a head teacher is adamant that a pupil should go, then the teacher/pupil ratio must be raised to your 'safe' level.

5 Go through your code of behaviour with the pupils.

6 If travelling by coach, anticipate travel sickness arrangements. Every child should take a spare plastic bag. The coach should also be provided with a bucket, toilet rolls, paper tissues, paper towel roll and air fresheners.

7 Check up on other medical arrangements – inhalers for asthmatics, etc.

8 Ensure that pupils are aware of any hazards, and that they know who to turn to in the event of a problem.

9 Remind pupils to bring suitable clothing, food and equipment.

Managing the fieldwork successfully on the day or residential journey

1 Be aware of the weather forecast.

2 Check names and numbers of pupils; see that all staff have a list of names.

3 Check that everyone is aware of the 'chain of command' – who has final responsibility during fieldwork.

4 Check that you have appropriate emergency contact numbers: for a day visit, school and head teacher at home; for a residential visit, the above, plus one of these – local adviser, inspector or director of education.

5 Check that pupils needing travel sickness pills have taken them and given all medication to you. Allocate seats at the front of the coach. Check that everyone has a spare plastic bag.

6 Check that you have remembered the whistle and the first aid kit; a small pocket kit is necessary on a local walking visit.

7 Have a cash float and/or cheques for entrance fees and emergencies.

8 Remind pupils of hazards and code of behaviour.

9 Check that pupils have equipment as organised.

10 Upon arrival, assess the site. Things may have changed since your pre-visit. Take contingency action if necessary.

11 *Have a safe, brilliantly organised and enjoyable field visit!*

And now you have successfully returned ...

1 Carry out planned follow-up work.

2 Write, or see that children write, any public relations thank you letters.

3 Evaluate with the children what you all learned from the visit.

4 Keep any useful materials, especially those which will cut down on work for the next time.

5 Communicate the result of your work to colleagues, other classes, parents and governors, as appropriate, to inform, encourage and celebrate successful work. Use displays in a central place in school, assemblies, parents' meetings, staff and governors' meetings, if appropriate.

Further details and advice about geographical fieldwork as it applies to the primary school can be found in The Geographical Association's *Geography Outside the Classroom* and in *Safety in Outdoor Education*, DES, 1989, a copy of which was sent to all schools by the DES in 1989. You may need to seek it out from your head teacher. It *should* be there somewhere.

Fieldwork skills and techniques

There is a strong link between mapwork skills and fieldwork skills. Many of the elements of mapwork skills needed for progression in mapwork have been dealt with in Chapter 7, for example direction and compass use. Fieldwork skills and techniques are concerned with the observation, use of equipment and recording data through the enquiry process. When guided by the right key questions, observation and recording will develop a sense of location, space and place and build up a knowledge of patterns which can be recognised in the physical and the human environment. Observation and recording will also lead pupils to recognise the processes which are taking place around them, thereby developing their understanding of patterns and processes through first-hand experiences of similarity and difference.

Progression in landscape sketching

In asking the key questions – How can I record what I see here? What is this building like? What can I see from this viewpoint? How is the land used in this place? – pupils will find the skill of landscape sketching helpful to record information.

Technically speaking, drawing a fieldwork sketch at its highest level – for example, 'an annotated sketch ... to record and interpret a landscape' – is not a statutory requirement until level 6 of the geography Statutory Order. However, this skill has a progression within it which starts at key stage 1 with an activity which many infant teachers will recognise – the sketching and labelling of a house. Many geographically- or artistically-minded teachers have always encouraged landscape sketching, so many primary school pupils transfer at age 11 well on the way to achieving this level 6 goal. A geographical landscape sketch is *not* a work of art. It is a sketched drawing of a view which – and here it differs from the artist's aim – will communicate to whoever looks at it the main features and use of the land sketched. Geographical vocabulary is used explicitly to label or annotate the sketch; this would be unlikely in a sketch which was purely artwork.

Landscape sketching is not an easy skill. Many simple steps can be practised in the local area on the way to landscape sketches which children can produce in contrasting environments on residential field trips. See Figure 8.4 and consider these points in relation to progression in landscape sketching:

- Increase the number and complexity of features in the views, but bring in 'outer limits' to the area to be sketched, as children will find that 'it won't all fit onto the paper'
- Children can make their own frame from card which has been subdivided so that they can concentrate on the view through each sector in turn
- Get children to focus on the horizons first; silhouettes first, detail last; details can always be drawn in school from a photograph taken on site or a commercial postcard, if one can be found showing the view from the same spot
- Make sure the feature and land use labels and positions are noted down – that won't be so easy to do back in school
- Encourage the oldest children to note down in which direction the sketch is orientated – use of the compass is reinforced yet again.

Progression in land use mapping – the 'quadrat' technique

In asking any of the key questions – What is the ground used for? What are the physical features of the area? What grows here? How is the land used? Is the land use different here from the use elsewhere? – pupils will need to make a map as well as talk about their observations.

The term 'land use' in geography means describing and identifying what kind of vegetation, rock, soil or buildings covers an area. It leads towards recognition of whether the land is used for industry, leisure or residential purposes, and so on. So land use mapping always relates to physical or human geography or, more likely, to both. A land use map can be the size of an actual footprint or represent a large area such as a city or a county.

The programme of study for key stage 1, paragraph 3C, requires pupils to:

"*Make and use maps of routes and sketch maps of small areas showing the main features and using symbols with keys.*"

Key stage 1, paragraphs 3 and 4 requires pupils:

"*to make representations of actual or imaginary places*"

and to:

"*make a map of a short route, showing main features in the correct order.*"

Like landscape sketching, the skill of sketch mapping, or free-hand map making in the field, needs a lot of practice. Again, it is the immensity of the sense of space that pupils find so difficult to commit to paper. 'I've gone off the edge of the paper', is a pupil's often-heard cry for help with free-hand map making.

By defining for children the limits the sketch map covers, we can help them to gain confidence in sketch mapping. A progression of activities over key stages 1 and 2 in the school grounds mapping land use will help them towards coping with less well-limited tasks in the upper junior age range.

The kinds of 'quadrat' activities described on page 95 will work towards achieving the programme of study requirements, as well

Figure 8.4

Progression in landscape sketching

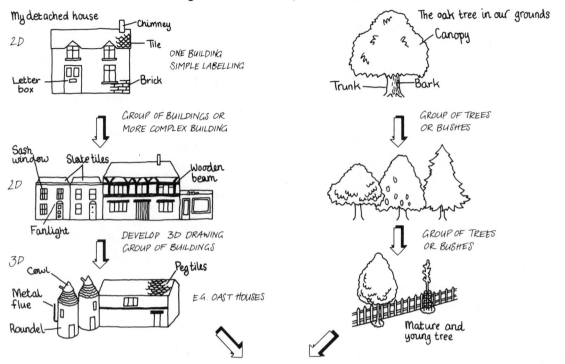

My detached house
2D
Chimney
Tile
Letter box
Brick

ONE BUILDING SIMPLE LABELLING

The oak tree in our grounds
Canopy
Trunk
Bark

GROUP OF BUILDINGS OR MORE COMPLEX BUILDING

GROUP OF TREES OR BUSHES

Sash window
Slate tiles
2D
Wooden beam
Fanlight

DEVELOP 3D DRAWING GROUP OF BUILDINGS

GROUP OF TREES OR BUSHES

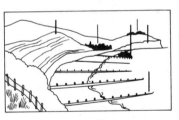

3D
Cowl
Metal flue
Roundel
Peg tiles

E.G. OAST HOUSES

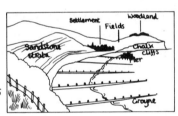

Mature and young tree

PARTLY COMPLETED SKETCHES

LABELS OMITTED. CHILDREN OBSERVE LANDSCAPE, IDENTIFY FEATURES AND LABEL ACCORDINGLY

LABELS PROVIDED BUT PARTS OF VIEW OMITTED. CHILDREN FOCUS ON SILHOUETTE OF FEATURES AND COMPLETE SKETCH

Settlement   Fields   Woodland
Sandstone strata   Chalk cliffs
Groyne

THIS KIND OF ACTIVITY CAN ALSO BE DONE STARTING WITH POSTCARD VIEWS AS PART OF THE PROGRESSION OR IF IT IS NOT POSSIBLE TO GET OUT TO A FIELD LOCATION

PUPIL SKETCHES AND LABELS WITH OR WITHOUT FRAME USE

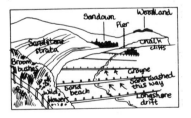

Sandown   Woodland
Pier
Sandstone strata   Chalk cliffs
Broom bushes   Groyne
Wild flowers   Sand beach   Sand washed this way   Longshore drift

"FREE" SKETCHING

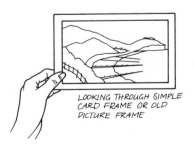

LOOKING THROUGH SIMPLE CARD FRAME OR OLD PICTURE FRAME

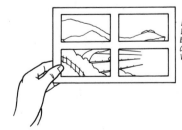

LOOKING THROUGH A DIVIDED FRAME ENABLES CONCENTRATION ON ONE SECTION OF THE VIEW AT A TIME

as the other mapping activities already described in Chapter 7.

The idea of the quadrat technique has been usefully adapted for primary school field-work. Usually found in secondary school biology or geography, a quadrat – a square-metre frame divided into four sectors – is traditionally used to find the number and type of different plant species grown in a small area. The square-metre frame is cast at random on the ground, and the number of plant species found counted or estimated. A series of quadrat examples can be taken else-where in the area at random, and the results averaged out to give a statistical result for the different type of plant cover.

For primary geography, it is not the number of plants which needs to be focused on, but the type and distribution of land use that pupils can observe. Using a square metre, with its connection with area work in maths, is for older pupils, but the progression map in Figure 8.5 shows how the technique can be developed at the primary school stage.

The school grounds provide the obvious environment for quadrat work, but it can be usefully done in the contrasting locality of a beach. Quadrat samples can be taken in different locations on the beach – along the high/low tide line, at the wave-cut platform, or on the wave-built terrace (see Glossary) – to build up a picture of the different rock/pebble, seaweed types and fauna dis-tribution in the shore zones. Any good children's book on the seashore will provide teachers with the information needed to put them ahead of their pupils.

Hand in hand with quadrat activities, pupils should be able to develop the land use mapping of larger but still confined areas in the school grounds, focusing on observa-tions, the representation of information, and the use of a key. The use of some quadrat activities should help children towards an easier, earlier grasp of land use recording and analysis.

A classroom extension of quadrat work for pupils who are mathematically able is to estimate land use from 1:25 000 or 1:50 000 maps. They can cover an area of the map with a plastic grid, shade different land use areas, and estimate residential coverage, and so on, in the local area.

Some further points about quadrats.

1   How to make a quadrat – see Figure 8.6.

2   The inside area can be divided into more than four. Dividing it into a 10 by 10 cm grid is an obvious choice, with each pupil mapping a different mini-grid to recreate the whole square metre in the classroom.

3   Use quadrats to reinforce the micro-climate plant growth connection. Take quadrats under trees, in an exposed site, on a flower bed and so on, to draw out contrasts.

4   Change in land use over time can be mapped with quadrat techniques – over the seasons or over several years, or if the school grounds are changing due to wild area growth or additional playground space.

5   Quadrat work should normally be inte-grated into work about the locality of the school. A geographical topic or a multi-subject-focused topic, drawing on science, environmental education and geography in the school grounds or the locality, are obvious ways of doing this.

6   Even an urban school with all-tarmac grounds can have a go at footstep and hoop quadrats – wet and dry tarmac or lichen- or moss-covered tarmac can be mapped. Try a vertical map – hold the shape against the wall.

Figure 8.5

Progression map for land use work

Footprint

In the classroom ask pupils to draw round their footprint and cut it out. Fold the paper in two to make the initial difficult cut.

Tell them to drop the footprint grid on the ground. They need to map what they observe in the space in the grid on to their cut-out footprint.

Replace the footprint in its grid frame. Record symbols for the land use on the frame.

A wire coat hanger bent out into a diamond shape is a useful size and also has the advantage of a handle.

KEY
GRASS
STONES
MUD

KEY
SAND
STONE
GRASS
BARK

Hoops

Use any circle shapes, all of which must be the same size. PE hoops are the obvious choice. Cast the hoop on the ground and map the land use inside on a circle of paper. Progression within this activity over time will be as follows:
1. Talk about what you see.
2. Pinpoint objects with markers without mapping.
3. Map - either on paper the same size as the hoop, or reduce the hoop size on the A4 paper.

KEY
CHESTNUT LEAVES
GRASS
MOSS
STONES

N

1 metre

Square-metre quadrats

An eight-year-old pupil's work from the Weald C.P. School, Kent
Context: map your garden.
Preparation: the class of top infants and eight-year-olds had looked at and discussed plan view and plan view representation in a variety of atlases and books. They were encouraged to view their garden from upstairs and work without parent help. The fact that moveable objects do not usually appear on maps was discussed. Pupils were encouraged to make up their own signs and symbols for their key.

Figure 8.6

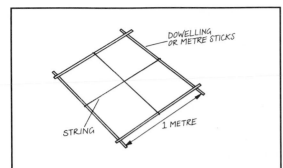

DOWELLING OR METRE STICKS

STRING

1 METRE

Pupils can make temporary or on the spot quadrat frames using four long sticks or skewers and four metres of string. More permanent quadrat frames can be made using dowelling and string. If dowelling is not available, four metre tapes can be laid on the ground with string to divide up the frame.

Progression in height-measuring, slope and gradient work

The ability to estimate and measure height, and an understanding of slope and gradient are part of physical and environmental geography, particularly at key stage 2. Estimating the height of features and trying to obtain a reasonable measurement of height by scale drawing from fieldwork, enables pupils to record patterns in rural and urban environments.

The programme of study for key stage 2 requires pupils to use a clinometer. Clinometers may be used to compare angles of slope and to measure height where it would otherwise be impossible, for example with a cliff, tree or building, but this technique and its use is currently a mystery to many teachers.

Lots of practice with a progression of simple activities built into key stage 1 and 2 work will lead to greater success in using and understanding the clinometer technique at the end of key stage 2. The progression map (Figure 8.7) is not intended to be exhaustive: you may have your own, similar tried and tested methods.

The context for this fieldwork height measurement technique is important. Sometimes it will need to be practised just as a skill to see that children can understand and use it in a different location, but often it can form part of an organised or incidental enquiry process. Here are some examples of ways in which it might be used:

● On a history field trip, a pupil asks the height of a castle wall while discussing attacking the castle's defences.
● If there are strong winds, would a particular tree fall on a particular part of the school, given a specific wind direction?
● If we planted a new tree in our school grounds, knowing the height it would grow to, would it dwarf the nearest tree?
● How high is the cliff on our local beach or in our field trip location? Can we make a scale transect – a cross-section – drawing of the cliff and beach as far as the low tideline?

Using a clinometer to measure steepness of slope

A clinometer can be used to used to find the angle of elevation of a slope. The larger the angles of elevation, the steeper the slope. Children can use the following method to obtain the angle of elevation for slope work.

Plant a rod at the top of the slope. Mark off a point on the pole at the same height from the ground as the observer's eye. From the bottom of the slope sight this point through the sighting tube or line of the clinometer (see Figure 8.8).

On a school-made clinometer (see page 99), the angle made by the weighted string or thread with 90° while sighting is equal to the angle of elevation of the slope. (For commercial clinometers, follow the maker's instructions.)

Figure 8.7

A progression of height estimating and measuring activities

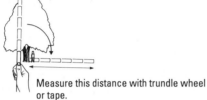

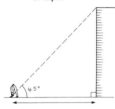

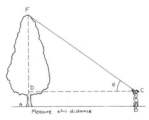

Measure this distance with trundle wheel or tape.

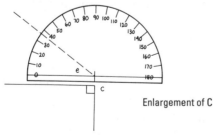

Measure this distance: *e* is the angle of elevation, the angle you look up through from the horizontal to site the top of cliff, building, tree, lamppost, etc.

Enlargement of C

Suitable for infants
Direct comparison
Compare heights visually. Which building is taller? Which tree is taller? A or B?

Infants Lower juniors
Estimating height compared to a known object
1 Measure your partner's height.
2 Your partner stands against base of tree or building.
3 Hold a pencil at arm's length.
4 Site your partner with your pencil and hold your pencil so partner height fits with section of pencil length.
5 Estimate how many pencil lengths fit the height of the tree by counting pencil lengths up the tree.
The tree is six times my partner's height or 6 x 1 metre, 6 x 1.5 m.

Top infants Lower juniors
An extension of this method answers the question: If the tree fell, how much ground would it cover?
1 Pencil estimate the height of the tree as before, but this time in addition visualise these 'partner heights' paced horizontally outwards from the base of the tree.
2 Send partner to point on the ground which marks the end of the sighting having counted out and noted the 'partner heights' horizontally.
3 Measure the distance from the base of the tree to partner with a trundle wheel or tape.

Using angles to find height
Walk away from the wall or tree until you can sight the top of it when you bend over and look back up at it through your legs. Mark where you are and measure the distance from there to the base of the building or tree. This distance is the same as the building or tree height because you are making a big isosceles triangle. You can use this method with or without the geometry for children if you wish.

Good upper juniors
Using field measurements, clinometer and scale drawing

On site
Children should work in pairs:
1 Estimate the height of the tree as a check for drawn results later.
2 Walk away from the base of the tree to a convenient point.
3 Measure distance A–B and note.
4 Measure height to eye level of pupil and record.
5 Sight the top of the tree, cliff, etc. with the clinometer and record the angle of elevation *(e)*.

Back in the classroom
1 Choose a simple scale, e.g. 1cm=1 m.
2 On suitable graph paper plot distance AB.
3 Plot the eye height of your partner.
4 Complete drawing the rectangle ABCD.
5 With a protractor draw the 'e' – the angle of elevation from C, with the protractor base along CD. 'e' will usually be between 20° and 30°, depending on your distance away from the feature in the field.
6 Extend the line from C through the angle of elevation constructed in the last step until it hits a vertical line extended up through line A–D. This vertical line represents the height of the tree.
7 Now measure this line A–F. Transfer this length back to real measurement using your scale, e.g. AF = 8.5 cms so tree is 8.5 m. high.

Equipment for slope and height work

For younger children estimating slope, gradient and height, no costly equipment is needed. For accurate work with upper juniors clinometers are necessary.

A clinometer is basically a 180 ° protractor, used with a plumbline suspended from the centre of its straight edge. Commercial ones are now widely available in educational catalogues for about £10. However, it is possible for children to make them at virtually no cost, by one of the following methods:

1 Photocopy a plastic protractor with white A4 paper behind it. Enlarge the image to the required size and cut it out. Stick it onto card, put a butterfly winged clip

Figure 8.8

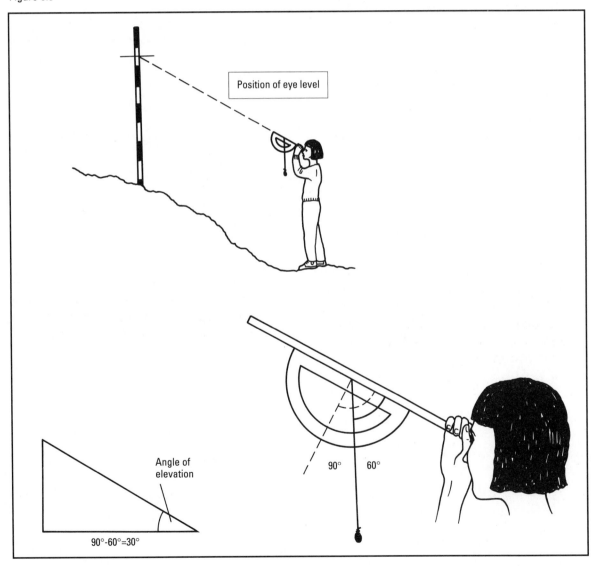

Position of eye level

Angle of elevation

90°-60°=30°

90°   60°

99

through the midpoint of the straight edge along the base line and attach a piece of string with a weight on the free end to form a plumb line.

2 Copy a protractor onto card, complete with angles marked in 5° divisions. Fix a plumb line as above, and stick a sighting, non-transparent straw along the straight edge base line.

3 Use your blackboard protractor in a similar way, turning it into a temporary or permanent clinometer.

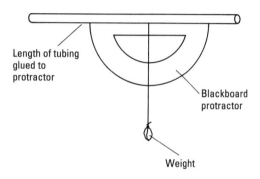

Length of tubing glued to protractor

Blackboard protractor

Weight

4 This method can be used with children who do not have geometry skills. Very little understanding of geometry is required, so it can be used with younger juniors or slower learners. Start with any piece of card.

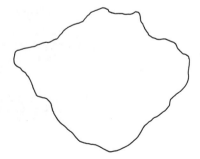

Rule a line across it to obtain one straight edge. Cut off the shaded area.

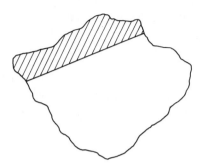

Roll up a sheet of paper to make a sighting tube. Stick it along the straight edge, with one of its ends at one end of the card.

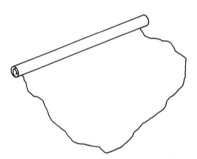

Pivot a piece of string on to the card at tube level half way along it, and put a weight, such as Blu-Tack®, on to the free end of the string. Sight the top of the tree or building and stand still.

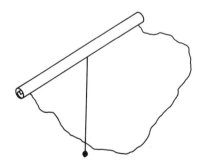

A partner tapes the end of the plumb line when it is steady at the vertical. This 'freezes', the angle. Complete other site measurements as necessary.

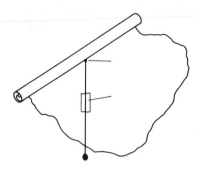

Back in the classroom, cut out the angle 'h' shape.

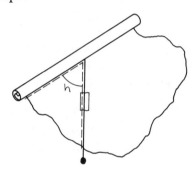

Either by folding along side *a* or by using a set square, obtain angle *e* and cut off the unwanted shaded section.

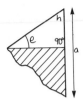

Use this angle like a template to mark the angle of elevation on squared paper. Draw on a scale such as 1 square = 1 m to obtain the height of the object sighted, as explained in Figure 8.7.

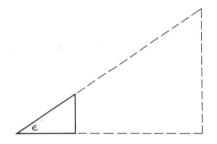

9

STUDYING PLACES

Of all the aspects of National Curriculum geography, it is 'place' that has caused most controversy. It is the difficulty of realistically assessing knowledge of places which is particularly problematical.

In Chapter 1, good practice in geography is described as much wider than the 'capes and bays approach' – the ability to name and locate places on the earth's surface. In Chapter 2, the authors noted that HMI (1989) found that primary geography demonstrated:

- Little work beyond the child's local area
- Limited work on other places in the British Isles
- Not enough use of atlases and globes.

It would seem that, although good work was being done relating to the local area, not enough was being done relating to distant places in either the narrow 'capes and bays' way or using the wider approach of good practice.

Balancing local and distant places

Good practice in teaching about places should balance a scale of development from local to global. The younger the children, the more they need experience of the local and therefore visible area. This does not mean that we should deprive them of learning about distant places because they cannot experience them by direct or first-hand experience. Breadth and balance must be the key to understanding places in geography. Children need to study local and distant places in order to develop a 'sense of place'. As this grows, their local, regional and country knowledge becomes a yardstick with which to compare the rest of the world.

The Geography Working Group was given the thankless task of trying to produce a broad and balanced 'place' framework for children aged 5 to 16. This framework was originally very specific as to the particular countries to be studied. Great protest greeted this prescription, which has been much modified. Teachers objected to being told which places to study. We can now have the option to choose which specific places we study: it is the type of place or general location of the place and the National Curriculum level for the place which have been prescribed. You may wish to refer back to the localities, regions and countries chart in Chapter 2, Figure 2.4 at this point.

The meaning of locality

Crucial to the type of place we need to study with children is an understanding of the word 'locality.' This means a focus, like that of a camera zoom lens, on a particular place in a country. That place covers 'a small area with distinctive features' (geography Statutory Order: programme of study, key stage 1, paragraph 5, page 31). This could mean a village, a small area of the countryside, a suburb, part of a large suburb, or a small town.

A locality does *not* mean a whole country, and it is important that we recognise the significance of this. There is a great risk that the specification in the Order to choose localities could concern us so much with the 'zoom lens' that we could forget to position these snapshots in their wider country context. Our children could end up with many detailed impressions of specific localities without ever relating them to the country or area in which they are located, as it is only implicit in the Order that the wider context is important. It is essential that we always help children to find the 'wide-angle lens view', as well. They need to know where the locality they are studying is situated in its country or area and how it links both to other places in that country or area and to where the pupil lives. This will, of course, be common-sense good practice to many colleagues, but to others who have not dealt with geography in the context of places very much, it needs reinforcing. This point will be returned to in the context of each locality type later.

Studying the local area

Include the school

The local area is a constant locality to be studied throughout key stages 1 and 2 until the end of level 4. It is defined as 'the immediate vicinity of the school or where the pupil lives' (PoS 1, paragraph 5).

If this is the definition, why did we include the classroom, school buildings and school grounds in our planning in Chapter 4? The early stages of National Curriculum geography made it quite clear that these areas were to be included. However, by omission, they are *implicit* in the Statutory Order, not stated under actual 'places' but cropping up only in incidental examples with certain statements of attainment. Some examples are:

- Gg 1, 2c follow a route or trail around the school site
- Gg 2, 1b identify activities carried out by parents and people who work in the school
- Gg 5, 3b describe improvements to the school grounds.

We need such examples to make it *explicit* that in good practice the school buildings and grounds do form part of our local area. Indeed, infant teachers always start with the geography of the classroom and school building because, until the children are familiar with those localities and can find their way about their classroom, further learning in any subject will be limited.

'Do we have to include the local area every year?' is a question teachers often ask when they plan a key stage. There cannot be a legal requirement to include the local area *every* year, but good practice indicates that teachers want to use the classroom, the school building and the area around the school as a place resource some time in each year. The amount of time for which they do so should depend on the type of geography work in the topics being undertaken and on knowledge of what children have done before in these areas, assuming good record-keeping has been passed on. Progression in the activities is crucial in both fieldwork and map skills as explained in Chapters 7 and 8. Progression in the depth of physical and human geography environment study in these areas, is also crucial. For vertically grouped schools it is likely that classroom, school building, school grounds, and local area will all have to be utilised in every class to secure adequate differentiation. For horizontally grouped classes it may only be possible to go beyond the school gates once in the infants, once in the lower juniors and once in the upper juniors. The authors would, however, like to stress that children should preferably be actively involved in investigating their local environment every year.

Using the classroom

The comparatively safe and limited spatial locality of the classroom has most potential for infants and for reinforcement activities for older, low ability learners.

Concepts relating to human geography and mapwork skills are the most useful areas of learning to be developed here.

The following suggestions for using the classroom locality may be useful.

- Children can locate 'services' in the classroom – Where are the scissors, paper, maths equipment and water supply kept? Children can describe the locations with geographical language or map them on a plan drawn by the teacher.
- Recognising the teacher's signs and symbols used to label these services is part of developing representational skills.
- Children can play 'signpost' mapping games (see Chapter 7).
- Children can plot their route around the classroom on their own maps or on the teacher's base map.
- Children can talk about the size and shape of the classroom compared to other classrooms or their rooms at home.
- Children can begin distance work with a scale drawing of the classroom (as in Chapter 7). Carpet or floor tiles can be

useful here for matching relative position and scale. If the classroom size is '10 rows' by '15 columns' of carpet tiles, then teacher or children can mark this off on squared paper or an overhead projector transparency grid and draw or position cut-out furniture, and so on, accordingly.

- Younger children can make sketch maps of their classroom, trying to get relative distance and positioning correct.

Using the school buildings

Again, this has greatest potential for key stage 1 pupils, although those children transferring to a separate junior school or to a different building on the same site will benefit from a quick revision and extension of activities already done at infant stage. They will need quickly to establish their new sense of place and space in the alternative environment.

The following suggestions for using the school buildings may be useful.

- Children can make up a trail inside the school building. They can then follow it themselves to check it, and ask another pair of children to follow it, too. Does the trail work or does it need improving? Is it a word trail, a photo trail, a map trail, or a puzzle trail? Can children escort visitors or other children to locations in the school? These obvious and important confidence-building activities are very geographical! Trails are referred to in more detail on page 111.
- Lay a series of signs around the school to develop a trail following and understanding signs and symbols: cut-out footsteps, arrows, etc. which will stick to the floor without damage, pictures on a theme placed along the walls.
- Can the children do a routeway survey in the school? Can they map their results?

Can they make recommendations in concluding, for example, which are the most used corridors?

- Explore the school as a workplace. Who works here? Where do they work? Map the results to record them on a plan of the school with colour codes. How many types of job are there? For example, caretaking; cleaning; teaching; classroom assistant; food preparation work; administrative work. Are they service jobs – do they help other people? Are the industrial jobs producing goods?
- How is the building itself used? Can children map it according to use or function? Use a colour key or picture symbols to show, for example, the kitchen areas, caretaker's room, administrative areas, teaching/learning areas. This is elementary work on land use.
- With older juniors, address microclimate within the building. Is one part of the building colder and damper than other parts? Carry out an enquiry to find out by measuring temperature, aspect (which direction the rooms face), trying to work out whether the walls are cavity walls or not. Is a room colder because of its location: because it is situated furthest away from the boiler; because of aspect, window size, poor insulation, or what?
- With children in school buildings of manageable size and shape, one-storey and flat roofs, can a scale model of the buildings be made to be fitted on a scale plan base of the grounds and building? Older children can make such a model to give to the infant department to develop plan view work.

Using the school grounds

The school grounds are a superb resource for geographical work whose potential is only just being explored thanks to the arrival of National Curriculum geography. Schools with fields and trees in their grounds will clearly be able to make wider use of their grounds than those schools with playground areas of concrete or tarmac only. Nevertheless, even the school which feels it has the most unstimulating grounds can deal with all aspects of school grounds geography – physical, human and environmental, except for soil and natural vegetation analysis and mapping.

The following suggestions for using the school grounds may be useful. First, let us look at the activities that can be done in the school grounds.

- Figure 9.1 indicates the wide range of activities possible to develop geography in the physical and human environments.
- All the mapping and fieldwork skills and techniques included in Chapters 7 and 8 can be used in the context of the school grounds to develop Physical or Human Geography themes, as well.
- Many enquiry process activities, including some of those listed in Chapter 1, can be undertaken in the school grounds, for example:
  - Where is the best place to site the new flower bed/seats/trees/compass rose drawn on the playground?
  - Are the school grounds and buildings a secure place?
  - How can we improve our grounds?
  - Can we make a trail for younger children to follow?
  - Where were those photographs taken from?

Second, let us look at the advantages of activities in the school grounds.

- Problems of supervision are alleviated.
- Often it is possible to set the children to work in groups within view of the teacher who is still able to work inside with the rest of the class.

Figure 9.1

Use of the school grounds from a geographical perspective		
Best use is made of any environment if the context is motivating, e.g. enquiry or issue-based. Some possible contexts: children need to know the best place to site new trees, tubs of flowers, compass rose, direction sign to office, KS2 children planning school grounds activities for KS1 children to use, etc. Map-making and using skills can be used throughout this work in context – see Figure 7.1.		
What natural environment work can we address?	**What human environment work can we address?**	**What specifically environmental issues can we address?**

Physical geography
 	
1 Soils and rocks
    Take soil samples and analyse. Compare to children's garden samples, samples taken from locality near school, etc.
2 Weather and climate
    Basic weather and seasonal change observation – including cloud cover and type.
    Micro climate studies – sun and shade site study – contrast in temperature, open aspect to wind, shelter from rain, etc.
3 Slope and run off (water) i.e. drainage
    Does the water from rain gather in certain places? Does it take longer to evaporate in some sites than others?
4 Vegetation
    Land use mapping.
    Transects, flower bed mapping.
    Quadrats, vegetation mapping.
	Human geography
	
	1 Built environment
	    School building, walls, playground: Natural or man made materials? Identification/classification.
	2 Human traffic
	    Examine traffic around the school site. Conduct surveys. Map pressure points.
	    Are there zones of greater/lesser use? Can they be mapped?
	    Concept of shortest route/best route. Are 'official' routes the most direct or are the 'unofficial' ones shortest?
	    Concept of barriers – detour linked with best route. Where are the barriers – steps, fences, car park areas, forbidden areas?
	3 Function
	    Map the function of different parts of the school, e.g. car park, office, etc.
	4 Services
	    Identify and trace service points around the school – telephone cables, drains, gas, electricity entry points. Safety issues: look, don't touch.
		1 Air pollution
		    Place filter paper in funnel of bottle – leave for a certain time. Test rain water and tree bark for acidity. Test for lichen and algae growth.
		2 Noise pollution
		    Develop a scale for testing noise pollution – lorries passing by, voices, aeroplanes, etc.
		3 Visual pollution
		    Mapping of litter or vandalism pollution, etc.
		4 Environmental improvement
		    Is there some project we can undertake to improve the grounds?

- Flexibility in timing the work is possible.
- The environment is a more limited, safe and controllable one.
- Skills can be safely and simply practised in a secure geographical context *before* being applied in a new and distant environment.

To ensure no overlap or unnecessary repetition, continuity and progression in the use of the school grounds as well as the classroom and buildings needs to be established by the geography coordinator and the staff by planning opportunities from the PoS for key stages 1 and 2, as suggested in Chapter 4.

Don't forget that many school grounds offer the opportunity to begin work on the vicinity of the school. In schools situated in a valley, whether urban or rural, or on a hill-top or slope, views out beyond the school grounds may offer the opportunity to do safe and easy work on the local area. In schools not hemmed in by high walls or other barriers over which children cannot see, just a walk around the perimeter of the grounds may enable land use and building form and function to be observed. Changes can also be observed through the fence (see Figure 9.2).

The local area: beyond the school

The Statutory Order defines the local area as 'the immediate vicinity of the school or of where the pupil lives' (programme of study, key stage 1, paragraph 5, page 31). This implies a fairly small area, suggesting a locality which is within walking distance of the school or the child's home, and therefore convenient for you to organise fieldwork in, as suggested in Chapter 8, Figure 8.1, at least once in each year. It is assumed that children's fieldwork and background knowledge will enable them to investigate this locality. We need to remember that fieldwork can be crucial for many children, as mobility is such that they may travel daily many miles by car to their school or be boarders and so have no 'sense of place' about the school locality.

Teachers, too, may commute many miles to work in a school about whose local area they have little knowledge, so it is important that the geography coordinator encourages staff to share knowledge about the local area and to come to a consensus about the suitability of various sites in it. This could be done in a

Figure 9.2

Looking out from the school grounds to the local area

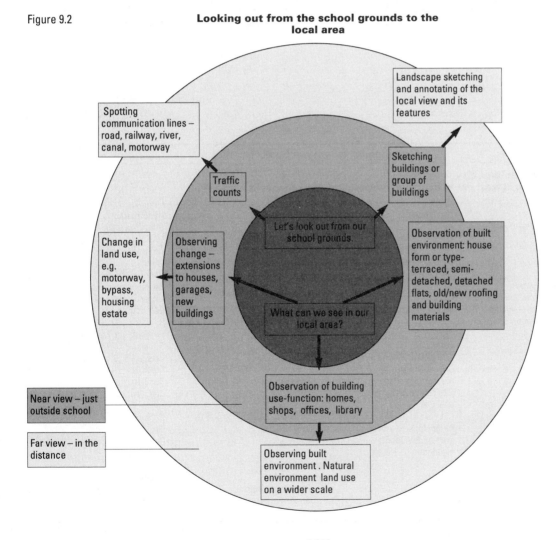

107

staff meeting or as an INSET activity. Figure 9.3 provides a list of the kind of sites and features you will need to think about and plan to use in your local area for children at some stage between ages 5 and 11.

Common sense tells us that sometimes we may need to extend the definition of the local area to something a little larger than the 'immediate vicinity of the school'. Here are some examples of when this may be sensible:

- Is your locality a very small village with limited features? Maybe you need to embrace a larger village or a nearby small town with which your village has strong links

- Is your locality very flat and featureless, or uniform, for example a very large, level housing estate? Maybe you could enlarge it to embrace the whole town area, including the town centre. In order to understand their locality the children need to see it in the context of the town of which it is a part.

Having established the potentially flexible extent of our local area, we can then plan in more detail which physical and human geography we will study with our children across the two key stages. Environmental geography should arise through the human and physical themes and local issues. Planning units of work on the local area

Figure 9.3

<table>
<tr><td colspan="4" align="center">**Checking up on your school's locality**</td></tr>
<tr><td colspan="4">**Which of these features do you have?**
Ideally you need at least one of each type for local area work for pupils ages 5–11</td></tr>
<tr>
<td>*Water features*
Stream, pond or lake
River
Estuary
Coastal area

Landscape features
Hills, valleys, cliffs, mountains, wood which show evidence of erosion or deposition by water, wind or ice

Physical features
for slopes, soil, rocks

Climate work sites
for weather surveys, micro-climate work (usually school grounds)</td>
<td>*Local issues*
By pass?
Road widening scheme?
Out-of-town shopping development?
New housing estate?
New reservoir?
Rubbish tip site?
Local improvement scheme?

Sites showing the origins of settlement
Crossing point of a river
A route centre
A defensive site
Site where water became available
Old core of modern settlement
Beginnings – growth/development – decline evidence</td>
<td>*Buildings*
House
Row of houses
Housing estate
Groups, rows of buildings to examine function

Transport
Safe place for traffic survey
Bus station
By-pass
Airport
Railway station

Industry
Farm
Business
Small manufacturing unit
Warehouse
Factory

Shops
Single shop
Parade of shops
Supermarket</td>
<td>Hypermarket
Shopping mall

Leisure facilities
Library
Park
Swimming pool
Leisure centre
Golf course

Settlements
House
Village
Town
Suburb
City – suburb

Services
Fire
Police
Ambulance
Hospital
Doctors
Refuse collection
Recycling plant</td>
</tr>
</table>

should revolve around the seven key questions shown in Figure 9.4, whether the units are purely geographical or form a smaller or minor part of a larger multi-subject-focused topic.

Asking these questions helps focus on the subject matter of geography. You will want to focus on the concepts behind settlement or the local landscape, for example, depending on which part of the programme of study you are developing in your units of work, and how they fit with other subjects.

Figure 9.4

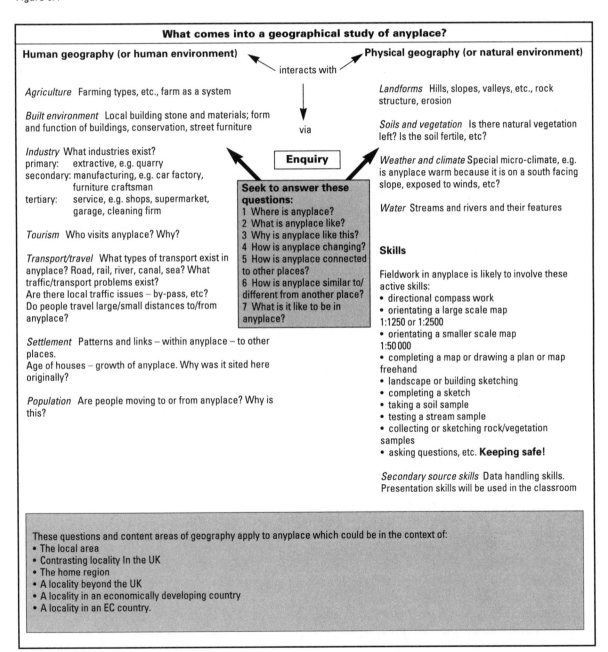

What comes into a geographical study of anyplace?

Human geography (or human environment) ← interacts with → **Physical geography (or natural environment)**

via

Agriculture Farming types, etc., farm as a system

Built environment Local building stone and materials; form and function of buildings, conservation, street furniture

Industry What industries exist?
primary: extractive, e.g. quarry
secondary: manufacturing, e.g. car factory, furniture craftsman
tertiary: service, e.g. shops, supermarket, garage, cleaning firm

Tourism Who visits anyplace? Why?

Transport/travel What types of transport exist in anyplace? Road, rail, river, canal, sea? What traffic/transport problems exist?
Are there local traffic issues – by-pass, etc?
Do people travel large/small distances to/from anyplace?

Settlement Patterns and links – within anyplace – to other places.
Age of houses – growth of anyplace. Why was it sited here originally?

Population Are people moving to or from anyplace? Why is this?

Enquiry

Seek to answer these questions:
1 Where is anyplace?
2 What is anyplace like?
3 Why is anyplace like this?
4 How is anyplace changing?
5 How is anyplace connected to other places?
6 How is anyplace similar to/ different from another place?
7 What is it like to be in anyplace?

Landforms Hills, slopes, valleys, etc., rock structure, erosion

Soils and vegetation Is there natural vegetation left? Is the soil fertile, etc?

Weather and climate Special micro-climate, e.g. is anyplace warm because it is on a south facing slope, exposed to winds, etc?

Water Streams and rivers and their features

Skills

Fieldwork in anyplace is likely to involve these active skills:
• directional compass work
• orientating a large scale map 1:1250 or 1:2500
• orientating a smaller scale map 1:50 000
• completing a map or drawing a plan or map freehand
• landscape or building sketching
• completing a sketch
• taking a soil sample
• testing a stream sample
• collecting or sketching rock/vegetation samples
• asking questions, etc. **Keeping safe!**

Secondary source skills Data handling skills. Presentation skills will be used in the classroom

These questions and content areas of geography apply to anyplace which could be in the context of:
• The local area
• Contrasting locality In the UK
• The home region
• A locality beyond the UK
• A locality in an economically developing country
• A locality in an EC country.

Progression in the local area

Teachers often ask for a model of study in the local area to show progression. As each locality is different and will have different resources, it is, unfortunately, not possible to provide such a model, but some guidelines may be useful.

- Beware of the large and complex environment. The larger the settlement, or area of a settlement, the richer yet more confusing it will be for the children. Your local row of shops may be less exciting than studying the Shambles in York or a hypermarket, but it is much more manageable for you and the pupils.
- The smaller the settlement, the easier it is for the children to get an overview of what goes on there.
- The younger the children, the fewer the features it is advisable to investigate at any one time. Form and function – what type, size and age the buildings are, and what they are used for – is a good illustration of this:
  - Top infants investigating their local homes could focus only on about three houses in a row. To begin with, it could be enough for them to identify what the houses seem to be built of, whether they are lived in or not, and the different colours of the houses' front doors. As both you and your children become more experienced, the enquiry can broaden
  - Lower juniors may consider a limited row of local shops – say six – and be asked to identify what kind of shops they are and note this on a large teacher-prepared map of an enlarged section of an OS map
  - Upper juniors may be divided into small groups, with each group being required to assess a defined section of a street according to ground-floor,

first-floor and any further floor's use. Their exercise may be in the context of an enquiry such as 'How has our High Street changed since 1840 in Victorian times?' whereas the infants may be answering the more limited key question 'What are the houses like around our school?'

- The younger the children, the more their geographical activities should be concerned with basic *observation* and *recognition* of features, with recording being secondary, although some data-recording can be done by the more able, or on a rotating basis.
- The older the child, the more observation and recognition should be speedy and used as a means of noticing changes, similarities and differences, and recording data in map or note form.

A suggestion for starting local area work

The following series of activities could be used to start off key stage 1 work in the local area in the context of a geographical or cross-curricular topic on 'My House', 'Homes' or 'My Family.' The difficult statement of attainment Gg 2/1c 'Know your address' needs to be dealt with in the context of local area work.

These activities, done by Kent teacher Sue Thomas with her class, turned 'Know your address', which could so easily be a boring, rote-learning exercise, into a constructive and active learning experience which children loved.

1 Children are asked to observe and sketch their front door at home. A discussion on 'My front door' then leads the children to talk about the materials, colours and fittings. As well as the design features they notice, some children will volunteer that their door has a name or a number.

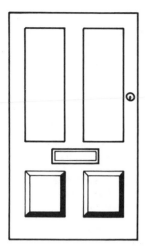

A further discussion on the various names and numbers of their houses lead to the reasons for identifying houses in this way. Each child can be given a numbered card to hold, and the class can arrange itself into a road, with odd numbers on one side and evens on the other. Other combinations can be tried out to simulate cul-de-sacs and 'walks.' Some children can act as post and milk delivery people, and show their delivery routes. Follow-up work could include drawing their door with a name or number and drawing a street with the post person's route marked.

2 The second session can be used to discuss all the different words used to describe roads – What is a lane, a close or a crescent? Photographs of different types of streets are a useful resource to show children that different places have different patterns of houses. A classroom display of the street names where each child lives is a useful follow-up activity.

Eldorado Road

3 From a starting point of whether we live in a village, town or city, a discussion on the characteristics of these three types of place will lead the children to talk about the names of their village, town or city and of nearby villages, towns or cities. They are able to talk about the differences in size of local places and also which way you have to go to reach them.

4 Making a signpost to local places and standing it up in the classroom or playground will help to strengthen this concept, and is a good introduction to work on direction.

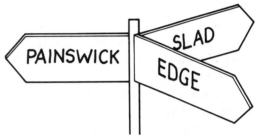

After these sessions, the children are ready to draw their house and to write or copy their address beside it, knowing the components and what each one means, and also understanding the usefulness of knowing people's addresses.

Further work can include making a poster for a lost dog which includes the owner's name and address, and addressing envelopes for special cards taken home after an art session, for example Mother's Day, Easter and Christmas.

Local Trails

Developing local trails is a tried and tested way of encouraging geographical and cross-curricular work. Teachers can develop them, but a good enquiry exercise is to get a class to develop one for other classes to use and for your own next year's class to refine. The aims and objectives of local trail work should be as shown overleaf.

1 To extend the children's knowledge about their own locality

2 To enable the children to develop the ideas of:
- Location
- Distribution
- Networks
- Distance
- Scale
- Similarity and difference
- Comparison
- Continuity and change
- Cause and effect
- Time.

3 To develop skills: written, spoken, numerical and graphical

4 To increase children's motivation and involvement through the use of first-hand experience

5 To encourage children to observe and be investigative

6 To increase environmental awareness by fostering an interest and concern for the quality of their local area.

Figure 9.5 suggests some ideas for use on local trails. Can you focus on these ideas and change them, or ask children to change them, into an enquiry to build up a trail?

Remember the following:

- Is the route safe?
- Variety in recording methods
- Green Cross Code
- Different eye levels. Look up, through, under or over
- Length of walk
- Arrange extra adults.

Teachers or children making up local trails may find the following tips useful.

1 See that the children are well briefed before they set out, have had a chance to read through the trail, and know what road behaviour is expected of them.

2 Arrange for parents or other adults to

Figure 9.5

Local trails	
Houses	Materials, doors, windows, types
Boundaries/ barriers	Fences, hedges, walls, council, safety
Underground	Gas, water, telephone, sewers
Patterns	Around, on different scales
Change	Over time, on-going
Development of the area	Over time, in the future
Pollution/litter	Source, cars, industrial, possible solutions
Trees	Different times of the year
Gardens	Type, size, colour
Habitats	Insects, birds
Shops	Hierarchy: Who uses them? What do they sell?
Feeling materials	At different places
Street furniture	What, where, why?
Words	What, where, why?
Transport	Evaluation, future possibilities
Good, bad and ugly	Evaluation
Maths trails	Number, measurement, symmetry
Park, wasteland	Use, design possibilities
Design	General small area, e.g. doors
Routes	Traffic or people flow, crossing points
Spotting trails	Photographs or sketches, useful for infants
Tourism	What should tourists stop at/visit? What would you want to show visiting friends?

help supervise the class during the outing. Inform your head teacher and complete any necessary paperwork, such as consent forms. Remember the safety guidelines provided in Chapter 8.

3 Decide exactly where you are going to cross roads – even busy streets are quite safe as long as the children are given clear instructions.

4 Don't always select the obvious route. If the trail leads down paths and alleyways, it is more likely to contain surprises and contrasts.

5 Choose a circular route, if possible, as this is most convenient and avoids a lengthy walk back to school.

6 Don't make the trail too long – eight stops are ideal – and always mark them clearly on the trail map.

7 Select the stops carefully, so that each one illustrates a single, definite idea.

8 Keep any text down to a minimum, so that the children do not spend too much time reading rather than working.

9 Include a range of recording techniques, such as surveys, diagrams, annotated sketches and mapwork exercises. Beware of questions which simply test the child's knowledge.

10 If possible, use illustrations to provide extra information, for example about the changes that have happened to a building or street.

Always bear in mind the following:

1 The urban environment is always changing. Be an opportunist and take advantage of chance events if they occur!

2 In the local area, whatever the age of the child, they will need to focus on these questions to do with description and analysis:
- Where is the place?
- What is it like?
- Why is it like this here?
- How is this place changing?
- How is this place similar to or different from other places we know?

Studying distant places

Distant places for primary school children are generally acknowledged by their teachers to be anywhere that is beyond the local area – indeed, anywhere beyond their personal experience at that moment. That is why these places can be:

- The home region
- A contrasting locality in the UK
- A contrasting locality beyond the UK
- A contrasting locality in an economically developing area
- A contrasting locality in an EC country.

The localities are all included in this section of the chapter. The same principles and strategies apply to teaching about all those localities of which the children have no, or very limited, first-hand experience.

The Statutory Order interprets 'distant' as anywhere beyond the UK – the foreign, international and global dimension – but primary teachers know that an environment five miles down the road can be as 'distant' as a locality in Outer Mongolia to most five-year-olds and, indeed, to many eleven-year-olds.

The home region (key stage 2, levels 4 and 5)

How do we define our 'home region?' The Statutory Order tells us that we are free to do so ourselves, unless we live in Wales, in which case the home region equates with the whole of Wales. The guidance for defining our home region says that we should:

> *"take into account the location of the school and the need to encompass an area which is substantial either in area or population."*

Programme of study for key stage 2, p. 36, paragraph 8

For most of us, our home region may well approximate to common regional definitions such as the South-West or the West Midlands. The school's location within that region may influence its extent. If the school is located on the edge of a region, it may make sense for it to see itself as part of two commonly recognised regions, and to take two parts of different regions as its home region. A school on the border of the West and East Midlands may find it makes more sense to make its own natural home region out of parts of both areas. Many regions are partly limited by the coast. Kent and Sussex fall into this category, although a forward-looking school in Dover in Kent may wish to encompass north-east France within its home region because communications and employment relate so much to links with France. Try to choose an area which gives a mixture of physical features, rural and urban environments, transport networks, settlement types and a range of economic activities. A school situated in Penzance may wish to regard Devon and Cornwall as its home region, rather than encompass the whole of the South-West as far as Somerset and Dorset.

It would be helpful for primary schools to liaise with secondary schools in the definition of the home region, as children continue to study it at key stage 3. A discussion with a consensus decision rather than a secondary geography department dictating the home region would be constructive.

There is great concern that for upper junior children working at levels 4 and 5, the home region will remain a largely taught, abstract type of geography more compatible with traditional secondary school learning. Some work about it will have to be done through indirect experience and secondary source material, but much valid work can be done in drawing on pupils' previous first-hand experience in their local area and in the home region.

The various places to be learned about rest within each other as shown in Figure 9.6. The local area work that has taken place in infant and lower junior levels and is still on-going at level 4 is the pivot for home region work. Children need to locate their local area on maps in relation to the home region – wall maps, UK atlas maps, regional maps – to help reinforce the notion that where they are is part of a wider area. This reinforces the 'zoom lens' altering to 'wide-angle lens' focus which is so important.

Every time children leave their local area for some fieldwork, be it a visit related to science, history, geography, or an arts visit to the theatre, they should locate where they are going on a map.

Teachers should draw on those visits made in the home region from infant age onwards to remind children that they have many 'snapshots' of their home region which can help piece together the different features and activities which go on there. An idea would be for the school to have a permanent 'home region' map in a central place where label flags are planted for every visit which occurs.

Teachers will also have to rely on the children's knowledge to build up home region work – an acknowledged problem where mobility and family outings are limited. Involve the class in questionnaires and map the results to get a picture of their knowledge and experience: Where do you go to the seaside for the day? Which is the biggest shopping centre you go to?

The key question and enquiry process approach is the most successful way to motivate work on the home region, along with investigating issues: What will the effects of building the motorway extension be? Where will it go to? Why is the superstore being built and what effects will it have on people living here?

Developing the human geography content in home region work is very important and the key stage 2 programme of study, paragraphs 16 and 17, should be looked at carefully with this in mind.

Don't forget to relate the position of the 'home region' to its position within the rest of the UK, building up the important relative position aspect of place knowledge.

A contrasting locality in the UK

All children at key stages 1 and 2 should learn about somewhere else in the UK.

What criteria should we apply to choosing these places? Figure 9.6 shows that the home region is part of the UK. Therefore, it can be argued that a visit to a contrasting locality in the home region may count as a contrasting locality in the UK. As we know from experience with young children, a visit to a seaport 30 miles away could just as easily be one to the other end of the country.

For an urban school, a field visit to a farm or a rural village will count as a look at a contrasting locality in either the home region or the UK, depending upon the level(s) at which children are working.

Figure 9.6

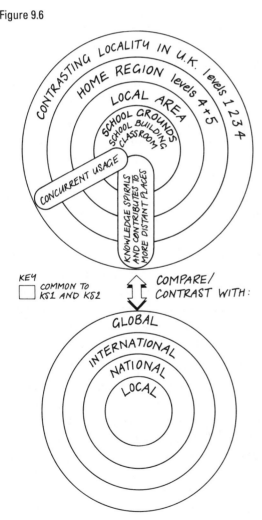

It is certainly preferable that all children have first-hand experience in a UK locality beyond their home region *at least once in their primary school career*, be it on a day trip or residential basis. We do know that for some children this cannot be a realistic target, and so secondary source material will be the only method they can use to study a contrasting locality in the UK. For guidance on this, refer to the section on page 119 on strategies for dealing with distant places.

A locality beyond the UK (key stage 1, levels 1–3)

Infant teachers have the advantage of being able to choose any locality in the world to study a camera zoom lens picture. They can therefore draw upon their own or their children's experience and resources if they choose a locality or localities beyond the UK, if they wish, as well as published resources.

A locality in an economically developing country (key stage 2, levels 2–5)

'How do we define an economically developing country?' most teachers ask. By common sense, is the pragmatic answer.

Technically, an 'economically developing country' is one whose gross national product falls below a certain figure in a table of statistics. The UK is considered to be an economically developed country, so it makes sense for children to study places with a contrasting lifestyle, which are not as developed. Values and attitudes are bound to surface in any such study and an open-minded approach is essential when comparing and contrasting 'developed' and 'developing' localities and countries.

An 'economically developing locality' was intended by the Geography Working Group to be located in the tropics, for example a

Caribbean island, a place in India or in a tropical African country. Nevertheless, since the opening-up of eastern Europe, it can be argued that some of these countries are economically developing compared with the UK. A primary school with twin school links in Czechoslovakia with a good exchange of geographical resource material should be encouraged to develop this link, not to drop it for a television programme on Barbados. Time should be allowed for both studies: the children's concept of distant places will be the wider.

A school may decide that its economically developing locality will be in Tunisia or Egypt because it has resources on such localities – this is then a valid criterion for choice.

The advice is then, to choose your own economically developing locality, according to resources and integration with other subjects, for example a history unit on Egypt.

A locality within an EC country outside the UK (key stage 2, level 5)

It is possible to take two differing approaches to this specific locality. In National Curriculum geography, the European locality comes at a high level in key stage 2: this implies that only a few children may have entitlement to it. Good practice indicates that many teachers already include work about European countries in the curriculum for key stage 2 pupils. To eliminate this would be to deprive children of what should be an equal entitlement to learn about the European dimension of life; attitudes and values are set by the time children reach secondary school. You may want to deal with the level 5 EC locality requirement in one of these broad ways:

1 Teach a multi-subject-focused topic on Europe or a geography-focused topic on Europe devised around physical and/or human environment themes, making up your own 'programme of study' for it at levels appropriate for your class, but enabling your group of children working towards level 5 to work on a particular EC locality within that topic

2 Enable the whole class to study a particular EC country with a 'wide-angle lens' approach, but quickly move your level 5 group into the locality study of that particular country.

Both groups will be able to feed back to and learn from each other at the end of the topic. Remember that children at key stage 3 have to study an EC country in depth, choosing between France, Germany, Italy or Spain, so it would make sense to avoid these countries. However, choosing a locality in one of these countries is fine if you give just a quick overview of the actual country before concentrating on the locality aspect.

Alternatively, if you really feel that you want to restrict the work on Europe to your group of level 5 children, if wider work relating to Europe has been done lower down the key stage, or if your school organisation and planning do not permit a wider approach, then follow these guidelines.

- Make sure that the children begin with a quick overview of Europe itself, then focus onto the European country in which they are going to study a locality.
- Then – the major part of the study – enable the children to study the locality – the 'zoom lens' view of the EC place.

Whichever approach you adopt, the locality chosen will depend on resources: it could be that each child in the group may have a different locality, because they have personal holiday experiences of it. There is also an argument to say that some EC localities could be considered as 'economically developing' in comparison with the UK, such as

116

Portugal and Greece. Again, it must surely be for the teacher, in conjunction with the geography coordinator, to make common sense decisions.

Issues relating to distant place work

The following issues relate to all distant place work in the UK and overseas.

Planning at key stage 1 It is crucial to plan distant place work from the programme of study, not the attainment targets, otherwise you could omit the contrasting UK locality and the locality beyond the UK. Examples of this error have been found! Place work is broader and more concerned with awareness-raising for infants, but there are also prescribed localities.

Planning at key stage 2 The greater number of prescribed localities, and the greater depth at which they need to be studied, will dominate lessons for juniors, but not all distant-place work can be directly linked to a locality study. You will need to check when planning key stage 2 that you are enabling children to:

- Learn why some parts of the world contain very few people, while other parts are densely populated (PoS, paragraph 16a)
- Examine and seek reasons for changes in the population size of regions and countries (PoS, pararaph 17a)
- Examine the global distribution of earthquakes and volcanoes and how this relates to the distribution of crustal plates (PoS, paragraph 15)
- Learn about weather conditions in different parts of the world, for example in polar, temperate, tropical desert and tropical forest regions (PoS, paragraph 14)
- Learn about seasonal patterns of temperature and rainfall over the British Isles (PoS, paragraph 15).

There are other statements from the thematic parts of the programme of study that could be studied in this wider distant place context, too. However, you have the choice to relate them to local work or home region work, if you wish:

> *"Pupils should be taught ways of extracting materials from the environment and how the natural extraction of natural resources affects the environments."*
>
> Programme of study for key stage 2, p. 38, paragraph 18

Children could equally well study the clearing of hardwoods from tropical rainforests or slate quarrying in their home region or local area.

The 'zoom lens' trap The danger of this issue has already been mentioned at the beginning of this chapter. For a strategy to help overcome it, refer to the next section.

'Cook's tour' syndrome Conversely, glib treatment of distant places will, one hopes, be discouraged by the geography Order. It is fine to include work on 'hats from different places' as in the technology non-statutory SATs, or 'songs from around the world' in infant cross-curricular work, but these do not fulfil the place requirements of the Orders for juniors any more than does a list of basic information on climate, population and famous monuments in a particular town or country.

'Infants can't understand work about distant places.' Some infant colleagues feel strongly that this is the case. Several arguments counteract this narrow view.

1 Infants are presented with distant-place images constantly via the media and through books. Often, the only people who will help them to understand these complex and confusing images will be their teachers, who will do so by careful planning and structuring of distant place work.

2 Many infants travel abroad: they have physically had experience of distant places in a holiday context. The teacher can capitalise on this and widen the limited mental picture which often results. Parents do not always do this.

3 Many of our children in multi-cultural areas have a heritage of distant place knowledge and culture. This may be first-hand, or transmitted as their cultural heritage by their families.

4 Attitude formation about other peoples, places and cultures takes place informally from a very young age. To help children develop informed and balanced attitudes we need to discuss other places, peoples and cultures from the youngest age poss-ible in school. This helps to counteract their received prejudice.

Stereotypical images It is important to avoid conveying or reinforcing stereotypical images. The following activity will illustrate the problem.

Task Which ten objects would you send in a box to the distant locality you are studying to show what *your* local area is like? The activity could have two different contexts in the classroom:

1 Developing links with a twin school in a contrasting locality in the UK or abroad
2 When studying a distant locality as a hypothetical exercise – what might we send them and what might we receive from them?

This task could be done either at the begin-ning or at the end of the unit of work. It can be done with children of any age or with teachers on in-service training. The out-comes will vary according to the age, experience and local knowledge of the participants.

There follows an example of the outcome of this task when done with year 6 children,

Our selected objects are:
1. a postcard of an oast house
2. a cluster of hops
3. an aerial photograph, showing our village
4. an estate agent's leaflet
5. a piece of sandstone
6. a sample of clay soil
7. a local newspaper
8. an Ordnance Survey 1:50,000 map
9. a photograph of our school
10. a tape of traffic noise, bird sound, our language.

once a class consensus was reached from initial group discussion.

Anyone receiving such a box of objects is likely to make a stereotypical image of our place. Because you have picked out things which illustrate your area best, you have transferred a stereotypical image. Your country will be viewed as a place where the agriculture is hop farming, or where the natural vegetation is hops growing in clay soil. The other items could similarly foster generalisations. Ten objects sent from North Wales would convey a different image from these from Kent. It is easy to understand where the 'Eskimos live in igloos' stereotype came from. Similarly, if we receive a set of ten photographs – oblique ones and ordi-nary ones – in a materials pack about Glasgow, which we are studying as a contrasting locality, we must be careful to ensure that the children do not assume that the whole of Scotland or northern UK is the same.

It is crucial for us to realise that when teach-ing about distant places we must raise awareness of stereotyping in children's learning and break it down, not reinforce it by accident.

Resources Because primary schools have paid scant attention to distant places in the past, we are finding a dearth of published resources. Where they exist, they are more likely to be appropriate as historical artefacts – text books from the fifties still lurk in some store cupboards! Many of the 'text book' resources from the 1980s are now inappropriate to the scale of locality study required in the Statutory Order.

Resources may be inadequate, but we can reassess what we already have available in our classrooms – postcards, pictures, artefacts from distant places – and look forward to educational broadcasters and publishers producing appropriate aids. We can also start collecting postcards and other materials to help ourselves.

Bias in resources All the resources we use contain a particular perspective or bias in their text. Travel brochures, often a wonderful source of climate statistics and pictures for a locality, present biased information because they concentrate only on the leisure and exotic nature of a locality. Biased information reinforces stereotypical images, for example, that indigenous people always and only do unskilled work such as waiting or room cleaning in hotels.

Some colleagues prefer not to use aid agency materials for the same reason. They suspect that images and facts have been selected to present the particular image that the agency wants. This attitude cuts off an important source of materials. It is better to be aware that such material could be biased and act accordingly. Examine the materials closely for bias. Ask children questions to bring out any bias; make sure that they are fully aware of that bias.

The photographs in the excellent Action Aid pack 'A Village in India' have a gender bias – most of the photographs show women (see Chapter 12). You need to read the background materials with the pupils and consider why this might be. Whatever their age might be, the majority of children are capable of opening out discussions on values.

Having explored the issues and concerns relating to distant place work, let's now consider the methods of making learning about them practical, motivating and meaningful.

Strategies for teaching and learning about distant places

Key questions The best way of approaching distant place work is to use the key question approach as advocated in Chapter 1, and refined in Chapter 5.

The central questions in Figure 9.4 can be applied to Physical or Human Geography content or to the interaction between both areas of content as shown in the chart. For example, from materials provided about a place in Dominica, it should be possible to answer the question 'What is it like to live here?' 'What kind of farming do the people do here?' could be one of the simple questions young juniors might answer.

You or your pupils can choose the broad key questions or refine them according to your/their experience and their age. The older the children, the greater the number and the more complex the nature of the questions to be asked. Figure 9.7 lists some suitable questions: you will want to select the most relevant and add others, as the list is not exhaustive.

Working towards answers to these questions will deal with the four strands of Gg 2:

- Knowledge of places
- An understanding of the distinctive features that give a place its identity

- An understanding of the similarities and differences between places
- An understanding of the relationship between themes and issues in particular locations.

The concept of similarity and difference is crucial to the study of distant places. The key question – 'How is this (distant) place the same as or different from our own area?' –' should be implicit or explicit in all our distant place work.

Children working at key stage 1 will concentrate on the local area, but will:

- Begin to discover about distant places
- Be able to describe distant places in terms of where they are and what their basic features are
- Be able to deal with mainly implicit, but sometimes explicit, comparisons between the local area and the distant place being considered.

Figure 9.7

Key questions for distant places	
General questions	**Specific questions**
Where is this place?	Which country, continent, part of the world is it in?
What is this place like?	What do people wear? What animals live there? What does it look like? What is the natural and built environment like? What plants grow here naturally? Who lives here? Where do the people live? What do people eat? What kind of homes do people live in? What do people do here? (work/leisure) What is the land being used for? (land use)
Why is it like this?	Why do people wear certain clothes? Why do people live here? Why do they live where they live? How have people made use of their environment? In what ways are people's activities and way of life influenced by what we have found out about it? Why do people come here?
How is it changing?	How have people changed this place? How are they changing it? Are there new buildings or schemes planned? How have new projects altered the landscape or people's lives?
How is it connected to other places?	How do people move about there? How do people get to other nearby towns or villages? To where do people send the goods they grow/produce? Do people go to work in nearby places?
How is it similar to/different from my own home village, town, settlement?	Is the weather the same as in ...? Is the landscape the same as in ...? Is the farming the same as in ...? Do the people travel mainly by car?
What is it like to be in...?	What do you feel about this place? Why do you think this? Do you think those living there think the changes are a good thing? Why?

In key stage 2, children will continue to study the local area, but will:

- Investigate more distant places
- Begin to analyse – 'How?' and 'Why?' as well as 'Where?' and 'What?'
- Compare and contrast their local area with the distant places being studied to assess similarities and differences between them – explicit comparison.

It is good practice to start with similarities and then proceed to differences. This coincides with the philosophy of Development Education (see Glossary). We all, wherever we live on the globe, have the following common basic needs:

- Shelter
- Water
- Energy sources
- Food.

We may obtain these needs differently, according to the geography and history of our country and culture. We need to emphasise similarity of needs, rather than stress the exotic or curious. Nevertheless, it is ultimately the differences which make geography fascinating. We all 'have' climate and scenery in the UK, but if that climate and scenery were identical to that of the Mediterranean, it is doubtful whether some of us would travel to Turkey or Majorca for a holiday!

A 'here and there' chart, an example of which is included as Figure 9.8, is a useful device for children to demonstrate their learning about distant places and for teachers to assess it. Variations on writing in the chart could include pupils' drawings, cutout pictures, photographs or postcards, and graphical representation according to age, special needs and your differentiation in task according to the children's ability. Note form or whole sentences can be used according to the type of English skills being practised.

Dealing with stereotypes The 'ten subjects in a box' activity described earlier raised the issue of stereotyping. We need to begin distant place work with our children with an awareness of what images or stereotypes they have of a country, for example Spain, part of a country, for example Somerset, or of a locality, for example a part of Calcutta. We need also to be aware of what images *we* have of those places, even before we establish our pupils' starting point, so that we can explore attitudes and values freely.

The following approach has been used by the authors:

- With teachers on INSET
- With children in classrooms
- With children to collect images of parents, relatives and other adults.

The approach can apply to any place, anywhere in the world. The more obscure the place, the less a concept of it, inaccurate or otherwise, will be held. The particular example here relates to introducing the Action Aid pack *Chembakolli – A Village in India* to teachers. They were asked to write down in groups of five what came to their minds when they were asked: 'What is it like to live in a village in India?' (See Figure 9.9.)

From the resulting brainstorms, you can see that the images are predominantly negative. Children in areas with little cultural contact with immigrants from the Indian subcontinent have similar images in a more simplified vocabulary.

Where do we get such images from?

- The media
  - television news (especially at times of catastrophe), documentaries, newspapers
- People:
  - acquaintances who have visited the area

121

FIGURE 9.8

	Here – a Yorkshire town	There – a village on a Caribbean island
Climate and Weather		
Landscape		
Vegetation		
Farming		
Industry		
Travel		
Any environmental concerns, projects		

This format can be given as guidance for children to discuss similarities and differences first, then to record individually later. Will they always need to record?

Infants can try the charts without the categories – just 'here' and 'there' columns.

Who decides the heading: pupil or teacher? How many headings?

The younger the child, the fewer the headings?

What form should the recording take? Note form? Sentences?

Could a combination of writing, drawings, stuck-on pictures, sketch maps or/and diagrams be appropriate?

What are the most appropriate methods of comparing here/there for younger pupils or special needs pupils: drawings, writing, etc?

Figure 9.9

Outcome of a brainstorm: 'What is it like to live in a village in India?'

poor hygiene, outdoor cooking, insects, under-nourished animals, primitive transport, poor schooling, religious or culture-based clothing

Images of India: positive? negative? neutral? fact? fiction? from the media? received images?

bikes, shanty towns, cows, sparse vegetation, lack of equipment, poor health, heat, no amenities (shops, sewage, electricity, water), dust, flies

begging, temples, working in fields, Mother Teresa, sacred cow, rice, tea, early death, dhoti, burning widows, silver jewellery, over-population, smelly, hot, wet

poor sanitation, no electricity, dust, dirt, barefoot, poverty, disease, hot, humid, communal living, extended family

- acquaintances who have lived there
- received images from people who have not visited or lived in the area
- peer group members.

Images of a contrasting locality of the UK could be similarly out of date, inaccurate or stereotypical, for example of South Wales: coal mining; pollution; coal dust; black; spoil heaps; small cramped houses; poverty; steel works; Welsh accents.

Having assessed our own and pupils' starting images of a distant place, we can then ask 'What is it really like to live in a village in India?' or 'What is it really like to live in the Scilly Isles?' By using key questions and up-to-date resources, we can hope both to provide children with a knowledge base from which they can reach a reasonably accurate picture of a distant locality and to shift negative, or even over-positive attitudes, towards an informed view. A useful self-assessment task is shown below.

- Ask children to record their image before starting work on the distant place. Maybe they know nothing because they have not heard of the place. They should also record the outcome of their personal brainstorming.

- Ask children to summarise their learning at the end of the unit of work now that they have some knowledge and understanding.

A format like Figure 9.10 can also be used for teacher assessment and as evaluation for you on the Gg2 section of the unit of work you are working through.

Twinning possibilities Twinning with a school in another place is often an effective way of promoting distant places work. Consider establishing a link with a school:

- in a contrasting UK locality
- in an EC locality
- in a locality in an economically developing country.

You may like to consider the following points about twinning procedure.

- It is best if twinning is a whole-school decision, even though only one year group may pursue it; otherwise the twinning may collapse when the teacher leaves or children go to secondary school.
- If you are nervous about possible language difficulties, remember that in Europe many adults speak good English. Many children in the EC begin to learn

Figure 9.10

Before	**After**
What I think about ....before I learn about it	What I know and think about .... now

English at primary school. Many developing countries in the Commonwealth still use English as their language of instruction.

- Links with developing countries are often made via aid agencies like Action Aid and church organisations, as then our values cannot directly damage the less materialistic values of children in developing countries.
- Schools in developing countries may have smaller budgets than British schools: they may have neither the technology nor the cash to respond with photographs, tapes or videos. Letters and drawings are often the most they can manage.

Once you've twinned, consider the range of possibilities in Figure 9.11.

If you are twinning with a school and intend to visit it as well as exchange materials, then it is essential that the contact time at the twin school should be very carefully programmed. The more contrasting the background and locality, the more carefully both sets of staff and children should be prepared. Contrasting backgrounds in the UK can cause culture shock if the meeting is not carefully managed. It is better if preparation work in the form of exchange letters and photographs has occurred as an absolute minimum, so that children have a specific 'twin' to relate to when they meet.

Figure 9.11

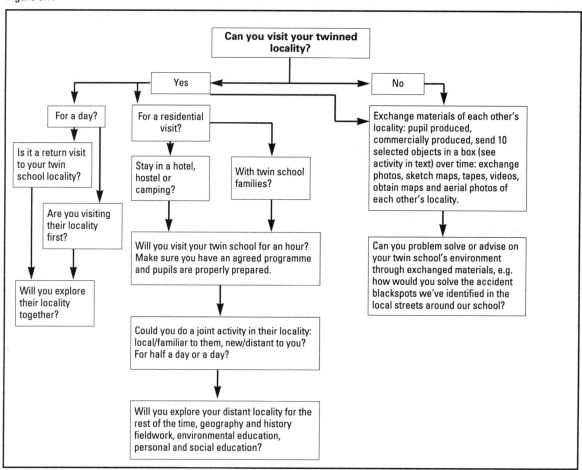

Here are some examples of particularly successful distant place activities achieved through twinning.

1 Two Y4 classes exchange within their home region.

   One school is located inland in a route-centre town with Norman origins, the other 60 miles away in a small coastal resort with Georgian seafront and some deep-sea fishing still taking place.

   Children did extensive project work on their own locality, shared it with parents, then sent it to the visiting school. The two schools used exchanged project work as the starting point for their visits, did further preparation on their distant locality, then were guided around their host school's locality with learning objectives relating to geography and history. Teachers and children were tremendously enthusiastic about the outcomes of the visit and the whole project.

2 An English school twins with a school for 9–16-year-olds in Bratislava, Czechoslovakia (eastern European economically developing area).

   An English Y5/6 vertically grouped class visited their local town centre, identified types of shops and mapped the layout of the interiors of some of the shops. Materials were sent to Czechoslovakia with the questions: 'Do you have similar shops to ours?' 'Are they stocked and laid out in the same way?' The written, graphed and mapped responses changed the English children's ideas: they found great similarity in the type and layout of shops, whereas they had expected differences. More goods were available in Bratislava than the media had led them to believe.

3 Two classes, one in a northern England urban location and one in a south west England rural location, could not visit each other, but exchanged materials with their IT resources and by electronic mail, which speeds up communication. Sketch maps and other graphical materials were sent on behalf of the school by fax, via two parents working from home with whom payment was negotiated.

Collecting and using appropriate resources
Michael Storm, a member of the Geography Working Group, has provided the following very helpful list which enables us to focus on the kinds of resources we need to gather.

To carry out locality studies, we need:

- A specific, named location (i.e. not India but Chembakolli, a village in India)
- Named people, preferably families
- A focus upon the lives of children
- Pictures of people, landscapes, buildings and unfamiliar artefacts, crops, etc.
- Maps and plans, from small-scale contextual locating maps (e.g. India, South India) to large-scale maps (e.g. Chembakolli village) and house plans
- The pattern of daily life – 24-hour time lines, etc.
- How income is earned, or subsistence organised;
- Diet, clothing, housing details
- Patterns of movement: work, school, trade
- Shopping, market, trade activities
- Leisure activities, festivities, special occasions
- Connections with the wider world through trade, travel, media
- Changes, recent/imminent, in landscape and life styles: aspirations and problems
- Data on climate, descriptions of weather
- Descriptive or imaginative literature set in the locality or its region.

Some characteristic pupil activities   In planning an imaginary journey to the locality (route, time, cost) children can be involved in the activities listed overleaf.

- Making posters to 'advertise' the locality
- Making pictures of the locality as envisaged
- Writing a letter home from an imagined visit to the locality
- Writing to a child who lives in the locality
- Writing a journal/diary entry for an imagined visit
- Writing a story set in the locality
- Making a map of the locality and its setting (using symbols, key, grid, index, scale)
- Making a model of the locality or a building within it
- Making diagrams (time-bar) of the daily rhythm of life
- Making calendar diagrams (pie chart) of the annual rhythm of life
- Making climate graphs for the locality
- Debating a proposed change in the locality
- Writing a letter to an envisaged local paper or enquiry
- Collecting and sorting other material about the country in which the locality is situated, e.g. pictures, stamps, coins, flags, products, etc.

Primary Geography Matters,
The Geographical Association, 1991

You probably have many resources which you will need for studying distant places, but will need further specific ones.

For key stage 1 resources, see Figure 9.12.

In addition:

- Children may be able to lend resources from home
- You may add to your own collection when you travel abroad
- Supermarkets and ethnic food stores are wonderful sources of fruit, vegetables, spices and other foods from distant locations
- A visitor or local contact from the distant locality invited into school has long been an excellent resource
- If you have a child in your class who is visiting relations abroad, enlist them and their parents to collect resources for you while they are there. They will probably be delighted to be of help, but remember to negotiate a budget for them. You will need to specify your requirements and decide whether it is feasible for them to collect some or all of them. Refer back to the checklist of optimum ingredients on page 125.

Remember to use your resources not just to develop work on the localities required in the part of the programme of study relating to Gg2, but also to develop awareness of the wider and more general range of places inferred in the theme attainment targets.

Figure 9.12

Resources for key stage 1 for studying distant places			
Photographs	your own and commercial	Maps	
Pictures	e.g. from calendars, posters	Artefacts,	e.g. pottery, hat, length of material, clothes
Postcards			
Stories	situated in distant locations	Travel brochures	useful, but biased
Information books	about countries, places, environments	Rock or fossil samples	
Slides	your own and commercial	Globe	
Radio/ TV programmes	best recorded for selective use	Big atlas	

Use photographs and/or slides to develop the recognition of:

- The *physical* environment in distant places
  - an earthquake photograph
  - a waterfall photograph
  - a volcano photograph
  - a wind photograph (for example a wind pump, a wind surfer)
  - a rain photograph (umbrella)
  - a sun photograph (an umbrella used as a parasol)
- *Human* environment activities
  - a work photograph (for example hand ploughing in a rice field)
  - a communications photograph (for example illustrating the use of bicycles)
  - a settlement photograph (an oblique aerial view of a village or part of a town).

Children talking about these photographs will develop their knowledge and understanding of vocabulary of:

- Aspects of distant places
- Geographical skills, such as direction finding and use of oblique aerial photographs, as many photographs and postcards are a form of oblique aerial photograph.

For key stage 2 a similar list of resources applies, but increasing numbers of the following are needed:

- Atlases
- Information books or 'text-type' books with details on localities
- Information packs on localities
- Larger-scale maps of localities (commercial or sketch maps).

Fiction and poetry are also important resources which could be listed as school resources for learning about distant places.

Fiction and distant places

We habitually read to our classes or encourage children to read fiction which is set in both time and place. With a little refocusing, we can capitalise on such fiction to develop history and geography work, while still ensuring that the enjoyment of the book for itself is most important.

All the fiction we read to children has some sort of 'place' background; but in some novels, it is especially relevant to heighten the sense of the place in which the novel is set. Fiction can enhance geographical learning, if:

- Children are encouraged to locate the place in the book and its surroundings in an atlas
- Descriptions of physical features or processes are made explicit and reinforced by the teacher, for example a volcano
- Descriptions of human processes and patterns are similarly clarified, for example farming
- The meaning of specific geographical vocabulary used in the book is checked up on and/or clarified by the teacher, for example a railway viaduct.

The following passage from *The Cay* by Theodore Taylor (Puffin), set on a tiny island in the Caribbean, illustrates the usefulness of fiction for geographical learning.

A description of erosion by water:

"He described the hole to me. It was about twenty feet in diameter and six to eight feet deep. The bottom was sandy, but mostly free of coral so that my hook would not snag. He said there was a 'mos' natural opening to the sea, so that the fish could swim in and out of this coral-walled pool.

"He took my hand to have me feel all around the edges of the hole. The coral had been

smoothed over by centuries of sea wash. Timothy said the sand in the sea water acted like a grindstone on the sharp edges of the coral. It was not completely smooth but there were no jagged edges sticking out."

It will be necessary to clarify geographical vocabulary: the 'cay' as in Florida Keys and 'volcano'.

"We often talked about the cay and what was on it. Timothy had not thought much about it. He took it for granted that the cay was always there, but I told him about geography, and how maybe a volcano could have caused the Devil's Mouth. He'd listen in fascination, almost speechless.

"We talked about how the little coral animals might have been building the foundations of the cay for thousands of years. I said, 'Then sand began to gather on it, and after more years, it was finally an island."

The passage also describes the process of coastal deposition, which could be contrasted with the process of erosion in the previous passage. Erosion and deposition occurs in KS2 programme of study 14.

Poetry can also be a very useful medium for teaching about distant places, as the following poem illustrates. Such a poem could be a small starting point for a great deal of geography about a Jamaican locality. Clearly maps, photographs and further details will be needed, but the essence of the effects of weather and climate on the island's human geography is here.

"Year in, year out, the land looks up and waits.
Year in, year out, the land is battered by the slanting rain
Which softens the brain, the earth, roots the sugar cane,
Washes away the top soil, breeds angry mosquitoes,

The land is flattened by hurricanes, like pneumatic drills,
Which uproot ancient trees, smash houses,
Splinter the sleepers on railway tracks.
Whiten the corners of hungry mouths,
And drown the population, given half the chance."

From a poem by a Jamaican poet. Preface to *Hurricane* by Andrew Salkey (Puffin).

Place study knowledge

The Statutory Order is quite specific in the programmes of study and attainment targets about the particular locational knowledge which children are expected to acquire by the end of levels 3 and 5.

This knowledge is expressed in the form of maps at the end of the programme of study with particular physical features and towns which children have to be able to identify:

- UK – Maps A and D
- Europe – Maps B and E
- World – Maps C and F.

The authors have tried to emphasise throughout this book that the approach to the acquisition of this place study knowledge should be developed through atlas and globe work in the context of human and physical environments, not as 'one-off' rote-learning.

The key question 'Where is the place?' and its related concept of location refers, of course, to both place study knowledge and the 'zoom lens out to wide-angle lens' focus issues described earlier in this chapter. It is important to know where places are, but part of that knowing should be understanding *where* a place is *relative* to another place or the region, country, continent or global sector in which it is situated. Learning about place is a process. Much of the formal locational knowledge required by the maps will be acquired when localities are studied if teachers adopt the approach advised here, locating each locality in its wider sphere and encouraging children to see how it is connected to other places, for example capital cities and other countries.

Children should also be aware of the process required to find out where a place is, including how to look up where that place is in an atlas via the contents list, index, latitude and longitude, and so on.

The pupil activity suggestions in Figures 9.13 and 9.15 could be modified/adapted to help children develop spatial and locational understanding while using atlases in context.

The essence of teaching about places

The points in Figure 9.14 will serve as a check-list for teaching about distant localities, within the UK or beyond.

Figure 9.13

Suggested questions to develop spatial and locational understanding

Direct experience

If the pupil has visited a place use these types of questions:

UK
1 How did you travel there?
2 What counties did you travel through?
3 Which county did you stay in?
4 If you stayed on the coast which sea did you swim in?
5 Which other countries were nearest to you and which seas surround the UK's coastline?

Abroad
1 How did you travel there?
2 Did you travel through or fly over any other countries?
3 Which seas did you cross?
4 If you visited an island which seas surrounded it?
5 If not, which countries were next to/bordered your holiday country and which seas washed its coasts?

Indirect experience

If the place being studied cannot be visited, adapt the questions in this way:

UK
1 How could you travel there?
2 Which route could you take from here?
3 In which county is the locality?
4 Which sea or lake is nearest to the locality?
5 Which other countries and seas border England/Wales/Scotland, and which seas surround its coastline?

Abroad
1 How could you travel there?
2 Which other countries would you be likely to fly over or travel through?
3 Which seas might you cross?
4 If an island, which seas surround it?
5 Which countries and seas border your distant locality?

Figure 9.14

Teaching about places

Why teach about places?
• worthwhile
• relevant
• enables balanced views to evolve
• reduces insularity

Try to ensure the study is
• realistic with real people and places
• linked to the child's own perception of local and distant places

Try to avoid
• bias and giving one-sided viewpoints
• stereotyped images
• token gestures
• 'Cook's tour' syndrome

Try to develop twinning
• locally
• nationally
• wider world
• links can be with individuals, schools, villages or visitors

Remember
• distant may be within the UK
• that a place study can arise from a theme
• a place study may be part of another subject-focused topic
• a place study may be a separate and discrete unit of work

Depth of study
• key stage 1 awareness/general
• key stage 2 greater understanding/prescription

Figure 9.15

Suggestions for pupil activity

1 Pupil shades or marks the country under discussion on a world map.

2 Pupil uses or leaves a map of Europe according to location of place being studied.

3 Pupil reinforces their own location by marking on a map of UK.

1.

2.

3.

 ↑To U.S.A

Cuba   Puerto Rico

To ← Mexico   Dominica

CARIBBEAN   Martinique

SEA   Barbados

Trinidad

Caracas   Venezuela

4.

<u>Where is Martinique?</u>
Martinique is one of the Windward Islands. It is in the Caribbean Sea, in the eastern part. Its east coast is washed by the Atlantic, the west coast by the Caribbean.
You have to travel south west from England to get there. The nearest big country is Venezuela in South America.
Its capital is Fort de France.

5.

4 Ask pupil to draw a sketch of the country the locality is situated in and to mark it on. Teacher or pupil sets detail required.

5 Ask pupil to write a variety of information according to their ability and age.
   You might consider directed/undirected activity.
   'Fill in the blanks' activity with vocabulary might be provided by teacher or chosen by child.

NB Maps 1, 2 and 3 are already on the worksheet, prepared by the teacher. 4 and 5 are completed by the children.

10

CROSS-CURRICULAR SKILLS IN GEOGRAPHY

This book stresses the first-hand experience and 'enquiry process' approach to geography as the one which leads to the most effective learning and teaching.

Primary geography also requires the use of many secondary sources to back up and develop fieldwork and to provide knowledge and understanding of people and places which it is impossible for children to visit.

As geography is the subject which bridges the gap between the arts and sciences, the possiblities for developing and reinforcing pupils' skills are limitless.

The skills of using secondary sources refer in some measure to all subjects across the curriculum. This chapter briefly outlines opportunities for developing them in a geographical context.

Research skills

Pupils will need, by the end of their primary years, to be able to read and extract information for a purpose from a range of written resources, including:

- Tourist leaflets
- Travel brochures
- Newspapers
- Information books
- Encyclopaedias
- Story books with a geographical setting.

They will need to work towards the development of higher reference and reading skills, such as:

- Using a contents page
- Using an index
- Extracting factual information from more than one book
- Scan reading
- Skimming text
- Summarising
- Detecting bias or stereotyping in text
- Detecting inaccuracies in text
- Ascertaining when a book was published.

The last is very relevant to geography, as many geographical reference books in class and in school libraries have themselves become historical documents: children need to know how up to date their information is!

Graphicacy skills

Geography uses graphicacy as a source of secondary information more than any other subject except maths.

Pupils will need to understand and extract information from:

- Graphs
  – block graphs

- bar-line graphs
- line graphs
- Charts
  - bar charts
  - tally charts
  - frequency charts
  - pie charts
  - flow charts
- Tables of various sets of data
- Maps of the many kinds already discussed.

Media sources

Educational television and radio, films, filmstrips and slides provide an important source of secondary information for pupils. Extracting the most useful information from these sources for geography can be a difficult skill. Pupils need to watch and listen, having been properly briefed on the programme. It may be appropriate for the children to watch with one or more key questions in mind to enable them to focus on a particular concept or area of content. Alternatively a useful technique with older children is to watch some programmes twice, the first time with no brief, but the second time with key questions in mind, or, for the more able children, a requirement to take some notes. This should not, however, be at the expense of watching, and the pause button should be used.

Some examples of key questions:

- What are the homes like there?
- What kind of work are people doing?
- How many different kinds of rock or landscape can you see? Note them down.

Whatever secondary sources have been used, teachers and children should know what the expected outcomes of the learning are. Information should be extracted not just *per se*, but to inform the pupils and to lead on to pupil comment, analysis and prediction, depending upon pupils' age and ability.

Data handling

Children collect information in the form of facts and figures from their fieldwork and secondary source enquiries. Traditionally, this data has been dealt with manually.

Findings are recorded, reflected on, questioned and so on by writing or using the various graphicacy skills. Some work will continue to be done like this but, whenever possible and appropriate, we need to encourage the use of IT as a key tool in both handling and presenting data. The presentation of data through electronic means is a bonus for geography, and helps pupils to spend more time on analysing their results than, say, drawing a block graph or pie chart.

The National Council for Educational Technology's *Focus on IT* states that handling data with computers should encourage the ability to:

- Plan, hypothesise and predict
- Design and carry out investigations
- Interpret results and findings
- Draw inferences
- Communicate ideas and findings
- Make decisions based on conclusions drawn from findings.

This list of aims could equally apply to geographical enquiry. IT provides the tool to handle the data or information generated by a geographical enquiry. Pupils will need to learn how to store, retrieve, correct, process and present information. Database packages like *Grass* and *Our Facts* are exceptionally good for primary age range children. *Our Facts* is a simple 'user friendly' package which can be used by pupils from Y1 on, as it can be set up with limited fields. It is also useful as an introduction for older pupils and teachers who have no previous experience of a database. *Grass* is a slightly more complicated package for pupils from about Y4 onwards. It has 16 fields, and can do complicated searches and mathematics. Both these programs are the box-file type of data package. Pupils can also be taught to access public data bases such as Ceefax, Teletext and library systems. Spread sheets can be used especially to plot field work data on and plan environments.

Touch Explorer Plus using the concept keyboard is more recent and is an excellent addition to the software available for juniors and special needs children. Its various files allow the graphic representation of data collected during fieldwork or secondary source research to be represented on a base plan of A3 or A4 size. The plan is divided up by a grid and information stored electronically under the plan at different 'levels'. These 'levels' can be drawn up to the screen by a 'touch' on a section of the plan or picture. This program allows for differentiation in levels of difficulty and/or type of information stored below the plan. For example, in a land use survey on a local high street, the first level of information could be the location of shops, the second could be the type of shop – for example butcher, estate agent, timber yard – and the third level would explain exactly what the shops did – for example estate agent, a service industry selling or renting houses; a timber yard, where you can buy woods, nails, fencing, and so on. The children can write the information to be stored in the different 'levels'. They can write for different audiences – for example classes lower down the school, different children in the same class and maybe adults.

The open-ended possibilities are too numerous to list here, but most aspects of data from physical and human geography or environmental considerations can be used. Publications of IT programs are given in chapter 12.

Presentation skills

Geographical work lends itself to every method of presentation. The following very varied methods of presentation should prove useful to teachers in the context of special needs children as well as mainstream pupils.

Depending on the special need in question, differing methods of presentation from those used by the majority of children can be used by a child to demonstrate understanding in geography.

Written presentation

- Children can record factual information with further analysis or comment.
- They can integrate factual information into creative writing – a story or a poem in a geographical context, for example a story in the geographical setting of an Amazon location after a project on the equatorial environment; 'I'm only a pebble on the beach': creative work tracking the historical and geographical progress of a flint pebble from cliff to stack to beach after work on coastal erosion and deposition.

Graphical presentation

Maps and plans are often needed to clarify written work or to serve the purpose of written work.

- IT will speed up many types of graphical presentation.
- Charts, graphs and diagrams can present data which has been collected and then

analysed. Flow charts, pie charts, here-and-there comparison charts for places are a few examples (see Chapter 9, Figure 9.8 for here-and-there charts).

- Landscape sketches and general drawings can be made.
- Use base maps as data collection sheets.

Spoken presentation

Spoken presentation can include:

- Straightforward reporting back on experience or evidence
- Tape recording
- Role play – in a geographical context, each child may play the part of a local resident or interested party to simulate a public enquiry surrounding a local issue, such as a bypass or reservoir scheme, to culminate work done on the issue and to demonstrate understanding.

Models

A great variety of models with art or design technology connections can be used to present and enhance geographical work.

Some examples are:

- 3D models of villages, streets, contour models, volcano models, cliff cross-section models
- Working models of water mills, weather instruments.

Photographic presentatation

Children's own photographs and postcards can be used to:

- Enhance a class or group display of geographical work
- Enhance their own project books.

They should be used for a purpose – annotated to explain children's understanding, and occasionally for fun, not just stuck in to fill space. One very full use of photographs is to mount them next to a rough sketch map which shows the location at which each one was taken and notes in which direction the camera was facing when it was taken. Pupils can annotate features, too, if appropriate.

On rare occasions, a video taken during fieldwork or in the classroom can be directed by the children.

11

CROSS-CURRICULAR THEMES AND DIMENSIONS IN GEOGRAPHY

'How does effective National Curriculum geography teaching deal with cross-curricular themes and dimensions without entailing further work?' This is a reasonable question which teachers have the right to ask.

To answer it we need to clarify what the themes and dimensions are; to recognise their relationship with geography and to focus on individual themes and plan them into geographical work where appropriate. This does not require a lot of extra work, but a heightening of our own awareness to bring out the explicit nature of the themes with pupils. Sometimes a change of focus within already planned work will be required to achieve this.

The cross-curricular themes

The five themes are:

- Economic and Industrial Understanding (NCC 4)
- Health Education (NCC 5)
- Careers Education (NCC 6)
- Environmental Education (NCC 7)
- Citizenship (NCC 8).

The Whole Curriculum, NCC 3, gives an outline of cross-curricular dimensions, skills and themes for quick reference.

For further, more detailed reference, the National Curriculum Council (NCC) sent one copy of all these Curriculum Guidance themes to all maintained schools between late 1989 and the end of 1990.

In many primary schools it is not unusual to find that these books have sunk without trace. However, to understand the concepts of each one in detail you will need to hunt them down and find the time to read them. Further copies are available from the National Curriculum Council in York. As a coordinator, this is a useful activity to build into your action plan (see Chapter 13), as someone in the school should have a deeper knowledge in order to advise others.

If you analyse these NCC guidance books in relation to *primary* geography you will see that the relationship between:

- Environmental Education and geography is very strong
- Economic and Industrial Understanding and geography is very strong
- Citizenship and geography is important
- Health Education and geography is contributory
- Careers Education and geography is contributory.

All the themes have a strong relationship with human geography because it is human action in and upon the environment which gives rise to the themes from the geography stance.

Environmental Education within geography

Environmental education is of great importance to geography. The geography Order has highlighted part of the human environment interaction with the physical environment content of the subject by pulling out these aspects and turning them into an attainment target: Environmental Geography.

One fifth of the geography Order in attainment target terms relates to the environment through these strands:

● Use and misuse of natural resources
● The quality and vulnerability of different environments
● The possibility of protecting and managing environments.

Environmental Education is defined as education:

● *In* the environment
  – active learning
  – fieldwork
● *About* the environment
  – to gather knowledge and understanding
● *For* the environment
  – in order to preserve, conserve and respect it.

(There are links with Gg2, 3, 4 and 5.)

The basic aims of geographical work share these ideas.

Economic and Industrial Understanding within geography

Economic and Industrial Understanding is concerned with:

● The nature of goods and services provided to customers
● How these goods and services are provided

● How some leisure activities harm areas of environmental value
● Economic activity – farming, industry, business and the world of work
● Industrial location – why certain economic activities are located near to a power source, workforce, raw materials, a transport network, consumer market or other resource
● The impact of industry on the local area
● The effect of economic change on the local area and people
● The economic importance of renewable and non-renewable resources
● The effects of extracting natural resources from the environment
● The impact of new industry on the environment.

(There are links with Gg2, 4, and 5.)

Citizenship within geography

Citizenship is concerned with:

● Similarities and differences in communities in different places and also on every scale
  – local area
  – home region
  – contrasting locality
  – countries
  – global
● Similarities and differences in the quality of life
● Decision-making processes
● Issues relating to change in settlements
● Attitudes and values and their effect on change.

(There are links with Gg2, 4 and 5.)

Health Education within geography

Health Education is concerned with:

● Hazard perception and safety in different fieldwork environments

136

- The prevention of pollution in water sources in the UK and in economically developing localities
- How the local physical geography and standards of wealth can affect the lives of people in different places
- The quality of environments and how this can affect the health of communities
- Conserving the Earth for our own health.

(There are links with Gg2, 4 and 5.)

Careers Education within geography

Careers Education is concerned with:

- Different types of work people do
- Differences in types of work, opportunities to work and reasons for this
- Environmental problems arising from industry.

(There are links with Gg4 and 5.)

Figure 11.1 relates each strand of the attainment targets to the various themes in more detail.

Some examples of activities which develop cross-curricular themes at key stages 1 and 2

Having recognised what the themes are and how they relate to primary geography, the following examples are given to illustrate how the themes can be highlighted in geographical work already being done. Many teachers are resistant to the themes at first glance because they do not feel, except perhaps for Environmental Education, that they are appropriate for young children. This is a limited view, as many of the activities which we are already doing with pupils involve the themes. We just need to recognise this and make it explicit, while, however, ensuring progression, of course. We can do this by extending our open-ended questioning of children's understanding and by slightly altering the focus of part of a topic.

Figure 11.1

Relating the geography Orders to cross-curricular themes at KS1 and KS2		Economic and industrial understanding	Environmental education	Citizenship	Health education	Careers education and guidance
Strands						
Gg1	Map use	Δ	Δ	Δ	Δ	Δ
	Fieldwork	Δ	•	Δ	Δ	Δ
Gg2	Knowledge of places	Δ	Δ		Δ	
	Understanding of distinctive features	•	Δ	Δ	Δ	
	Similarities/differences	•	Δ	•	Δ	
	Themes/issues	•	•	•	Δ	
Gg3	Weather and climate		Δ		Δ	
	Seas and oceans		Δ			
	Rivers, river basins	Δ	•	Δ	Δ	
	Landforms		Δ			
	Animals, plants, soils		•			
Gg4	Population	Δ	•		Δ	
	Settlement	Δ	•		Δ	
	Communication and movement	Δ	Δ			
	Economic activities	•	•	•	Δ	Δ
Gg5	Use/misuse of natural resources	Δ	•	Δ		
	Quality and vulnerability of environments	Δ	•			
	Protecting/managing environments	Δ	•	Δ		
	Δ = links • = strong links					

137

Environmental Education
Key stage 1
- Children can map the worst litter zones in the school grounds and around the school, or
- plan a scheme to improve the school grounds: working with environmental awareness.

Key stage 2
- In an ongoing topic relating to the change in use of a local site, pupils can monitor the restoration of the landscape on and around the site over a period of time.

Economic and Industrial Understanding
Key stage 1

Infants frequently set up shops and businesses in the classroom and may visit real ones as fieldwork experience.

- Set up a travel agency with top infants as a way of beginning work on a particular locality beyond the UK, using the globe to locate countries and differentiate between land and sea. Have pupils make mock cheques for fictitious or real costs, depending on their place value concepts, for their journeys or package tours.
- When visiting a dairy farm, make sure that the children understand that farmers need to buy and sell calves or cows and buy feedstuffs in order to produce the milk pupils see.

Key stage 2
- Children preparing for a residential journey for fieldwork can be involved in the costing of those activities, including alternative transport costings against distance. They can compare the group entrance fees for places they will visit and consider the difference in likely maintenance costings for different places, for example which costs more to run – a castle or a National Park visitors' centre?

Local issues
- Pupils examining the issue of alternative by-pass routes, actual or fictitious, can contact the local highways department to discover construction costs per mile over different land types, so that they can make a more informed decision about the costs and benefits of the alternatives in their public enquiry simulation.

Global issues
- Upper juniors studying an economically developing locality in an equatorial or tropical zone need to be made aware of, and consider both sides of, the deforestation problem. Conservation, world climate and soil erosion versus the economic pressures on tropical governments to export hardwood to keep part of their population employed and to trade with other governments are important issues. Bringing in much needed foreign currency resources benefits the population and needs to be considered.
  Here the area of economic needs as opposed to wants, costs and benefits, environmental and social issues associated with economic activity, is developed.
- Within a topic on conservation is a focus on animal conservation in the Arctic. It could address the issues that some Inuit need to hunt to make a living and that it is appropriate for indigenous people to dress in fur clothing in the sub-zero temperature zones of the world.

Economic and Industrial Understanding is often considered a particularly difficult theme for primary pupils. The above suggestions should disprove that theory. After all, infants able to understand that if there are not enough pairs of scissors in their class for one pair each then they must share are already understanding the concept of scarcity of resources, a concept central to

138

economics. Similarly, juniors can understand that when the money inputs of a car manufacturing industry fall because customers cannot afford to buy cars, then car workers are laid off.

Economic and Industrial Understanding can enhance geographical work because the two lend themselves to the involvement of Adults Other than Teachers (AOTs). The teacher does not and cannot be expected to know the details of other people's work which could enhance their pupils' learning.

Pupils engaged in a geographical enquiry can gain invaluable benefits from either visiting professionals or asking them into school to help with the enquiry. Professionals, however, should *not* just act as one-off deliverers of information. As part of their enquiry, pupils need to design questions to which professionals will respond. These questions and answers will aid pupils in completing their enquiry more effectively, thereby learning more. Both public and private industry employees can be of great assistance as long as they have been properly briefed before working with pupils.

For example, in a multi-subject focus topic on road safety in the local area, involving science, design technology and geography, children are asked to identify through fieldwork local pedestrian and traffic blackspots around their school. Then they are asked in groups to design and make models of solutions to one of these blackspots. They brainstorm possibilities, but need to have these confirmed by an 'expert'. A highways engineer explains the different types of solutions and their costings which the department has to consider when making an improvement. The children learn that the safest solution is sometimes the most expensive, by the AOT bringing to their attention the cost factor which they had not considered before. As a result, some of them make

compromises to their model solutions, and weigh up the advantages and disadvantages, the costs and benefits, financial, social and in terms of safety.

Citizenship
Key stage 1

- The fire officer, police officer or librarian who visits school or whom pupils may visit on their work site can be used to identify public services which we all depend on.
- Use the study of the local area with the locational knowledge which grows from it – knowing your address, where you live locally and within the UK – to develop the idea of community.
- When studying other places, the similarities and differences concept of geography develops the pluralism concept of citizenship: it is natural for others to speak different languages, have different roles and other differences in their way of life.

Key stage 2
At this key stage, citizenship forms part of geography from the point of view of attitudes, values and issues, and similarities and differences.

- Work on any local issue such as a proposition for changes in land use by building a supermarket or more housing, lends itself to developing the concept of democracy. Pupils can collect data on the range of opinions about the proposed development through questionnaires via parents and/or fieldwork interviewing. They can ask the professionals involved for information and see how plans are put to the public and how and when the need for a public enquiry arises. They could also role play a public enquiry simulation.

Health Education
Key stage 1

- Deal with basic road safety relating to local road features or blackspots as one focus in part of a 'Transport' or 'Journeys' topic.
- Whenever pupils visit another environment, discuss the hazards which could affect them in that environment.

Key stage 2

- Develop increased personal awareness of safety issues on fieldwork in different types of environment, for example the top of a castle or by the sea.
- Overlaps between Health Education, Environmental Education and Economic and Industrial Understanding are highlighted in developing localities:
  – Encourage pupils to see the cause and effect relationship between health and the lack of service provision in some localities. If there is a lack of doctors, hospitals and sewage disposal in an area, people's health and general expectations are bound to be affected.
  – The availability and management of water and food resources can be compared 'here' and 'there'.
  – Consider the health issues involved in supplying water to pupils' homes and the removal of waste water.

Careers Education

There is considerable overlap with EIU here, because recognising jobs relates to economic activity.

Fieldwork activities described in Chapter 8 develop understanding of ideas about roles and work.

- Map the different work areas of the school and graph the results of a survey to see how many different job types exist in the school.
- Do some fieldwork in the local area to spot different workplaces and associated job types.
- Visit a workplace such as a supermarket and question people about their roles as part of a team. This, of course, would be only part of the focus for the visit.
- Settlement in the local area: from fieldwork experience, maps and a correlated aerial photograph, pupils can work out and map which parts of the area are predominantly residential and where and what the workplaces are. As part of a local history project, the current situation could be compared to sources of information about the past.

Cross-curricular dimensions

Cross-curricular dimensions are concerned with all aspects of equal opportunities:

- Gender
- Race
- Religion
- Ability
- Culture.

The school's attitude to these should be indicated in the whole-school policy statement. Geography should play an important part in the multi-cultural dimension.

Multi-cultural education

Although the school's policy statement should ensure that this dimension permeates the whole curriculum, primary geography is a wonderful vehicle to open it up.

For those pupils living in multi-cultural areas, learning with peers whose cultural heritage is part British and part distant places makes learning about those distant places more relevant.

For those pupils in schools where multi-cultural contacts are rare, geography is one subject area which brings in the dimension naturally. Studying distant places and learning to value other people's cultures and environments widen pupils' horizons.

Planning for cross-curricular themes and dimensions

In Chapter 3, the links which geography has with other subjects was explored. Ideally, links with cross-curricular themes should also be explored before planning key stages. The dimensions certainly need to be considered by the staff as part of the whole-school ethos at the level of whole-school policy development.

However, because there is a limit to what we can cope with at any one time, it is suggested that until you are familiar with the themes and know how they relate to the geography parts of a topic, you should plan themes in at the unit of study stage. Ask yourself how the themes relate to the focus questions planned and make a note of which ones you will be dealing with, as shown in the focus-planning examples in Chapter 5.

As you grow in experience, you will find that you are able to see the links more clearly and develop the cross-curricular themes and dimensions more deeply through geography, planning them in explicitly first of all at focus planning level, but later bearing them in mind at key stage planning level when reviewing takes place.

12
RESONANCES

To teach primary geography well a wide range of resources is necessary. Most schools will have some resources, however limited, and in the Appendix a resources audit list for National Curriculum geography, key stages 1 and 2, is provided which will help you to evaluate your current position. Resources which have been referred to in previous chapters will be found listed here.

The resources listed are not the only ones available, but are some that the authors have found useful for classroom teaching. New resources are constantly being produced, and it is recommended that you send for inspection copies where possible, to check for usefulness and value for money. Will the resources be relevant to your key stage plan and its units of work?

Books and resources

Text books and schemes

The purchasing of one set of text books as a 'scheme of work' to satisfy National Curriculum requirements is not recommended. No one scheme can fit a primary school's individual approach to geography within the context of its own curriculum. However, it is recognised that text books can be extremely useful if used as resources in a variety of ways.

1 By using certain pages, sections and chapters of the book as a group or class activity to support planned units of work from the key stage plan.
2 To give teachers information and ideas to use with pupils.
3 To be used by pupils for their own enquiry.

However, there are times when coordinators may find it useful to have a set of text books available to guide and support teachers who feel uncertain in this curriculum area, as long as the books are relevant to the appropriate units of work.

Many of the current schemes are being rewritten in light of the Order. Others are being replaced, and many completely new schemes are coming onto the market. Schemes listed here have been published after 1990 unless otherwise indicated.

Schemes

Ginn Key stage 1 and 2 Geography, Bill Chambers and Wendy Morgan, Ginn, 1991.

Into Geography (being revised), Patricia Harrison, Steve Harrison and Mike Pearson, Arnold-Wheaton, 1987.

Keystart (see Atlases below), Collins Longman, 1991.

Oliver & Boyd Key Stage 1 and 2, W.E. and V. Marsden, Oliver & Boyd, 1991.

Schoolbase Geography, Stephen Scoffham, Colin Bridge and Terry Jewson, Schofield & Sims, 1986.

Sunshine Geography (part of Sunshine Books key stage 1), Heinemann, 1991.

Time and Place, Patricia Harrison and Steve Harrison, Simon & Schuster, 1992.

The Young Geographer Investigates, Terry Jennings, OUP, 1986.

Text books for mapwork

Discover Maps, Patricia Harrison and Steve Harrison, Collins Educational/OS, 1988.

Mapping Skills, Tom A. Dodd, OUP, 1985.

Mapskills Activity Book, OUP, 1985.

The Mapskills Atlas, work book and copymasters, Collins Longman, 1992.

Mapstart Books 1–3, Simon Catling, Collins Longman, 1985.

OS Mapstart, Simon Catling, Collins Longman, 1989.

Mapwork 1, David Flint and Mandy Suhr, Wayland, 1992.

Master Maps, Patricia Harrison and Steve Harrison, Holmes McDougall/OS, 1988.

OS Resource File, Patricia Harrison and Steve Harrison, Collins Educational, 1989.

Philp's Children's Atlas, 1992.

Another related map book:

Moving Into Maps, Heinemann, 1983.

Atlases

Most of the main publishers have a range of atlases in their lists. Some interesting atlases include:

For young children:

Atlas One, Heinemann, 1986.

A First Atlas of the World, Schofield & Sims, 1992.

Rainbow Atlas, OUP, 1987.

Going up the age range for key stage 2:

Atlas 2, Collins Longman, 1980.

The World Today Schofield & Sims, 1992.

The Whole World Now, Schofield & Sims, 1992.

The Folens OS World Atlas, Folens, 1991.

A recent trend is to incorporate an atlas and text book into one. Examples are:

Keystart UK Atlas, Collins Longman, 1991.

Keystart World Atlas, Collins Longman, 1991.

The main atlas publishers are:

Arnold Wheaton
Collins Longman
Heinemann
OUP
Phillips
Schofield & Sims.

There is no perfect atlas. Consider these criteria when choosing:

Audience Is the atlas appropriate for its intended age and ability range?

Function What kind of atlas is it?

Is it a working atlas? Does it have activities, copy masters, outline maps, gazetteer?

Is a range of atlas skills covered?

Publication date When was this edition published?

How up-to-date is it?

Remember that an atlas will probably be out of date as soon as you buy it. Part of the skill in using an atlas is noticing and discussing changed boundaries and altered countries.

Details Do you like a lot of pictures or

photographs around the maps?

Do you prefer clear, uncluttered maps?

Do you want a map of the whole of the UK on one page?

Do you want your area of the UK shown fairly large?

Do you want a map which shows southern England or the whole of the UK and northern France and Belgium on the same page to emphasise connections with continental Europe?

Do you want a map which shows the current counties of the UK?

Is the text/size/density of the text appropriate for the intended age range?

Have the maps been oversimplified at the expense of accuracy?

Are the symbols used explained to the pupils?

If abbreviations are used, are they also in the key?

Is the difference between towns, cities and countries clearly indicated by the size difference in the print?

Ease of use Is there a contents page and an index?

Are the page numbers, grid systems or latitude and longitude used to refer to places?

Which of these is most suitable for the age of your pupils?

Projections and orientations Are you told which map projection is being used?

Is it Mercator, Peter's, Eckert, Winkel's (see Glossary)?

Are two or more projections presented on pages for comparison?

Are the world maps all Euro-centred, or are some centred on the North Pole, etc.?

Do aerial photographs and satellite images support the maps?

Images of places How is the sense of place conveyed: by words, through photographs, through sketch drawings?

Do the pictures reflect contrasts within the country or continent?

Are the stereotypical images challenged or reinforced? (For example desert = camel; tundra = igloo.)

Are people of both genders from varying ethnic and cultural backgrounds shown in a range of roles?

Map clarity Does each map need and have: a title, a key, a scale, a compass pointer?

Are both metric and imperial units of measurement shown, or only one?

Do foreign place names have English or native language spelling, for example Brussels/Bruxelles? Which do you require?

Is the colour key helpful? For example does green show lowland or vegetation?

Cost Is the cost reasonable?

Format and durability Is the atlas attractive to children?

How durable is it?

Look at the binding, cover lamination, etc.

Geographical work in Primary and Middle Schools, Appendix 4, has a more detailed set of criteria to which you may wish to refer when choosing an atlas.

Maps and plans

When using materials to support mapwork a major resource will be that of maps and plans. The following list shows the variety.

- Street maps
- Road maps
- Postcard maps
- Maps on stamps
- Maps in adverts
- Road sign maps
- Housing estate maps
- Town centre maps
- Tourist maps
- Trail maps
- Ordnance Survey maps
- Bus maps
- Rail maps
- Underground maps
- Building plans
- Room plans
- Board game maps
- Guide book maps
- Picture maps
- Atlas maps
- 'Antique' maps
- Microchip circuit 'maps'
- Wall chart maps
- Walkers' maps
- Land use maps
- Sketch maps
- Globe maps
- Architects' plans
- Developers' plans
- Maps in stories

The types of OS maps needed and the key stage to which they are appropriate has been described in detail in Chapter 7.

Mapwork General details about sources for OS maps were also given in Chapter 7. Information and price lists on all OS maps and wall charts can be obtained from:

Information Department
Ordnance Survey
Romsey Road
Maybush
SOUTHAMPTON
SO9 4DH
Tel. (0703) 792000

The National Map Centre
22-24 Caxton Street
LONDON
SW1H OQU
Tel. (071) 222 2466

and Stanfords, listed under Globes.

Ordnance Survey now have many listed regional and local suppliers for large scale maps as well as smaller scale ones. Check their catalogue for your nearest supplier.

A full range of OS products is also available through Chas. E. Goad, as well as their own town centre plans. Goad plans are accurate plans of shopping centres and high streets. These plans show in detail the layout of the shops, the retailer and what they trade in. They are updated, some annually and others once every two years, so comparisons can be made of the shops now, when the plan was drawn and some number of years ago. It is possible to buy the copyright for £2, which enables the buyer to reproduce parts of the plans for pupils' worksheets. There is also a primary pack to help teachers develop work in shopping centres using the plans (for ages 7 to 11) – *Education Pack A: Good Shopping Centre Plans in Junior Schools.*

Chas. E. Goad
8–12 Salisbury Square
OLD HATFIELD
Herfordshire
AJ9 5BJ
Tel. (0707) 271171

Globes

Globes are either physical – showing land forms – or political – showing countries. They can be bought from many stationers, for example W.H. Smith, high street shops such as the Early Learning Centre, and through educational catalogues, for example Phillips, Hestair Hope, E.J. Arnold.

Stanfords,
12–14 Long Acre
LONDON
WC2E 9LP
Tel. (071) 836 1321

Stanfords has an extensive globe catalogue.

If you are buying a hard globe, it sometimes pays to buy one with a metal arm, as these last longer with children leaning on them. Good-quality globes are expensive; inflatable globes provide a viable and inexpensive alternative. They start around £4, and can be bought from Chas. E. Goad and:

Cambridge Publishing Services
PO Box 62
CAMBRIDGE
CB3 9NA

Other equipment

Compasses, clinometers and weather-measuring instruments can be obtained through educational suppliers. For more specific help on weather studies, including weather forecast logging maps, contact:

The Meteorological Office
Marketing Services
Sutton Building
London Road
BRACKNELL
Berks
RG12 2SZ
Tel. (0344) 854 818

Collect your own rocks and fossils. Commercial packs are available, for example Primary Core Pack (key stage 2) from:

Earth Works
Geography Supplies Limited
16 Station Road
Chapeltown
SHEFFIELD
S3O 4XH
Tel. (0742) 455746

Vertical aerial photograph sources

Sources   Local newspapers have aerial photographs, usually in black and white.

Local flying clubs may have members who are prepared to overfly your area and take photographs if you cover costs.

Local flying centres may be approached for a hire service and local hot air balloon enthusiasts/clubs can be hired or paid costs.

Commercial aerial photograph companies offer varying packages. Check that their service is a colour one, and that they will laminate photographs. This service costs extra, but extends the use and life of photographs and is well worth it.

Reputable companies   Geonex UK Ltd has an education officer. INSET sessions can be provided for primary teachers.

Geonex UK Ltd
92-94 Church Road
MITCHAM
Surrey
CR4 3TD
Tel. (081) 685 9393

Photoair
191A Main Street
Yaxley
PETERBOROUGH
PE7 3LD
Tel. (0733) 241850

Hunting Aerofilms
Gate Studios
Station Road
BOREHAM WOOD
Herts
WD6 1EJ
Tel. (081) 207 0666

Ask your local secondary school for its discarded GCSE oblique and vertical aerial photographs. You may be given sets, although they are unlikely to be of your area.

Figure 12.1

Geographical software			
Software type	Package	Company	Availability
Word processing packages	Pen Down	Longman Logotron	A
	Desktop Folio	ESM	A
	Folio	ESM	BBC
	Stylus	Mape	BBC, N
	Magpie	Longman Logotron	A
	Caxton Press	Newman College	480Z
	Front Page Extra	Newman College	A, BBC, N
	Caption		BBC
	Developing Tray	Inner London Education Computing Centre	
Communication with other schools	Email		
	Fax Machines		
Data handling packages	Our Facts Sorting Game Notice Board Datashow Branch	NCET data handling pack	BBC, N, 480Z
	Notice Board	Newman College	BBC
	Grass		BBC, N
	Grasshopper		BBC, N
	Datasuite		A
	Graph It		BBC
	Touch Explorer Plus	NCET	BBC, N
Directional packages	Logo (version 1)	Longman Logotron	A, BBC
	Logo (version 2)	Research Machines	N
	Tiny Logo	Topologica	A, N
	Turtle	Valiant or Jessop	A, BBC, N
	Roamer	Valiant	freestanding
	Pip	through Fernleaf from Swallow Systems	freestanding
Data logging packages	First Sense	Philip Harris	
	Weather Reporter	Advisory Unit for Microtechnology in Education	
	Sensing Science Pack	NCET	
Software designed to support geography specifically (key stage 2)	Mapventure	Sherston Software	BBC, N
	Viewpoints	Sherston Software	A
	Mapping Skills	ESM	BBC
	SMILE maths	Inner London Education Computing Centre	
	Whatley Quarry	NCET	
	List Explorer	NCET	BBC Master
	World Atlas	Software Toolworks	
	World Wise	Bourne Educational	
	Domesday Interactive Video Disc	Cumana	BBC
		(A = Archimedes) (BBC = BBC) (N = Nimbus) (480Z = Research Machines)	

Specific books for the school library which are suitable for infants and juniors include:

The Aerofilms Book of Britain from the Air
The Aerofilms Book of England from the Air
The Aerofilms Book of Scotland from the Air
The Aerofilms Book of Ireland from the Air
Yorkshire from the Air
The Changing Face of Britain

(available from Hunting Aerofilms);

Above London, Editors: Robert Cameron and Alistair Cooke, Andre Deutsch
Above Paris, Salinger, Andre Deutsch
are obtainable from bookshops.

Information technology

New software is being developed all the time; the range available for National Curriculum geography has suddenly grown.

All the open-ended software available for communicating and handling information is extremely useful for geography. Concept keyboard overlays are useful to promote geographical vocabulary. See Figure 12.1 for full information on software availability.

The Domesday disc assists National Curriculum local area history and geography. It can also be used as a resource for a contrasting UK locality study providing screen maps, photographs and data.

Two recent publications from NCET are helpful in promoting the integration of IT into geographical work, they are: *Focus on IT*, and *Primary Humanities and IT in the National Curriculum*.

NCET
Sir William Lyons Road
University of Warwick Science Park
COVENTRY
CV4 7EQ
Tel. (0203) 416994

Another useful address for IT follows.

The Advisory Unit for Microtechnology in Education
Endymion Road
HATFIELD
Hertfordshire
Tel. (0707) 265443

Media and audio visual aids

Media Educational broadcasts are a very useful resource for geography work. Both television and radio programmes for schools come with professional and usually detailed teacher's notes and often with relevant worksheets.

Programmes should be used as a resource, not the rationale, for the unit of work. Television can help particularly in the provision of up-to-date material on distant places, both UK and wider world. Watch out for programmes which help locality studies. Ideally teachers should preview programmes.

- Programmes should be recorded to provide a resource bank and to facilitate appropriate use.
- It may only be appropriate to draw on one or two programmes from a series. Take care to choose only those which supplement or form a focus for some part of pupils' work. Sequences can be chosen from a programme to make a particular point.
- Often the best use of a programme is made by seeing or listening to the programme once then replaying key sequences to reinforce an idea. Pupils can interact with the material, having been guided by the teacher to focus on particular aspects or answer specific questions.
- Small group viewing and listening can be used for further differentiation.
- Don't forget that the pause or freeze-frame button can be very useful in clarifying parts of the programme.

Useful programmes

- *Our World*, key stage 1, ITV
- *Geography – Start Here*, key stage 1 and 2, ITV
- *Search*, key stage 2, ITV
- *Environments*, key stage 2, ITV
- *Going Places*, key stage 2, ITV
- *Watch*, key stage 1, BBC
- *Landmarks*, key stage 2, BBC

Individual programmes from a wider range of series can complement your work; check the programme titles and synopses.

Audio visual aids BBC's *Teaching Today* series, prepared for in-service training, has issued a video comprising two programmes on key stages 1 and 2 primary geography. There is a further one on Environmental Education in primary schools. The videos have an accompanying booklet to help head teachers or coordinators who wish to use them with the whole school staff for school focused staff development.

You can borrow or hire videos from many of the organisations already listed. The *Environmental Review* video from Ark is very useful for upper juniors. Filmstrips and slide sets can be purchased from similar organisations. Remember to check the age range for which they are designed before ordering.

Ark
489–500 Harrow Road
LONDON W9
Tel. (081) 968 6780

Useful addresses for UK studies

Conservation Trust
National Centre for Environmental Education, George Palmer Site
Northumberland Avenue
READING
RG2 7PW
Tel. (0734) 868442

Council for Environmental Education
School of Education
University of Reading
London Road
READING
RG1 5AQ
Tel. (0734) 318921

Council for the Protection of Rural England
Warwick House
25–27 Buckingham Palace Road
LONDON
SW1W 0PP
Tel. (071) 976 6433

Countryside Commission
John Dower House
Crescent Place
CHELTENHAM
GL50 3RA
Tel. (0242) 521381

English Heritage
Fortress House
23 Saville Row
LONDON
W1X 2HE
Tel. (071) 973 3498

Field Studies Council
Preston Montford
Montfort Bridge
SHREWSBURY
SY4 1HW
Tel. (0743) 850674

Forestry Commission
231 Costorphine Road
EDINBURGH
EH12 7AT
Tel. (031) 334 0303

Learning through Landscapes
Third Floor
Southside Offices
The Law Courts
WINCHESTER
Hampshire
SO23 7DU
Tel. (0962) 846258

National Association for Environmental
Education
Wolverhampton Polytechnic
Gorway Road
WALSALL
WS1 3BD
Tel. (0922) 31200

National Trust
36 Queen Anne's Gate
LONDON
SW1H 9AS
Tel. (071) 222 9251

National Conservancy Council
Northminster House
PETERBOROUGH
PE1 1YA
Tel. (0733) 40345

Ramblers Association
1-5 Wandsworth Road
LONDON
SW8 2IJ
Tel. (071) 582 6878

Royal Society for the Protection of Birds
The Lodge
SANDY
Bedfordshire
SG19 2DL
Tel. (0767) 80551

Soil Association
86–88 Colston Street
BRISTOL
BS1 5BB
Tel. (0272) 290661

Tidy Britain Group
The Pier
WIGAN
WN3 4EX
Tel. (0942)824620

Town and Country Planning Association
17 Carlton House Terrace
LONDON
SW1Y 5AS
Tel. (071) 930 8903

Woodland Trust
Autumn Park
Dysart Road
GRANTHAM
Lincolnshire
NG31 6LL
Tel. (0476)74297

Useful addresses for distant places studies

Action Aid
Hamlyn House
Archway
LONDON
N19 5PG
Tel. (071) 281 4101

British Red Cross
9 Grosvenor Crescent
LONDON
SW1X 7EJ
Tel. (071) 235 5454

Catholic Institute for International Relations
22 Coleman Fields
LONDON
N1 7AF
Tel. (071) 354 0883

Catholic Fund for Overseas Development
2 Romero Close
Stockwell Road
LONDON
SW9 9TY
Tel. (071) 733 7900

Centre for Alternative Technology
Llwyngwern
MACHYNLLETH
Powys
SY20 9AZ
Tel. (0654) 702400 and 703409
(Education Office) 703743
(Bookshop) 702948

Centre for Global Education
Longwith College
University of York
YORK
YO1 5DD
Tel. (0904) 413267

Centre for World Development Education
Regent's College
Inner Circle
Regent's Park
LONDON
NW1 4NS
Tel. (071) 487 7410

Centre for World Development Education
1 Catton Street
LONDON
WC1R 4AB
Tel. (071) 487 7410

Christian Aid
PO Box 100
LONDON
SE1 7RT
Tel. (071) 620 4444

Commonwealth Institute
Kensington High Street
LONDON
W8 6NQ
Tel. (081) 603 4535

Council for Education in World Citizenship
Seymour Mews House
Seymour Mews
LONDON
W1H 9PE
Tel. (071) 935 1752

Development Education Centre
Gillott Centre
Bristol Road
BIRMINGHAM
B29 9LQ
Tel. (021) 472 3255

Latin American Bureau
1 Amwell Street
LONDON
EC1R 1UL
Tel. (071) 278 2829

National Association of Development
Centres
8 Endsleigh Street
LONDON
WC1H 0DX
Tel. (071) 388 2670

National Geographic Society
PO Box 19
GUILDFORD
Surrey
GU3 3NY
Tel. (0483) 33161

Oxfam
274 Banbury Road
OXFORD
OX2 7GZ
Tel. (0865) 56777

Save the Children
Mary Datchelor House
17 Grove Lane
Camberwell
LONDON
SE5 8RD
Tel. (071) 703 5400

Scottish Catholic International Aid Fund
5 Oswald Street
GLASGOW
C1 4QR
Tel. (041) 221 4446

Scottish Education and Action for
Development
29 Nicolson Square
EDINBURGH
EH8 9BX
Tel. (031) 667 0120

UNICEF
55–56 Lincoln's Inn Fields
LONDON
WC2A 3NB
Tel. (071) 405 5592

Welsh Centre for International Affairs
Temple of Peace
Cathays Park
CARDIFF
CF1 3AP
Tel. (0222) 384912

World Education Development Group
Canterbury Centre
St Alphege Lane
CANTERBURY
Kent
Tel. (0227) 766552

World Wide Fund for Nature (WWF)
Panda House
Weyside Park
GODALMING
Surrey
GU7 1XR
Tel. (0483) 426444

Packs

Useful packs on distant places

1 A pack, suitable for key stage 2, on a contrasting UK locality is *The Lake District Work and Leisure Pack* , issued by the Lake District National Park:

   Lake District National Park Authority
   Blencathra Centre
   Threlkeld
   KESWICK
   Cumbria
   CA12 4SG
   Tel. (059) 683 601

   Other National Parks are also producing resources.

2 *Chembakolli – A Village in India*
   Bambamarca – A Town in Peru
   Nairobi – A Kenyan City
   Kapsokwony – Rural Kenya

These excellent and value-for-money packs for key stage 2 are available from:

   Action Aid
   Old Church House
   Church Steps
   FROME
   Somerset
   BA11 1PL 01460 238000
   Tel. (0373) 452292

3 *Dominica – A Small Caribbean Island*. This pack (for key stages 2 and 3) comes with resource sheets, video and computer software. It provides many links with cross-curricular themes and geography. It

is published and distributed by:

Development Education in Dorset (DEED)
East Dorset Professional Education Centre
Lowther Road
BOURNEMOUTH
BH8 8NR
Tel. (0202) 296701

4   *An Arctic Child* (Labrador and Norway)

Rainforest Child (various rainforest locations with tapes)

A Mountain Child (Bolivia) are packs for the 8-to-13 age range and are published by Lyle and Roberts. They look at various aspects of global physical and environmental geography, and two of them are studies of economically developing localities. They can be obtained from:

Greenlight Publications
Ty Bryn
Comb Gardens
Llangynog
CARMARTHEN
Dyfed
SA33 5AY
Tel. (026) 783 332

An optional video to be used with all the packs can be obtained from:

Jeff Forster
Yorkshire Television
Kirkstal Road
LEEDS
Tel. (0532) 438283

The photopack *A Tale of Two Cities: London and Calcutta* is good for home region/distant place, or contrasting locality in the UK/contrasting locality in an economically developing country, similarity and difference work. It is also good for rural/urban contrast work, for example to contrast with the *Village in India* pack. It is aimed at the 5-to-19 age range and is available from the World Wide Fund for Nature.

The Geographical Association

The Geographical Association is a vital resource for primary school teachers via its publishing department. Primary and secondary classroom teachers, advisory teachers, inspectors and geographers involved in teacher training and in research institutes write voluntarily for the GA. Its publications seek to advise and inform on the teaching of geography in both primary and secondary education. It holds an annual three-day conference, of which at least one day is now targeted at primary teachers. You can become a personal member of the GA, or your school can become a corporate member. Publications are available more cheaply to members. Publications and membership details can be obtained from The Geographical Association.

The Geographical Association
343 Fulwood Road
SHEFFIELD
S10 3BP
Tel. (0742) 670666

The following publications are of direct relevance to primary teachers. Coordinators should certainly consider purchasing copies of the first two for themselves and their school. New primary publications and resource packs are constantly being added.

Geographical Work in Primary and Middle Schools (new revised edition), edited by David Mills, 1988.

Local Studies 5–13. Suggestions for the Non-specialist Teacher, updated 1991.

A Guide to the GA's Geographical Work in Primary and Middle Schools. Wendy Morgan (accompanies the major work).

Planning for key stage 2, Wendy Morgan.

Geography IT and the National Curriculum – Case Studies Booklet.

Geography Through Topics in Primary and Middle Schools Including the Application of Information Technology, 1989.

Primary Geography Matters: Inequalities Resources from Workshops and Keynote Lectures: Annual Conference, 1991.

Primary Geographer (a magazine produced four times a year, obtained automatically when you become a GA subscriber).

Teacher's books

The Outdoor Classroom: Educational Use, Landscape Design and Management of School Grounds, (DES publication,) Southgate Publishers.

Teaching Children Through the Environment, Hodder & Stoughton.

Using the School Surroundings, Stephen Scoffham, Ward Lock Educational.

Developing Topic Work in the Primary School, Sarah Tann (ed), The Falmer Press.

World Studies 8–13, Simon Fisher and David Hicks, Oliver & Boyd, 1985.

Making Global Connections, David Hicks and Miriam Steiner (eds) Oliver & Boyd, 1989.

An Eye on the Environment, H.B. Joicey, Bell & Hyman.

Curriculum Leadership and Co-ordination in the Primary School: a Handbook for Teachers, Steve Harrison and Ken Theaker, Guild House Press, Guild House, Mitton Road, WHALLEY, Lancs.

Individual county or borough curriculum guidelines, geography sections.

Who's Who in the Environment: England (an

excellent reference directory), The Environment Council, 80 York Way, LONDON, Tel. (071) 837 9688.

Discovering Geology, Patrick H. Armstrong, Shire Publications.

HMI publications

Geography from 5–16: HMI Curriculum Matters Series (No. 7),

Environmental Education 5–16: HMI Curriculum Matters Series (No. 13).

Teaching and Learning of History and Geography: HMI Aspects of Primary Education Series.

These titles are available from:

HMSO
15 Whitehall
LONDON
SW1A 2DD
Tel. (071) 839 7426

PO Box 276 *(for London post orders)*
LONDON
SW8 5DT
Tel. (071) 622 3316

HMSO publications are also available or can be ordered from provincial shops in certain towns and cities.

Magazines

Child Education and *Junior Education* (published monthly, sometimes contain articles relevant to geography).

Junior Projects (a bi-monthly magazine for Primary Teachers).

Primary file (a termly subscription service sometimes containing relevant articles).

Primary Geographer (see Geographical Association section).

Story books

The list indicates just a few of many books available to enhance geographical work.

Mainly for infants

The Lighthouse Keeper's Catastrophe, Ronda and David Armitage, Puffin Books.

Shaker Lane, Alice and Martin Provenson, Walker Books.

Little Red Riding Hood,: many versions are available.

Rainforest, Helen Cowcher, Andre Deutsch.

Antarctica, Helen Cowcher, Andre Deutsch.

Window, Jeannie Baker, Julia MacRae Books.

Dear Daddy, Philippe Dupasquier, Picture Puffins.

Morning Mollie, Shirley Hughes, Picture Lions.

Kim and the Watermelon, Miriam Smith, Picture Puffins.

The Journey Home, Joanne Findall, Walker Books.

The Great Round the World Balloon Race, Sue Scullard, Macmillan.

Little Polar Bear and the Brave Little Hare, Hans de Beer, North South Books.

Our House on the Hill, Philippe Dupasquier, Anderson Press

Beyond the UK for key stage 2

I am David, Anne Holm, Mammoth.

The Cay, Theodore Taylor, Puffin.

Hurricane, Andrew Salkey, Puffin.

Carefully chosen extracts from Laurie Lee's books for adults provide superb geographical descriptions of landscapes in the UK and Spain. Such extracts can be used successfully in the context of UK work and EC (Spain) work with older juniors. The books are not modern, but many of the descriptions still hold good, or provide a basis for discussing development and change in the landscape, rural and urban:

Cider with Rosie, Laurie Lee, Penguin

As I Walked Out One Midsummer Morning, Laurie Lee, Penguin

A Rose for Winter, Laurie Lee, Penguin.

Action plan for resources

1 Audit resources (see Resource Audit Sheet, see Appendix).
2 Prioritise collection and purchase needs.
3 Discuss budget for geography resources with head teacher within the School Development Plan context.
4 Obtain as many free posters, information packs, etc. as possible from the various organisations.
5 Involve pupils and staff in collecting postcards, pictures, photographsand other suitable materials.
6 Consider storage of resources. A central resource bank makes financial sense *but* classroom-based resources make for most effective use with pupils.

Central resource bank
● Cheaper
● Is there a borrowing book?
● Who tidies it?
● A lot of time wasted fetching and returning items.

Classroom resources
● Instant access
● Permanent access
● Greater cost to school.

A compromise system is usually best, with master OS maps and supplementary compasses centrally stored, for example, and atlases and some compasses in the classroom.

7 Always involve all or relevant staff when reviewing/assessing which published/commercial resources to buy.

8 Consider sharing more expensive resources if you work in a small group of schools. In theory, this is economic and helpful; but the practicalities of time and transport to fetch and return things need to be seriously considered. Fieldwork equipment, such as a soil augur or commercial clinometer, will not be used a lot. Control technology, such as a Roamer, could be a shared purchase by six rural schools used for a half-term in each school over the year. Similarly, very expensive equipment, such as Weather Reporter, could be shared. It is better to plan use for half a term than not to have one at all.

9 Save yourself and your colleagues work by building up resource boxes or files on certain themes or localities. Key stage planning and keeping units of work within topics for several cycles of learning make for stability and less work in the end.

13

COORDINATING GEOGRAPHY IN THE SCHOOL

Whole-school plans

The context and timetable for the development of geography should be defined within the Whole School Development Plan, along with the plans for other subjects. There should be a section on the development of teacher assessment skills, techniques and moderation in geography within the whole school assessment policy (see Figure 13.1).

Figure 13.1

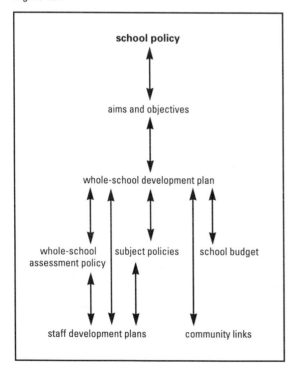

The role of the coordinator

As schools and school plans vary widely, so will the title and position of the person responsible for the teaching and learning of geography in the school. This person might be called coordinator, postholder, teacher responsible for geography or the unlucky teacher that was 'dumped' with geography! Throughout the book we have referred to the person in this crucial role as the coordinator because we feel it carries the important message that you work with other teachers, not on them, or at them, to bring about change.

The role of coordinator has sharpened in focus since the implementation of the geography Order. The role has developed from that of someone who knew where the topic resources were kept, what atlases and maps were in school, the geography of the local area, and so on, into a far more complex one:

● Developing the subject on all levels – skills, concepts, knowledge and understanding
● Designing a curriculum to fit National Curriculum requirements while maintaining a balance within the whole primary curriculum
● Guiding colleagues on teacher assessment, unit planning and what the document really means!

Your main task as a coordinator is to see that, with, and through, your colleagues, the school develops good practice in primary geography teaching and learning.

All schools will be at different stages. You have to evaluate where you are, then move forward in small achievable steps, always keeping in mind an overview of your aim.

The role of coordinator can be broken down into five main areas:

- Communication
- Designing the curriculum
- Resources
- Assessment, evaluation and monitoring
- Staff development.

Communication

Communication involves:

- Motivating, directing, aiding and assisting the whole school staff to develop geography teaching and learning.
- Being a role model to encourage methods of good practice
- Sharing good work by spotting good displays in colleagues' rooms and redisplaying them in central places
- Labelling your own displays for children and adults
- Team teaching and group teaching with a colleague
- Helping other non-specialists
- Talking to parents and govenors
- Cross-phase links.

Designing the curriculum

Curriculum planning involves:

- Designing, directing and overseeing the development of a key stage plan
- Implementing and supporting the key stage plan
- Helping teachers to develop medium-term plans for units of work

- Advising on lesson plans and strategies
- Integrating IT into geography plans
- Integrating the cross-curricular themes into geography plans.
- Developing a geography policy
- Developing a fieldwork health and safety policy
- Collecting SEN ideas for geography
- Key stage 1, 2 and 2, 3 liaison
- Monitoring teachers' plans.

Resources

Managing resources involves:

- Auditing the resources
- Consulting with colleagues on needs
- Organising the resources
- Checking new resources
- Budgeting for resources.

Assessment, evaluation and monitoring

These involve:

- Auditing where your school is now
- Advising on assessment
- Encouraging agreement trials
- Collecting a folder of moderated work as school examples
- Having an overview of the geography recording/records
- Possibly having a role in records for cross-phase liaison
- Monitoring children's achievement in geography in the school.

Staff development

The coordinator's role in staff development involves:

- Advising on staff INSET needs
- Attending courses to update and improve your knowledge
- Feeding information back from courses to the staff

● Working through school-focused staff development.

As the coordinator you will need to keep up to date with changes in National Curriculum documentation and geographical teaching to feed back to your colleagues. This will involve going on courses and inviting specialists into school to help you. Advisory services offer a range of courses on planning and teaching geography. There might also be a 20-day professional development course available through a university or teacher training college. It may be up to you to make sure that other teachers in the school are aware of any courses that would be of use to them, funds and continuing access to Local Authority training facilities being available.

The following are some areas you might like to consider for future INSET needs in your school:

● Planning from focus questions
● Using open-ended IT programmes in geography
● Using specific geography IT programmes
● Using the concept keyboard for geography
● Physical geography of the home region
● Progression in the use of the local area, through active learning, fieldwork, secondary sources and by drawing on pupils' own knowledge
● SEN and geography
● Progression in mapping
● Teaching distant places.

Sometimes if you are in a new school or new to the role you will need to have clarified for you:

● How much authority and responsibility the head teacher will offer you
● How much non-contact time, if any, the head teacher will be able to organise for you to develop your role

● How much INSET time and Grant for Educational Support and Training (GEST) funds will be available for geography
● Where geography fits within your appraisal targets
● Whether the head teacher will enable you to *lead* through workshops, meetings, INSET activities, etc.
● What the (unlikely) scope is for possible specialist exchange and non-contact time to help you to develop the subject more thoroughly.

There is not room here to discuss in detail the skills and strategies needed by coordinators. Various books address this issue for those new to the role, or new to it in the context of the National Curriculum, and who would like to read more (see Chapter 12 and the Bibliography). Not all strategies and skills are unique to the role of geography coordinator and many can be applied in other primary curriculum areas, too.

Tackling the role

To help get yourself started negotiate an action plan with the head based on the school's three-year development plan which should already have been developed as part of the wider school policy. Decide:

● What you have to do
● How you are going to do it
● Who might help you
● How long the job will take you (be realistic)
● How to prioritise the tasks (remember you have a class as well)
● On an action plan and write it.

Figure 13.2 suggests examples of what your action plan might look like.

Figure 13.2

Geography coordinator's action plan				April 92 Improving skills
Action	**How**	**By whom**	**By when**	**Further action**
Lead staff meeting on pre-mapping skills / progression in mapwork.	Collect mapwork examples from my class and any others, prepare some notes using Child Education and Primary Geographer articles. Run workshop.	Co	July	Ask teachers to plan mapwork into next year's topics.
Ensure that Yr 2 children do mapping activities.	Check that Yr 2 teachers have mapping activities incorporated in "Our School" topic	Co with colleagues	Sept.	Ask for maps to be displayed in hall after half term.
Audit infant map-work resources.	Teachers to use my audit sheet provided.	Colleagues	Mid Oct.	
Prioritise acquisition of new equipment.	Examine audit sheets.	Co	End Oct.	Pass list to head-teacher - check it goes into school development plan eventually!
Review Yr 2 colleagues' mapwork	Staff meeting sharing	Co and Staff	End Nov.	Keep good examples of mapwork for school geography agreement trialling folder.

Geography coordinator's action plan				June 92
Action	**How**	**By whom**	**By when**	**Further action**
Audit geography in schools' existing 'Topics'.	Fill in a geography audit sheet for topics covered over last academic year.	Co	June	
Develop a Key Stage plan to implement National Curriculum geography	Draft plan Present to staff Support staff in its implementation	Co. + Dep. Head Whole Staff Co.	June July 12th Sept. →	Amend plan if necessary Evaluate plan 1st year, amend if necessary, evaluate again.
Help staff to develop a key question approach to topic / unit planning	Go on planning course. School development day on developing medium term planning of geographical units	Co. AT + Co. Whole staff	Nov. Jan. 6th	Try to develop own unit Share with other staff Build up a bank of plans and work sheets to support Key Stage plan.

Co. = Co-ordinator
AT = Advisory Teacher

160

Curriculum documentation

Why do we need a geography policy?

The reasons we need a geography policy are:

- To state the school's aims for implementing and developing geographical education for its pupils and to ensure it is carried out
- To inform teachers, new teachers, long-term supply teachers, governors, LEAs, HMI and parents of the ways in which this will be achieved
- To define long-term, medium-term and short-term planning objectives for geography
- To ensure that all members of staff are fully informed at any time of the school's geography policy
- So people know where they stand if verbal interpretations are unclear
- To provide a basis for review and evaluation at all scales of planning
- To ensure continuity of geography's curricular development within the school as staff changes occur.

What should go into a geography policy?

A geography policy should form part of the whole-school planning process and documentation. Once the overall aims, ethos and curriculum policy of the school have been clarified it is up to the geography coordinator, or a small planning team or the whole staff in a small rural school, to develop a policy for consideration by the whole staff. Their draft policy can be modified in the light of discussion with the whole staff. A sense of ownership of the school policies by the whole staff is important. They need to know why certain things have to be done in certain ways and they can often clarify issues for the policy developer who may be too close to the document to see an error or ambiguity.

The policy should not run to too many pages but be a short, concise statement of intentions, plans and ways to implement them which is usable by teachers – in short, a working document. Writing the policy will help the coordinator to think through and develop their own action plans to develop the subject over the next two to three years.

It should contain:

- The aims of teaching and learning in geography
- An action plan for the development of geography in the school
- The skills, concepts, attitudes and knowledge to be covered
- The teaching and learning approaches to use in geography
  - the enquiry approach
  - key questions
  - fieldwork
  - issues
  - role-play and simulations
- A statement regarding the time allocation
- Integration of the subject into the whole primary curriculum
- Links with other subjects in the primary curriculum
- Long-term planning which shows how geography will be covered over a key stage
- Medium-term planning, units of work, a blank planning form and completed examples showing differentiation
- School assessment policy and marking schemes
- Recording techniques and the records required for pupils and teachers
- The place of cross-curricular themes and dimensions
- Fieldwork organisation, permission forms, health and safety requirements

- Reference to the school policies on equal opportunities, multi-cultural education and how they affect the teaching of geography
- Information about resources: amounts and location
- Special needs in geography
- Provision for evaluation of the planning and review of the document.

Evaluation of the policy

With so many changes happening in the primary curriculum, we have to be prepared to take a step backwards and review what is happening at all levels and stages in the teaching and learning of geography. By introducing the National Curriculum we have made substantial changes in the long-, medium- and short-term planning. These innovations need to be worked through, then reviewed and evaluated and adapted where necessary. As the whole staff will be involved in the implementation of the plans, they must also be involved in the evaluation. You can do this by reviewing different sections of the planning at different times. A teacher can quickly review a unit of work at the end and jot down any relevant comments such as 'Groups were too large', 'This key question worked well', 'This was a very heavy geography unit against a very heavy history unit'. Then, at the end of the year, the staff could get together and discuss how the units fitted into the whole primary curriculum and any changes that may need to be made.

The coordinator can collect and keep as a central resource the unit of work plans and any relevant work sheets. These resource can then provide a model for a teacher who has changed years, or a teacher new to the school. They do not need to be adhered to slavishly but will be useful as indicators of where things can be improved or changed. It means there is a starting point for medium- and short-term planning and we don't have to spend hours re-inventing the wheel. Traditionally teachers have enjoyed teaching new topics and units of work but we know that the precise planning required by the National Curriculum and teachers' work loads do not allow for this. Furthermore, it is a good idea to let planned units of work run for, say, three years or several cycles.

Year 1

- It's new – you run it through
- See how it could be improved
- Start collecting resources.

Year 2

- Refine the units
- Feel more comfortable with them
- Sort out any snags within the overall plan
- The resource collection grows.

Year 3

- Everything is now to hand
- There is little time spent on planning
- Look forward to minor changes or a different focus in the next year.

Any changes will obviously have to reflect national changes as well as school ones. With a structured plan it is possible to target the purchasing and collecting of new resources, which help in these times of financial constraints.

The success of a policy is visible, tangible evidence of it in practice in everyday school life, being internalised or as a working document – not a folder gathering dust on a shelf, to which only lip service is paid. The long-term final proof of the success of the policy will be in the pupils' enhanced achievements.

POSTSCRIPT

What is the benefit of National Curriculum geography?

If National Curriculum geography disappeared tomorrow, what would we have learned?

How would we have benefited from its implementation?

It would have highlighted:

- The importance of the rigour of focusing on geographical concepts, skills and vocabulary
- The rigour needed when planning one subject within the whole primary framework
- That geography is not, and should not, be an isolated subject – during planning you are forced to isolate it and identify its links with the whole primary curriculum
- That when you have a criterion-referenced assessment system, you need good practice and enquiry to fulfil it
- That careful planning, athough time-consuming, actually *saves* time in the end because learning outcomes have been anticipated
- That an enquiry approach to learning is relevant to geography
- That primary children can enjoy learning about people and places near and far
- That children of all ages are fascinated by maps and globes
- That good practice in primary geography, which existed in part in many schools before the National Curriculum, is wider than the Order
- That fieldwork in geography is essential.

Good luck!

APPENDIX

The charts on pages 164–7 are intended to be photocopied for use in your school; permission is hereby granted for purchasing institutions to copy freely these three pages. You will find that if you copy at 130% magnification you will have an A4 form.

Geography National Curriculum audit by statements of attainment levels 1–5

ATs \ Level	1	2	3	4	5
1 Geographical skills	a b	a b c d e	a b c d	a b c d e f	a b c d e
2 Knowledge and understanding of places	a b c d e	a b c d	a b c d e f	a b c d e	a b c
3 Physical geography	a	a b	a b c	a b c d e	a b c d e
4 Human geography	a b c	a b c	a b c d	a b c d e	a b c d e
5 Environmental geography	a b	a b	a b	a b c	a b

A1

A

Resource audit for National Curriculum geography key stages 1 and 2

	R	Y1	Y2	Y3	Y4	Y5	Y6	

Computer plus relevant software
Directional compasses
Pictorial maps
(poster sizes, in story books, etc.)
 	
Photographs, postcards, pictures of geographical places
Photographs, postcards, pictures of geographical features
 	
Objects to provide plan view and to draw round – standard 3D maths shapes, play mats, Brio® tracks and houses
 	
Tourist maps and plans
OS maps 1:1250 scale
and/or 1:2500 scale
Plan of school site
Oblique aerial photographs (can include postcards and photographs)
 	
Objects/artefacts from different places
 	
Videos
Atlases
Globe
Wall map of UK
Wall map of world
Access to soil and rock samples
Sand
Reference books relating to countries, places, themes – such as journeys, etc.
Story books with a place context
Reference materials relating to localities in:
    areas beyond the UK
contrasting localities in UK
    local area
Text books
								Applicable at key stages 1 and 2, levels 1–5

Tape measures – metres, surveyor's
Rain gauges
Clinometers
Stop watch
Wind speed gauges
Weather vane
Thermometers – a variety of types
Callipers
OS maps 1:25 000 scale
OS maps 1:50 000 scale
Vertical aerial photographs
Reference materials relating to localities in:
    home region
    Europe
    economically developing country
								Key stage 2 only

A2

Geography coordinator's action plan

Action	How	By whom	By when	Further action

The mathematics/geography links

Maths SoA	Geographical activities	Geography SoA
Ma1, 2b talk about work or ask questions using appropriate mathematical language. Ma1, 2c respond appropriately to the question 'What would I happen if?'	talk about how they decided to collect information on how children travel to school and discuss a resulting block graph; respond to the question 'How would the graph change if the school bus couldn't run tomorrow?'	
Ma1, 3b use or interpret mathematical terms and mathematical aspects of everyday language in a precise way.	describe the weather vane and its functions using appropriate directional vocabulary.	
Ma1, 3c present results in a clear organised way.	keep a record of the weather over a period of time; display the results in a chart.	Gg1, 2d record weather observations made over a short period.
Ma1, 4b interpret situations mathematically, using appropriate symbols or diagrams.	use coordinates to record the classroom layout; use a street map to locate your home; give coordinates of hidden treasure on an imaginary island map.	Gg1, 3a use letter/number coordinates to locate features on a map.
Ma1, 4d make generalisations or a simple hypothesis.	observe from temperature data collected that temperatures around the school building and grounds will tend to be lower on north-facing sites than on south facing sites.	
Ma2, 2d recognise the need for standard units measurement.	talk about distances measured in metres, miles, kilometres	
Ma2, 3e interpret a range of numbers in the context of measurement.	read a thermometer, rain gauge, measuring cylinder in weather-recording work	Gg1, 4d measure and record weather using direct observation and simple equipment.
Ma2, 5b Find fractions or percentages of quantities (understanding the notion of scale in maps and plans).	Use a ratio of 1:50 for drawing a plan of the classroom	
	measure the distance between home and school, home and shops, etc. using a simple linear scale.	Gg1, 4b measure the straight line distance between two points on a plan.
Ma3, 4c use coordinates in the first quadrant	draw graphs – line and bar – showing temperature, daily sunshine hours for a locality	
Ma4, 1a talk about models they have made.	talk about looking down on 3D shapes of a model village they have made and discuss the plan view shapes they see.	
Ma4, 1b follow or give instructions related to movement and position.	follow directions around the classroom, to the school secretary's office; programme toy like Roamer	Gg1, 1a follow directions
Ma4, 2a use mathematical terms to describe common 2D and 3D shapes.	talk about the shapes they see when looking down on 3D objects in the classroom; from an upstairs window or a viewpoint.	
Ma4, 3c use the eight points of the compass to show direction.	describe locations in the school grounds or area beyond the school sites using the compass points.	KS1 PoS3, level 3 use the eight points of a compass
Ma4, 4b specify location.	record the coordinates of a wood, lake or motorway junction on a 1:50 000 OS map.	Gg1, 4a use four-figure coordinates to locate features on a map.
Ma4, 5c use networks to solve problems.	find the shortest route from one point to another on a map, e.g. for a delivery van, taxi, pedestrian.	
Ma4	Handling Data strands (i) collecting and processing and (ii) representing and interpreting: all statements levels 1–5 can be applied in a geographical context. The examples given alongside the mathematics statements of attainment are largely geographical in nature, e.g. block graph of means of transport to school, bar chart of hours of sunshine, handling weather statistics, interpreting pie charts on farming data, designing an observation sheet to collect data on car occupancy.	

A4

BIBLIOGRAPHY

DES, *Geography In the National Curriculum*, HMSO 1991

DES, *National Curriculum Geography for Ages 5 - 16 Final Report*, HMSO 1990

DES, *Science in the National Curriculum*, HMSO 1989

DES, *History in the National Curriculum*, HMSO 1991

DES, *Safety in Outdoor Education*, HMSO 1989

GA, *Geography Outside the Classroom*, Geographical Association 1989

Harrison, Steve and Thacker, Ken, *Curriculum Leadership and Co-ordination in the Primary school*, Guild House Press 1991

HMI *Aspects of Primary Education: The teaching and learning of History and Geography*, HMSO 1989

HMI, *Geography from 5-16*, HMSO 1986

HMI, *Matters for Discussion 5: The Teaching of Ideas in Geography*, HMSO 1978

HMI, *Mathematics Key stages 1 & 2- A Report by HMI on the First Year 1989-90.* DES 1991

Mills, David, editor, *Geographical Work in the Primary and Middle Schools*, Geographical Association 1988

National Council for Educational Technology, *Focus on IT* NCET 1991

NCC, *Careers Education NCC 6*, NCC 1990

NCC, *Citizenship NCC 8*, NCC 1991

NCC, *Economic and Industrial Understanding NCC 4*, NCC1990

NCC, *Environmental Education NCC 7*, NCC 1990

NCC, *Health Education NCC 5*, NCC 1990

NCC, *The Whole Curriculum NCC 3*, NCC 1989

Playfoot, D., Skelton, M., Southworth, G., *The Primary School Management Book*, MGP 1989

Sutton, Ruth, *Assessment a Framework for Teaching*, NFER/Nelson 1991

TGAT, *Task Group for Assessment and Testing Report* 1988

GLOSSARY

alternative technology small scale, environmentally-friendly technology

anemometer an instrument to measure wind speed

barometer an instrument to measure air pressure

barrier a physical or mental obstacle to communication, e.g. mountain, safety fence, 'no go area'

'capes and bays' geography knowing facts, figures and names

cay an area formed by the deposition of sand, e.g. Florida Keys

clinometer an instrument for measuring angles to calculate the height of objects

contour lines lines on a map which join points of equal height

cycle a series of events which happen repeatedly in a certain order

data words, figures, any type of collected information on a given theme

deposition the laying down of eroded or weathered material

development education is about common issues which connect our own localities with other localities

Eckert's projection an elliptical map projection where the poles are shown by lines half the length of the Equator to minimise distortion of land area in the temperate latitudes

EDC Economically developing country

EC European Community

EIU Economic and Industrial Understanding

empathy appreciating the reasons for the actions of others in certain situations

enquiry questions a series of questions which lead pupils to investigate an issue or idea using primary or secondary sources

erosion the action of material carried by ice sea rivers and wind to change the shape of the land

fieldwork work outside the classroom

form the shape and layout of a settlement

function the services and goods provided by a settlement

GNP Gross National Product: the amount a country 'earns' in a year

graphicacy representing information in a non-written form, e.g. maps diagrams, charts, tables, graphs

grid north the north imposed on a map by cartographers

grid a system of lines that are used to clarify or explain ideas

hazard perception the ability to predict the potential dangers of a site

igneous rock formed by heat within the earth's crust, e.g. granite

'in the field' anywhere outside the classroom-school grounds local street, etc.

INSET In-Service Education and Training

land use the way humans use the land to live or work, e.g. recreation, farming

locality a small area with distinctive features

location where something is to be found

magnetic north this is the north to which the compass needle points; it moves a fraction of a degree every year

matrix a diagrammatic lined format on which you develop ideas

Mercator's projection a map projection where the lines of latitude get further apart towards the poles, so the northern hemisphere countries appear larger than they are

metamorphic   igneous or sedimentary rocks which have been changed by pressure, e.g. slate

micro-climate   the variations in climatic details on different parts of a site, e.g. shade and humidity

migration   the movement of people from one place to another

networks   links between places in the landscape, e.g. bus route, telephone system, post person's rounds

OS   Ordnance Survey

Peters projection   a map projection showing countries according to their true area with accurate directions

pie chart   a circle divided proportionally to show the equivalent value of the segments

primary industry   the extraction of materials from the ground, e.g. mining quarrying

primary sources   first hand experience

process   a series of events which cause a change

quadrat   an area of land enclosed within a square for data collection

relief   the difference in height of the Earth's surface

SAT   standard assessment task

scan reading   fast reading to pick out a particular fact or detail

secondary industry   manufacture of goods, e.g. cars, paint

secondary sources   pupils working from material collected by other people and presented in many forms

sedimentary   rocks formed from sediments often laid down in warm shallow seas, e.g. sandstone

skimming   fast reading to get an overall impression of a text

soil auger   special giant screw-like tool for taking soil samples

spatial patterns   patterns made in the landscape by places, features and people, e.g. transport, settlement,shopping

stack   a stump of eroded rock in the sea, e.g. the Needles, Isle of Wight

systems   separate parts which connect to make a whole, e.g. transport,river system

tertiary industry   a service activity helping other industries and people, e.g. travel agent, dry cleaners, distribution warehouse

true north   is the same as polar north, the North Pole on the globe

unit of study   sequence of work relating to a particular topic, theme or issue

wave built terrace   the area of the beach where material has been deposited

wave cut platform   the area of the beach worn away and cleared by erosion

weathering   the wearing away of the landscape by the elements of the weather – rain, frost, sun, wind

wide-angle-lens view   study or overview of a region or country in which a locality is found

Winkelsche projection   a map projection with a rounded grid so that directions are distorted, as are the shapes of countries on the edge of the map

zoom lens view   study of the details of a locality